PARADOX FOR THE PROGRAMMER

PARADOX FOR THE PROGRAMMER

Nelson T. Dinerstein

Computer Science Department
Utah State University

SCOTT, FORESMAN AND COMPANY
GLENVIEW, ILLINOIS LONDON

Printed in the United States of America.

Library of Congress Cataloging-in-Publication Data
Dinerstein, Nelson T.
Paradox for the programmer.

Includes index.
1. Data base management. 2. Paradox (Computer program) 3. PAL (Computer program language) I. Title.
QA76.9.D3D546 1986 005.75'6 86-10022
ISBN 0-673-18569-9
1 2 3 4 5 6-KPF-91 90 89 88 87 86

Scott, Foresman Professional Publishing Group books are available for bulk sales at quantity discounts. For information, please contact Marketing Manager, Professional Books, Professional Publishing Group, Scott, Foresman and Company, 1900 East Lake Avenue, Glenview, IL 60025.

CONTENTS

PARADOX FOR THE PROGRAMMER

CHAPTER

1

INTRODUCTION

1.1 BACKGROUND

Paradox is a product of Ansa. It has many of the features of dBASE II and dBASE III, but it also contains a number of features not found in either of these languages. This book is presented from the point of view that you already know how to program in some language, but not necessarily in Paradox.

Paradox has been written especially for the 16-bit machine. The first release of Paradox was for the IBM PC and 100 percent IBM PC compatible computers. It is expected that future releases of Paradox will be for the 16-bit machines that are not 100 percent IBM PC compatible.

1.2 SYSTEM REQUIREMENTS

In order for Paradox to run on your 16-bit microcomputer, you will need a minimum of 512K bytes of main memory and either

1. Two 360K floppy disk drives, or
2. One 360K floppy disk drive and a hard disk drive.

You will also need an operating system equivalent to MS/PC DOS version 2.0 or later.

It is true that you can make Paradox work with two floppy disk drives, but it is so much more convenient with a hard disk that I strongly recommend using a machine with a hard disk.

WARNING: You really need a hard disk machine if you are going to use Paradox.

1.3 SETTING UP YOUR HARD DISK TO USE PARADOX

When you receive Paradox from your dealer, you will receive four or five disks, possibly including two copies of SYSTEM DISK I. The disks are: SYSTEM DISK I, SYSTEM DISK II, SAMPLE TABLES, and the INSTALLATION DISK.

To set up your system with one floppy disk drive (drive A) and one hard disk (disk C), use the following procedure. If your drives are named differently, modify the statements to match your specific drive names.

1. Boot your computer.
2. Place your INSTALLATION DISK in drive A and close the door.
3. Enter the following DOS command

   ```
   A: INSTALL C:
   ```

   At this point, you will be asked a number of questions and will be given instructions concerning the insertion of Paradox disks into drive A. Follow the instructions that appear on the screen.

   WARNING: If you have an AUTOEXEC.BAT file on your root directory that calls a memory-resident program, you may find that you cannot install Paradox. In this case, you will need to boot in a manner that does not use the AUTOEXEC.BAT file. Either boot from the original DOS floppy system disk or change the name of the AUTOEXEC.BAT file and then reboot.

4. The installation program will install the Paradox system for you on your hard disk and modify or create, as necessary, the CONFIG.SYS file in the root directory. The installation procedure automatically copies all the necessary files to your current directory on drive C. You may wish to create a new directory especially for Paradox, make that directory the current directory, and then change to drive A before the installation process. Version 1.1 creates a new directory for you.
5. Version 1.0 of Paradox is stored on the original floppy distribution disk in a manner that allows you to install it on another disk, but not to copy it using the standard COPY and COPYDISK functions. When you run the installation program, a counter on the distribution disk is reset from 1 to 0. You will not be able to install the system on another disk until you uninstall it first. To uninstall the system, follow the procedure described above, but enter the command

   ```
   A: UNINSTAL C:
   ```

Once Paradox has been uninstalled, it can be installed at any time on another disk. Once you uninstall Paradox the copy that you had on your hard disk can no longer be used. It will be necessary to install it again on the hard disk before it can be used. Version 1.1 can be copied in the usual manner; that is, it is not copy-protected.

6. Since the CONFIG.SYS file has potentially been changed, it is a good idea to reboot the system before you attempt to use Paradox.
7. If you have successfully installed Paradox and, if necessary, rebooted your system, initiate Paradox by entering the command

   PARADOX

   If the installation has been performed successfully, you will see the Paradox logo on the screen, the message that Paradox is loading, and, finally, the Paradox main menu at the top of the screen. To exit from Paradox, either move the highlight to the word Exit on the screen and then press RETURN, or simply enter the letter E. Answer Y to the question asked by Paradox to confirm your desire to exit from Paradox, and control will pass to DOS.

CHAPTER

2

A PARADOX PRIMER

2.1 INTRODUCTION

This primer is designed to provide a brief introduction to some of the language elements of Paradox. If you are already familiar with Paradox, you might prefer to skip this chapter. In the following text, examples are provided for the more frequently used language elements.

Paradox offers both the ability to manipulate database files both interactively and through the use of programs. It is a self-contained system in that it provides both data management facilities and a complete programming language. The calls to the database functions are an integral part of the programming language and do not require special subroutine calls.

2.1.1 Files

The files used by or created by Paradox may be categorized by families. The families are shown in the following table.

FILE TYPE	VERSION	USE
Form	.F or .Fn	Settings for an input form
Image settings	.SET	Image setting save file
Primary index	.PX	Fast access to data
Procedure library	.LIB	Fast access to procedures
Report format	.R or .Rn	Format for a report
Script (program)	.SC	Application programs
Secondary index	.Xn or .Yn	Fast access to data
Table (database)	.DB	Storage of data
Validity checks	.VAL	Storage of validity rules

where n represents one or two digits in the above table.

2.1.2 Variables and Constants

Paradox allows the use of both program variables and database records. Variable names and names of fields in records must satisfy the following restrictions: the first character must be a letter, the characters ., $, !, and _ may be used in a name, and the maximum length of a name is 132 characters.

There are six types of data objects (types) in Paradox. They are alphanumeric (character string), numeric, dollar, date, short number, and logical. Variables and fields can be of any data type except logical. Only constants and functions may have the values True and False.

1. Character string
   Character strings are delimited by quotes (“ ”). The maximum length of a string (alphanumeric data type) is 255 characters. The delimiters are not counted as part of the string. If you wish to include a special character in a string, precede the character with a backslash (\).
2. Numbers
   Paradox has two types of numbers, regular and short. The regular numbers are real numbers (floating point) and have approximately 15 digits of precision, with numbers ranging from $\pm10^{-307}$ to $\pm10^{308}$. Short numbers are integers, with numbers ranging from –32,767 to +32,767. Both the regular and the short numbers can be formatted for output purposes.
3. Dollars
   Objects of type dollar can be used in virtually all places where numbers are allowed. The major difference between dollars and numbers is the manner in which they are displayed. When dollars are output, they are automatically rounded to two decimal places, commas are used to separate the three-digit groups, and negative numbers are enclosed in parentheses (no minus sign is used).
4. Dates
   Dates can be entered either in the form MM/DD/YY, MM/DD/YYYY, or in the form DD-MMM-YYYY. When a date has been stored in a variable or in a field in a database record, it can be displayed in a variety of formats (not just in the format used when it was entered). Dates can also be used in conjunction with arithmetic computations.

For example, if today's date is 01/01/87, then 01/01/87 + 10 is the date 01/11/87. Notice that dates are entered without any quotation marks. Dates must be in the range of Jan 1, 100 through December 31, 9999.

5. Logicals
The logical constants are True and False.

A variable is defined (allocated) dynamically. The type of the variable is determined when you assign a value to the variable. If you later assign another value, the type of the variable is redetermined.

To access a field in a table record, enclose the name in square brackets [ ]. The function # can be used to obtain the record number of a display image or the first field of a query image. To access a field in a record in a table other than the current table, prefix the name of the field with the name of the table in the following form

[TABLENAME —> FIELDNAME].

A complete list of techniques for accessing data in a database (table) is given below.

SPECIFIER	MEANING
[]	The current field in the current image
[T —>]	The current field in the image named T
[T(n) —>]	The current field in the nth display image of the table T
[T(Q) —>]	The current field in the query image of the table T
[F]	The field named F in the current image
[T —> F]	The field named F in the image T
[T(n) —> F]	The field named F in the nth display image of the table T
[T(Q) —> F]	The field named F in the query image of the table T

PAL (Paradox Application Language) supports arrays. Each of the elements of an array is treated as a separate variable, allowing you to have different types of data stored in an array. To declare an array, use the ARRAY command. Only one-dimensional arrays are allowed. If the name of the ARRAY is X, then access to an element of X is done with a name of the form X[exp], where exp evaluates to an integer between 1 and the size of the array. The COPYTOARRAY command can be used to copy data from a record in a table to an array. Similarly, the COPYFROMARRAY command can be used to copy data from an array to a table record. If the data in an array has been obtained from a table record (through the use of the COPYFROMARRAY command), then the individual elements in the array are available through the use of the field name. For example, if X is the name of the array and NAME is one of the fields in the table record, then X["NAME"] allows access to the desired array element. Notice that, unlike ordinary field names, when a field named is used as a subscript, then it must be enclosed in quotes.

2.1.3 Functions

PAL has a rich set of functions built right into the language. Each of the functions available in the language are examined in this section. Some of the examples use constants, and some of the examples use variables, showing a wide variety of usage. In most cases, you may select either a constant or a variable for use with a function, depending on your circumstances. Functions may require the use of parameters. In this case, the function is followed by parentheses with the types and numbers of the parameters indicated. Some functions do not use parameters. In this case, the function is followed by an empty set of parentheses. For example, the function TODAY( ) is always followed by a set of parentheses, but you never include any information between the parentheses when you use this function in a program.

ABS–absolute value

SYNTAX: ABS(<numeric expression>)

DESCRIPTION: Remove the sign from a number.

EXAMPLES:

ABS(-1) is 1
ABS(0) is 0
ABS(1) is 1

Table 2.1 FUNCTION TABLE

TYPE	NAME	DESCRIPTION
Date and time	BLANKDATE DAY DOW MONTH MOY TIME TODAY YEAR	Generate a blank date Day of the month Day of the week Numeric value of the month The month as a character string The current time Today's date Four-digit year
Financial	CNPV FV PMT PV	Compute net present value Compute future value Compute mortgage payments Compute present value
Input/Output	CHARWAITING GETCHAR	Test input buffer Get a character from the keyboard
Mathematical	ABS ACOS ASIN ATAN ATAN2 BLANKNUM COS EXP INT LN LOG MOD PI POW RAND ROUND SIN SQRT TAN	Absolute value of a number Arc cosine of a number Arc sine of a number 2-quadrant arc tangent of a number 4-quadrant arc tangent of a number Generate a blank number Cosine of an angle Raise e to a given power The integer portion of a number Natural logarithm Log base 10 Modulus Return the value of pi Raise a number to a power Random number generator Round a number Sine of an angle Compute the square root Tangent of an angle
Query	ARRAYSIZE ISASSIGNED ISBLANK ISEMPTY ISFILE ISTABLE TYPE	The size of an array Determine whether a variable has a value Test for a blank value Test for empty table Test for the existence of a file Test for the existence of a table Determine the type of a data object
Statistical	CAVERAGE CCOUNT CMAX CMIN CSTD CSUM CVAR MAX MIN	Average of values in a column Count of nonblank fields in a column Find maximum value in column Find minimum value in column Standard deviation of numbers in a column Sum of numbers in a column Variance of the numbers in a column Determine the maximum of two numbers Determine the minimum of two numbers

Table 2.1 FUNCTION TABLE (*continued*)

TYPE	NAME	DESCRIPTION
Status	ATFIRST	Test for first record
	ATLAST	Test for last record
	BANDINFO	Report Generator Band indicator
	BOT	Test for beginning of table
	COL	Find the current column position
	COLNO	Find the current column number
	CURSORCHAR	Find the current character
	EOT	Test for end of table
	FIELD	Find the name of the current column
	FIELDNO	Find the number of the current column
	FIELDINFO	Find the name of the current field
	IMAGENO	Find the number of the current image
	IMAGETYPE	Find the type of the current image
	ISFIELDVIEW	Test for Field view
	ISFORMVIEW	Test for Form view
	ISINSERTMODE	Test for Insert mode
	NFIELDS	Find the number of fields in a table
	NIMAGES	Find the number of images being used
	NKEYFIELDS	Find the number of key fields
	NPAGES	Find the number of pages
	NRECORDS	Find the number of records in a table
	NROWS	Find the number of rows
	PAGENO	Find the page number
	PAGEWIDTH	Find the current page width
	RECNO	Find number of current record
	ROW	Find the current row position
	ROWNO	Find the current row number
	TABLE	Find the name of the current table
String manipulation	ASC	ASCII code for a character
	CHR	Convert ASCII code to character
	DATEVAL	Convert a string to a date
	FILL	Repeat a character
	FORMAT	Specify output format
	LEN	Find the length of a string
	LOWER	Convert to lowercase
	MATCH	Test a string against a pattern
	MENUCHOICE	Return name of menu item
	NUMVAL	Convert a character string to a number
	SEARCH	Substring search
	SPACES	Generate a blank string
	STRVAL	Convert any data type to a string
	SUBSTR	Extract a substring
	UPPER	Convert to uppercase
	WINDOW	Return current window message
System	DIRECTORY	Find the name of the current directory
	DRIVESPACE	Check available disk space
	DRIVESTATUS	Determine if disk drive is available
	MONITOR	Determine the type of the monitor
	PRINTERSTATUS	Determine if printer is ready
	SYSMODE	Determine the current Paradox mode

ACOS–arc cosine

SYNTAX: ACOS(<numeric expression>)

DESCRIPTION: Return the angle in radians (between 0 and PI) whose cosine has the value of <numeric expression>.

ARRAYSIZE–array size

SYNTAX: ARRAYSIZE(<object name>)

DESCRIPTION: Return the maximum number of elements in the object. If the object is not an array, then this function returns the value 0. You may therefore use this function to determine if the named object is an array.

EXAMPLES:

```
ARRAY A[10]
B = 1
@ 1,1 ?? ARRAYSIZE(A)
```

displays the value 10, but

```
@ 2,1 ?? ARRAYSIZE(B)
```

displays the value 0.

ASC–convert a character to an ASCII code

SYNTAX: ASC(<character>)

DESCRIPTION: This function returns the ASCII code for any of the allowable keystrokes of the extended IBM code. If the keystroke represents a character in the normal ASCII character set, then the decimal code is returned as a non-negative number. If the keystroke represents a character in the extended set, then the decimal code is returned as a negative number. The list of characters and their decimal codes are given in Appendix B of the PAL User's Guide. Note that <character> may be a string containing a single character or the name of a key (such as **PgUp**).

EXAMPLES:

@ 1,1 ?? ASC("A")

displays the value 65

@ 2,1 ?? ASC("O")

displays the value 48

@ 3,1 ?? ASC ("END")

displays the value -79

@ 4,1 ?? ASC("F1")

displays the value -59

ASIN–arc sine

SYNTAX: ASIN(<numeric expression>), where <numeric expression> evaluates to a number between -1 and 1.

DESCRIPTION: Return the arc (in radian measurements) whose sine has the value of <numeric expression>.

ATAN–2-quadrant arc tangent

SYNTAX: ATAN(<numeric expression>)

DESCRIPTION: The arc in radians whose tangent is the value of <numeric expression>. The value returned by this function is between -PI/2 and PI/2.

ATAN2–4-quadrant arc tangent

SYNTAX: ATAN2(<numeric expression 1>, <numeric expression 2>)

DESCRIPTION: This function returns the arc in radians whose cosine has the value of <numeric expression 1> and whose sine has the value of <numeric expression 2>. This function returns values in all four quadrants.

ATFIRST–determine if at first record of the current table

SYNTAX: ATFIRST()

DESCRIPTION: If the current row of the table is the first row, then this function returns True; otherwise it returns False.

EXAMPLE:

```
VIEW "MYTABLE"
@ 1,1 ?? ATFIRST()
```

displays the value True

NOTES: If the table has no records in it, then ATFIRST() returns the value True.

ATLAST–determine if at last record of the current table

SYNTAX: ATLAST( )

DESCRIPTION: If the current row of the table is the last row, then this function returns True; otherwise it returns False.

EXAMPLE:

```
VIEW "MYTABLE"
END
@ 1,1 ?? ATLAST( )
```

displays the value True

NOTES: If the table has no records in it, then ATLAST( ) returns the value True.

BANDINFO–obtain the contents of the Report Generator band indicator

SYNTAX: BANDINFO( )

DESCRIPTION: You must be in Report mode to use this function. The report specification is divided into bands, or parts. This function indicates which band currently contains the cursor. Typical values returned by this function are: **Report Header, Page Header,** and **Form Band.**

BLANKDATE–generate a blank date

SYNTAX: BLANKDATE( )

DESCRIPTION: Use this function to initialize a blank date variable or field or to test whether an object of type date contains a value.

EXAMPLE:

```
NEWDATE = BLANKDATE( )
            .
            .
            .
IF ISBLANK(X)
   THEN
         <perform then clause>
   ELSE
         <perform else clause>
ENDIF
```

BLANKNUM–generate a blank number

SYNTAX: BLANKNUM( )

DESCRIPTION: Use this function to initialize a blank numeric variable or field or to test whether a numeric object contains a value.

EXAMPLE:

```
NUMBER_ORDERED = BLANKNUM( )
```

NOTE: A blank numeric variable does not have the value 0.

BOT–test for beginning of table

SYNTAX: BOT( )

DESCRIPTION: Use this function when you are performing a sequential scan from the current position back to the beginning of the table.

EXAMPLE:

```
WHILE NOT BOT( )
   PGUP
        .
        .
        .
ENDWHILE
```

CAVERAGE–compute the average of the values in a table column

SYNTAX: CAVERAGE (<"table name">, <"field name">)

DESCRIPTION: Note that the names of the table and the field must either be character string constants or variables. When the computation is performed, blank entries in the column are skipped. They do not participate either in the sum or the count.

EXAMPLE:

```
CAVERAGE("MYTABLE", "AMOUNT_OWED")
```

NOTE: This function should only be used on a column that is numeric.

CCOUNT–count the number of nonblank entries in a table column

SYNTAX: CCOUNT(<"table name">, <"field name">)

DESCRIPTION: Note that the names of the column and the field must be either character string constants or variables. When the count is performed, blank entries in the named column are not included.

EXAMPLE:

```
CCOUNT("MYTABLE", "AMOUNT_OWED")
```

NOTE: This function can be used with columns of any type.

CHARWAITING–determine if a character remains in the input buffer

SYNTAX: CHARWAITING( )

DESCRIPTION: Use this function to determine if a character has been entered at the keyboard, placed in the buffer, but not yet retrieved from the buffer. If there is a character in the buffer, this function returns the value True; otherwise it returns the value False.

EXAMPLE:

```
INVAR = GETCHAR( )
        .
        .
        .
IF CHARWAITING( )
   THEN
        <perform then clause>
   ELSE
        <perform else clause>
ENDIF
```

CHR–convert an ASCII decimal code to a character

SYNTAX: CHR(<decimal number>)

DESCRIPTION: The parameter <decimal number> may be any arithmetic expression that evaluates to an integer between 0 and 255. The function returns the printable character associated with the given decimal code.

EXAMPLES:

```
CHR(65)
```

returns the letter A

```
CHR(20)
```

returns the Greek symbol for pi

```
@ 14,0 CODE = CHR(GETCHAR( ))
@ 14,0 ?? CODE
```

CMAX–find the largest numeric value in a table column

SYNTAX: CMAX(<"table name">, <"field name">)

DESCRIPTION: Both the table and the field names may be character string constants or variables. When the search of the column is performed, blank entries are ignored.

EXAMPLE:

```
CMAX("MYTABLE", "AMOUNT_OWED")
```

NOTES: The column being searched must be numeric. The column must contain at least one nonblank entry.

CMIN–find the smallest numeric value in a table column

SYNTAX: CMIN(<"table name">, <"field name">)

DESCRIPTION: Both the table and the field names may be character string constants or variables. When the search of the column is performed, blank entries are ignored.

EXAMPLE:

```
CMIN("MYTABLE", "AMOUNT_OWED")
```

NOTES: The column being searched must be numeric. The column must contain at least one nonblank entry.

CNPV–compute the net present value of the entries in a table column

SYNTAX: CNPV(<"table name">, <"field name">, <interest rate>)

DESCRIPTION: Both the table and the field names may be character string constants or variables.

NOTES: The column being searched must be numeric. Blank entries in the column are ignored.

COL–determine the current position of the cursor on the screen

SYNTAX: COL( )

DESCRIPTION: The value returned by this function is an integer between 0 and 79, where 0 indicates the first column. You may find this function useful when you wish to display information in a nonstandard position on the screen, i.e., in a position that depends on a user response. This function is often used in conjunction with the function ROW( ).

EXAMPLE 1:

```
<previous user response>
@ ROW( )+1, COL( )+5 ?? <your response>
```

EXAMPLE 2:

```
? SPACES(20), [CHCHECKNO], SPACES(29-COL( ) ), [CHDATE]
```

COLNO–determine the number of the current data column

SYNTAX: COLNO( )

DESCRIPTION: This function returns values that are context dependent. For example, if the cursor is currently within an image, then the column number is returned. If the cursor is currently within a program being edited, then it returns the column number as shown at the top of the screen.

EXAMPLE:

If an image of the table MYTABLE is currently displayed on the screen, then

```
COLNO( )
```

will return the value 1 if the cursor is in the column containing the record numbers, and will return the value 2 if the cursor is in the first (leftmost) data column.

COS–the cosine of an angle

SYNTAX: COS(<numeric expression>)

DESCRIPTION: The parameter <numeric expression> is an angle expressed in radians. COS returns a value between -1 and 1.

EXAMPLE:

```
X = 0
COS(X)
```

returns the value 1, and so does

COS(0)

CSTD–compute the standard deviation of entries in a table column

SYNTAX: CSTD(<"table name">, <"field name">)

DESCRIPTION: Both the names of the table and the field may be character string constants or variables. When the computation is performed, blank entries are ignored.

EXAMPLE:

```
CSTD("MYTABLE", "AMT_OWED")
```

NOTE: The column must be numeric and there must be at least one nonblank entry in the column.

CSUM–compute the arithmetic sum of the entries in a table column

SYNTAX: CSUM(<"table name">, <"field name">)

DESCRIPTION: Both the names of the table and the field may be character string constants or variables. When the computation is performed, blank fields are ignored.

EXAMPLE:

```
CSUM("MYTABLE", "AMT_OWED")
```

NOTES: The column must be numeric.

CURSORCHAR–return a copy of the character under the cursor

SYNTAX: CURSORCHAR( )

DESCRIPTION: This function can only be used when in one of the following modes: Form, Report, or Script Editor.

CVAR–compute the variance of entries in a table column

SYNTAX: CVAR(<"table name">, <"field name">)

DESCRIPTION: Both the names of the table and the field may be character string constants or variables. When the computation is performed, blank entries are ignored.

EXAMPLE:

```
CVAR("MYTABLE", "AMT_OWED")
```

NOTE: The column must be numeric and there must be at least one nonblank entry in the column.

DATEVAL–convert a character string to a date

SYNTAX: DATEVAL(<"date string">)

DESCRIPTION: The parameter <"date string"> must be a character string constant or variable in one of the following forms: MM/DD/YY, MM/DD/YYYY, or DD-MMM-YYYY.

EXAMPLES:

```
DATEVAL("01/01/87")
DATEVAL("1/01/87")
DATEVAL("1/1/1987")
DATEVAL("1-JAN-1987")
```

DAY–day of the month as an integer between 1 and 31

SYNTAX: DAY(<date>)

DESCRIPTION: The day of the month is extracted from the object of type date and returned as an integer.

EXAMPLE:

If today's date is January 1, 1987, then

```
DAY(TODAY())
```

will return the number 1.

DIRECTORY–determine the name of the current directory

SYNTAX: DIRECTORY()

DESCRIPTION: The complete name of the current directory is returned as a character string.

EXAMPLE:

If the name of the current directory is \PARADOX on drive C:, then

```
DIRECTORY()
```

returns a character string with the content

```
c:\paradox\
```

DOW–day of the week as a three-character string

SYNTAX: DOW(<date>)

DESCRIPTION: The day of the week is extracted from the object of the type date and returned as a three-character name.

EXAMPLE:

```
DOW(01/01/87)
```

returns the value **Thu**

DRIVESPACE–return the available space on the disk

SYNTAX: DRIVESPACE(<name of the drive>)

DESCRIPTION: Compute the number of bytes available on the indicated drive.

EXAMPLE:

```
DRIVESPACE("A")
```

DRIVESTATUS–determine the ready status of the indicated drive

SYNTAX: DRIVESTATUS(<"drive name">)

DESCRIPTION: The parameter <"drive name"> may be either a character string constant or variable containing a single character.

EXAMPLE:

```
DRIVESTATUS("A")
```

returns the value True if the door is closed and a disk of the correct format has been properly inserted; otherwise it returns the value False

EOT–test for end of table

SYNTAX: EOT( )

DESCRIPTION: Use this function when you are performing a sequential scan from the current position to the end of the table.

EXAMPLE:

```
WHILE NOT EOT( )
   PGDN
       .
       .
       .
ENDWHILE
```

EXP–raise e to the indicated power

SYNTAX: EXP(<numeric expression>)

DESCRIPTION: This function computes e (approximately 2.7182845905) raised to the power indicated by the parameter <numeric expression>.

FIELD–determine the name of the current field

SYNTAX: FIELD( )

DESCRIPTION: This function returns the name of the current column of the current image.

NOTE: If the current column is the leftmost column, then the name "#" is returned.

FIELDINFO–return a copy of the contents of the field indicator

SYNTAX: FIELDINFO( )

DESCRIPTION: The field indicator is located in the upper right-hand corner of the screen when either a report or a form is being designed. This indicator contains the name of a placed field if the cursor is currently in such a position, otherwise it contains a blank.

FIELDNO–determine the number of the current field in the table

SYNTAX: FIELDNO(<"field name">, <"table name">)

DESCRIPTION: Both the table and the field names may be character string constants or variables.

NOTES: The order of the parameters is unusual in this function, since the field name comes before the table name. Another important observation is that the number that is returned reflects the actual data column. For example, if the named field is the first data column in the table, then the number 1 is returned. This differs from the function COLNO, which adds the number 1 to the actual position of the column in the table.

FILL–create a character string that contains copies of a character

SYNTAX: FILL(<"character">, <length>)

DESCRIPTION: The first character of the first parameter is duplicated as many times as specified by the number <length>.

EXAMPLES:

FILL("X", 3)

produces the string "XXX"

FILL("XYZ", 3)

produces the string "XYZ"

FILL("X", 0)

produces the null string

LEN(FILL("X", 0))

is 0

NOTE: The length of the new string may not exceed 255 characters. If the length is 0, then the new string is the null string.

FORMAT–set specifications for output format

SYNTAX: FORMAT(<"format list">, <print object>)

DESCRIPTION: The first parameter is a string that contains a list of the format options. The second parameter specifies the object to be printed. The format function allows you to specify, among other things, field width, justification, alignment, case, date format, numeric formatting, sign control, and the form of the logical constants. The specific objects that may appear in the format list are shown in the Table 2.2.

Table 2.2 FORMAT SPECIFICATIONS

PURPOSE	SPECIFIER	DESCRIPTION	OBJECT TYPE
Width	Wn Wn.m	Width of field Width of real number	All N, D
Alignment	AL AR AC	Left justify Right justify Center within field	All All All
Case	CU CL CC	Upper case Lower case Capitalize first letter of each word	All All All
Edit	E$ EC EZ EB E*	Floating dollar sign Insert comma in appropriate place Print leading zeros Suppress leading zeros Replace leading zeros with asterisks	N,S,$ N,S,$ N,S,$ N,S,$ N,S,$
Sign	S+ S- SC SD SP	Print leading + or - sign Print leading - sign Print trailing CR if negative Print CR if positive, DB if negative Enclose in parentheses if negative	N,S,$ N,S,$ N,S,$ N,S,$ N,S,$
Dates	D1 D2 D3 D4 D5 D6 D7 D8	MM/DD/YY Month DD, YYYY MM, DD MM/YY DD-Month Mon YY DD-Mon-YYYY MM/DD/YYYY	D D D D D D D D
Logical	LY LO	Use Yes/No instead of True/False Use On/Off instead of True/False	L L

EXAMPLES:

@ 1,1 ?? FORMAT("W8.2", 1234.567)

produces the value 1234.57

@ 2,1 ?? FORMAT("W20, AL", "Learning Paradox")

left justifies the string in the output field

NOTES: When a width specification of the form Wn.m is used, the last decimal place is rounded, not chopped. When sign and width specifications are both used, the width specification should come first. There must always be two parameters. If the specifier Wn is used, real numbers print as integers. The specifier Wn.0 prints a trailing decimal point. None of the sign specifiers seem to work. In addition, CC does not seem to work.

FV–compute future value of a series of cash flows

SYNTAX: FV(<payment>, <rate>, <number of periods>)

DESCRIPTION: The accumulated value of the investment, where equal payments are made for the indicated number of payments, and where rate is the interest rate. The value is given by the formula

payment * (POW(1 + rate, number of periods) – 1) /rate

GETCHAR–get a character from the keyboard

SYNTAX: GETCHAR()

DESCRIPTION: Paradox waits until a keystroke is entered at the keyboard, captures the keystroke, and then returns the ASCII value of the keystroke. If the keystroke is in the extended character set, then a negative value is returned. This keystroke is particularly handy when you wish to *freeze* the screen, i.e., when you wish to display output on the screen until a keystroke is entered by the user.

EXAMPLE:

```
@ 1,1 ?? "Your message goes here."
X = GETCHAR()
```

IMAGENO–return the number of the current image

SYNTAX: IMAGENO( )

DESCRIPTION: The images are arranged on the screen from top to bottom. The images are numbered consecutively from 1. If no images are displayed on the screen, then this function returns the value 0, otherwise it returns the number of the current image. This function can be used to move to a higher level or to a lower level image.

EXAMPLES:

```
WHILE IMAGENO( ) > 1
    UPIMAGE
ENDWHILE
```

or

```
WHILE IMAGENO( ) < 5
    DOWNIMAGE
ENDWHILE
```

IMAGETYPE–determine the type of the current image

SYNTAX: IMAGETYPE( )

DESCRIPTION: The type of the current image is returned as a character string. The possible types are: Display, Query, and None. You can use this function to determine if there already is an image on the screen.

INT–extract the integer portion of a number

SYNTAX: INT(<numeric expression>)

DESCRIPTION: This function discards the fractional part of a number and returns the integer portion.

EXAMPLES:

@ 1,1 ?? INT(1.9)

displays the value 1

@ 2,1 ?? INT(1.1)

displays the value 1

@ 3,1 ?? INT(-1.9)

displays the value -1

ISASSIGNED–determine if a variable or array element has had a value assigned to it yet

SYNTAX: ISASSIGNED(<object name>)

DESCRIPTION: Use this function to see if a value is currently assigned to the object, i.e., to see if the object is currently defined. If the object contains a value, then True is returned; otherwise False is returned. Ordinarily, if you reference an object before it has been defined, an error will occur.

EXAMPLES:

```
ISASSIGNED(X)
ISASSIGNED(A[5])
```

ISBLANK–determine if an object has a blank value

SYNTAX: ISBLANK(<object name>)

DESCRIPTION: If the object is blank, then the value True is returned, otherwise the value False is returned. This function may be helpful in determining if the object has a blank value (after using the BLANKNUM or the BLANKDATE functions). If you set a variable, field, or an array element to blank, you can test its value later to see if any data has been entered yet.

EXAMPLES:

```
@ 1,1 ?? ISBLANK(X)
@ 2,1 ?? ISBLANK([A])
@ 3,1 ?? ISBLANK(B[1])
```

ANOTHER EXAMPLE:

```
@ 1,0 ACCEPT "A5" TO MEMENTER
IF ISBLANK(MEMENTER) THEN RETURN ENDIF
```

NOTES: This function returns the value True if the object contains the null string.

ISEMPTY–determine if a table is empty (contains no rows)

SYNTAX: ISEMPTY(<"table name">)

DESCRIPTION: If the table contains no records, then the value True is returned; otherwise False is returned.

EXAMPLE:

```
ISEMPTY("MYTABLE")
```

NOTE: If the table does not exist in the current directory, then an error will occur.

ISFIELDVIEW–determine if the current image is being viewed in Field view

SYNTAX: ISFIELDVIEW( )

DESCRIPTION: In the cases where Field view is not possible, such as in Form or Report modes, the value False is always returned. This function returns the value True if the image is currently in Field view; otherwise it returns the value False.

EXAMPLE:

```
MESSAGE ISFIELDVIEW( )
```

ISFILE–determine if the named files exist

SYNTAX: ISFILE(<"file name">)

DESCRIPTION: The file name may contain complete path information, as well as the actual name of the file. Always give a complete specification for the name of the file (including the extension).

EXAMPLE:

```
ISFILE("C:\\AUTOEXEC.BAT:")
```

NOTES: Note the use of the double backslash (\\) in the example. In a number of situations, Paradox uses the backslash to indicate that the next character is to be taken literally. It is most unusual that the backslash is used in this manner within a character string.

WARNING: This function should not be used to determine whether a table created during the current session of Paradox is on the disk.

ISFORMVIEW–determine if the current image is being viewed in Form view

SYNTAX: ISFORMVIEW( )

DESCRIPTION: If the current image is being displayed in Form view, then it returns the value True; otherwise it returns the value False.

EXAMPLE:

```
ISFORMVIEW( )
```

NOTE: If Paradox is not in Main mode or in Edit mode, then an error will occur.

ISINSERTMODE–determine if Paradox is in Insert mode

SYNTAX: ISINSERTMODE( )

DESCRIPTION: Insert mode is used when reports, forms, and programs are being edited. If current mode is not Insert, you may wish to warn the user that typeover rather than insert will occur.

EXAMPLE:

```
IF NOT ISINSERTMODE( )
   THEN
         <display warning>
   ELSE
         <continue with normal processing>
ENDIF
```

ISTABLE–determine if a Paradox table of the given name exists

SYNTAX: ISTABLE(<"table name">)

DESCRIPTION: Always use this function, rather than ISFILE, to determine if the specified table exists. This function will determine two things: does the file exist, and is the file actually a Paradox table. The value True is returned only if both conditions are True.

EXAMPLES:

```
ISTABLE("MYTABLE")
ISTABLE("A:\\YOURTABLE")
```

LEN–compute the length of a character string

SYNTAX: LEN(<expression>)

DESCRIPTION: This function first examines the parameter for its type. If the parameter is not a character string, it is converted to a string. Then the string is examined for its length.

EXAMPLES:

```
X="ABC"
LEN(X)
```

returns the value 3

```
X=SPACES(5)
LEN(X)
```

returns the value 0

```
LEN(10)
```

returns the value 2

NOTES: This function does not change the type of the original variable when a numeric expression is changed to a character string. For example, if X contains the number 10, then LEN(X) returns the value 2, but X is still numeric. The length of a field in a table is determined by its contents, not by its original definition. For example, if a field has been defined as a character string of length 10, but is currently empty, then the length is 0, not 10.

LN–compute the natural logarithm of a number

SYNTAX: LN(<numeric expression>)

DESCRIPTION: The value of the <numeric expression> must be positive. The value returned is POW(e, <numeric expression>). If <numeric expression> evaluates to a number less than or equal to 0, then the value **error** is returned.

EXAMPLE:

```
LN(2.5)
```

LOG–compute the logarithm base 10 of a number

SYNTAX: LOG(<numeric expression>)

DESCRIPTION: The value of <numeric expression> must be positive. The value returned is POW(10, <numeric expression>). If

<numeric expression> evaluates to a number less than or equal to 0, then the value **error** is returned.

EXAMPLE:

LOG(2.5)

LOWER–convert characters to lowercase

SYNTAX: LOWER(<expression>)

DESCRIPTION: If necessary, first convert to a character string, and then convert each letter to lowercase.

EXAMPLES:

LOWER("ABC")

produces the result **abc**

LOWER(123)

produces the result **123**

MATCH–test a substring against a pattern

SYNTAX: MATCH(<"string">,<"pattern">, [,<list of variable names>])

DESCRIPTION: The parameter <"string"> is a character string that is to be matched against the pattern. The parameter <"pattern"> is a character string that contains a mixture of ordinary characters and wild card characters. The wild card characters are .. and @. The character .. will match any collection of characters, including the empty collection. The character @ will match any single character. If a match occurs, then the function returns the value True; otherwise it returns the value False. If optional variable names are provided as parameters, then the matching substrings are captured in the named variables. The assignment takes place from left to right until there are no more substrings to capture or until there are no more variables left to store the captured substring. This function ignores case.

EXAMPLES:

MATCH("Paradox", "p. .r@d. .", s1, s2, s3, s4)

returns the value True, stores **a** in s1, **a** in s2, **ox** in s3, and leaves s4 unchanged

MATCH([NAME], ". .,. .", LAST, FIRST)

will extract the two parts of the name and store them in different variables, if [NAME] is of the form "last name, first name"

NOTE: A pattern of the form ". .x", for any character x, always fails to match the character string.

MAX–find the larger of two numbers

SYNTAX: MAX(<numeric expression 1>, <numeric expression 2>)

DESCRIPTION: Return the larger of the two given values.

EXAMPLE:

MAX(NUM1, NUM2)

MENUCHOICE–return the name of the current menu item

SYNTAX: MENUCHOICE( )

DESCRIPTION: The name of the currently selected menu item is returned as a character string. If no item is currently selected, an error occurs. Note that the parameter list is always empty.

MIN–find the smaller of two numbers

SYNTAX: MIN(<numeric expression 1>, <numeric expression 2>)

DESCRIPTION: Return the smaller of two given values.

EXAMPLE:

MIN(NUM1, NUM2)

MOD–compute the modules

SYNTAX: MOD(<numeric expression 1>, <numeric expression 2>)

DESCRIPTION: Return the remainder obtained by dividing the first expression by the second.

EXAMPLES:

MOD(5,2)

returns the value 1

MOD(6,3)

returns the value 0

NOTE: If the value of the second expression is 0, then the function returns the value 0.

MONITOR–determine the type of the current monitor

SYNTAX: MONITOR( )

DESCRIPTION: This function actually looks at the video board to determine how the output will appear on the screen. If the output that is sent to a monochrome monitor has color characteristics, then it is often hard to read the screen. Similarly, if output that is sent to a color monitor has monochrome attributes, then many of the useful functions of a color monitor would not be used. You may test for the type of monitor to determine the desirable display attributes. See also the STYLE statement described later in this chapter. The style attributes appear in Appendix A of the PAL User's Guide.

EXAMPLE:

```
IF MONITOR( ) = "Color"
   THEN
         <set one type of attribute>
   ELSE
         <set another type of attribute>
ENDIF
```

NOTE: The possible values returned by this function are Mono, B&W, and Color.

MONTH–return the month as a number

SYNTAX: MONTH(<date>)

DESCRIPTION: Return the month as a number between 1 and 12.

EXAMPLE:

If today's date were January 10, 1987, then

```
MONTH(TODAY())
```

would return the value 1.

MOY–return the month as a character string of length 3

SYNTAX: MOY(<date>)

DESCRIPTION: The choice of names for the months is: Jan, Feb, Mar, Apr, May, Jun, Jul, Aug, Sep, Oct, Nov, and Dec.

EXAMPLE:

If today's date were January 10, 1987, then

```
MOY(TODAY())
```

would return the value **Jan.**

NFIELDS–count the number of fields in a table

SYNTAX: NFIELDS(<"table name">)

DESCRIPTION: The number returned is the actual number of fields (columns) in the table.

EXAMPLE:

```
NFIELDS("MYTABLE")
```

NOTE: If the named table is not on the disk, then an error occurs.

NIMAGES–count the number of images currently on the screen

SYNTAX: NIMAGES( )

DESCRIPTION: This function returns the number of images currently on the screen (in the workspace). If there are no images on the screen, then the number 0 is returned.

EXAMPLE:

This function can be used to remove all but the desired number of images from the screen in the following manner:

```
WHILE NIMAGES > 4
    CLEARIMAGE
ENDWHILE
```

NKEYFIELDS–count the number of keys (key fields) in a table

SYNTAX: NKEYFIELDS(<"table name">)

DESCRIPTION: If the table has no key fields, then the number 0 is returned. If the table is not on the disk, then an error occurs.

EXAMPLE:

```
NKEYFIELDS("MYTABLE")
```

NPAGES–count the number of pages

SYNTAX: NPAGES( )

DESCRIPTION: This function counts the number of pages, but with respect to the current environment (context). When in Report mode, the number of pagewidths is returned. In Form or Main mode, then number of pages is returned.

EXAMPLE:

```
NPAGES( )
```

NRECORDS–count the number of records in a table

SYNTAX: NRECORDS(<“table name”>)

DESCRIPTION: Count the number of records in the indicated table. If the table is not on the disk, then an error occurs. This function may be useful in conjunction with a counter-controlled search of the records in the data file.

EXAMPLE:

```
NRECORDS("MYTABLE")
```

NROWS–count the number of rows

SYNTAX: NROWS( )

DESCRIPTION: The current image or report specification is examined. This function can only be used in Main and Edit modes, and the current image may be either a display or a query image. A display image must be in Table view. The function returns the number of rows in the image or the number of rows in the specification.

EXAMPLE:

```
VIEW "MYTABLE"
MENU {IMAGE} {TABLESIZE} DOWN
MESSAGE NROWS( )
```

adds one row to the display size and then shows the new count

NOTES: The display size of a table image is controlled through the selection of the TABLESIZE option. After this option has been selected, the cursor movement keys (up arrow and down arrow) are used to change the number of rows displayed on the screen. The default number of rows displayed in a table image is 22.

NUMVAL–convert a character string to a number

SYNTAX: NUMVAL(<“character string”>)

DESCRIPTION: The form of the number returned is automatically determined by the string version of the number, so no indication of the number of decimal places is required.

EXAMPLES:

NUMVAL(“15.223”)

returns the number 15.223

NUMVAL(“-12.2”)

returns the number -12.2

NOTE: This function takes any numeric string that is legal in Paradox and converts it. In particular, parentheses are used (in some cases) to indicate a negative number, so NUMVAL(“(125)”) returns the number -125.

PAGENO–return the current page number

SYNTAX: PAGENO( )

DESCRIPTION: In Report mode, this function returns the number of the current pagewidth. In Form and Main mode, it returns the number of the current page.

EXAMPLE:

PAGENO( )

PAGEWIDTH–count the number of characters in the current page width

SYNTAX: PAGEWIDTH( )

DESCRIPTION: This function returns the width of a report page.

EXAMPLE:

```
PAGEWIDTH( )
```

PI–return the value for pi

SYNTAX: PI( )

DESCRIPTION: This function returns the real value for pi. The value, approximately, is 3.14159265358979.

EXAMPLE:

```
SIN(PI( ))
```

returns the value 0, correct to 15 decimal places

PMT–compute mortgage payments

SYNTAX: PMT(<principle>, <interest>, <number of periods>)

DESCRIPTION: This function computes the amount of the loan to be paid each period, except (possibly) for the last payment. Each payment is to be paid at the end of the period, and the interest rate is for the fixed-length period. The equation for the computation is

PMT = principal * (interest/(1 – POW(1 + interest, – number of periods)))

EXAMPLE:

```
PMT(40000, .01, 360)
```

returns (approximately) the value 411, the interest payment on a $40,000 loan, at 12% per year, with a loan period of 20 years.

NOTE: The interest is entered in the form .12 for 12%.

POW–raise a number to a power

SYNTAX: POW(<base>, <exponent>)

DESCRIPTION: It seems strange to me that Paradox implements exponentiation as an individual function rather than as a simple operator, but they are equivalent.

EXAMPLES:

```
@ 1,1 ?? pow(3,2)
```

returns the value 5

```
@ 2,1 ?? pow(2, .5)
```

returns the value 1.4142135623731

```
@ 3,1 ?? pow(2, -1)
```

returns the value .5

PRINTERSTATUS–determine if printer is ready

SYNTAX: PRINTERSTATUS( )

DESCRIPTION: This function returns the value True if the printer is connected and ready for use; otherwise it returns the value False.

EXAMPLE:

```
IF NOT PRINTERSTATUS( )
  THEN
        MESSAGE "The printer is not ready"
ENDIF
```

PV–compute the present value of a series of equal payments

SYNTAX: PV(<payment>, <rate>, <number of periods>)

DESCRIPTION: The formula used to compute the present value is

PV = payment * (1 – POW(1 + rate, – number of periods))/rate

RAND–generate a random number between 0 and 1

SYNTAX: RAND( )

DESCRIPTION: The numbers returned by this function are uniformly distributed between 0 and 1. In all cases, 0 <= RAND( ) < 1.

EXAMPLE:

```
RAND()
```

RECNO–determine the position of the current record

SYNTAX: RECNO( )

DESCRIPTION: There must currently be a display image on the screen.

EXAMPLE:

```
IF RECNO() <> 1
   THEN
          MOVETO RECORD 1
ENDIF
```

ROUND–round a number to the indicated number of digits

SYNTAX: ROUND(<numeric expression>, <number of digits>)

DESCRIPTION: If <number of digits> is positive, then rounding takes place at the specified digit to the right of the decimal point. If <number of digits> is negative, then rounding takes place at the indicated digit to the left of the decimal point.

EXAMPLES:

```
@ 1,1 ?? ROUND(123.45,3)
```

returns the value 123.45

```
@ 2,1 ?? ROUND(123.45,2)
```

returns the value 123.45

```
@ 3,1 ?? ROUND(123.45,1)
```

returns the value 123.5

```
@ 4,1 ?? ROUND(123.45,0)
```

returns the value 123

```
@ 5,1 ?? ROUND(123.45,-1)
```

returns the value 120

```
@ 6,1 ?? ROUND(-123.45,1)
```

returns the value -123.4

ROW–determine the current row number of the cursor

SYNTAX: ROW( )

DESCRIPTION: The rows on the screen are numbered from 0 to 24, where 0 is the number of the first row. This function may be useful when you desire to display information starting at a point determined by an arbitrary response from the user.

EXAMPLE: See the function COL for an example.

ROWNO–determine the current row number

SYNTAX: ROWNO( )

DESCRIPTION: If Paradox is in Main or Edit mode, then the value returned (row number) is the number of the current row. The row number may not equal the record number, since tables are displayed in groups of records that fit on the screen. If Paradox is in Report mode, then the value returned is the number of the current row of the report specification.

EXAMPLE:

```
ROWNO()
```

SEARCH–find a substring

SYNTAX: SEARCH(<substring>, <string>)

DESCRIPTION: If necessary, each of the two parameters is converted to a character string. If a match is found, then the position of the first character of the match in the string is returned. If no match is found, then the value 0 is returned.

EXAMPLE:

SEARCH("doxa", "PARADOX")

returns the value 0

SEARCH("DOX", "PARADOX")

returns the value 5

SEARCH(1, 20013.25)

returns the value 4

NOTE: Uppercase and lowercase are ignored when the substring is compared with the string.

WARNING: If you attempt to use the function with parameters such as

SEARCH(DOX, PARADOX)

Paradox looks for variables with the names DOX and PARADOX. You should therefore enclose all non-numeric parameters in quotation marks.

SIN–compute the sine of an angle

SYNTAX: SIN(<numeric expression>)

DESCRIPTION: The parameter is an angle expressed in radians. The value returned by this function is the sine of the given angle.

EXAMPLE:

```
SIN(PI( ))
```

returns the value 0 (correct to 15 decimal places)

```
SIN(PI( )/2)
```

returns the value 1

```
SIN(PI( )/4)
```

returns the value .7071067811186547

SPACES–create a character string consisting of the given number of blanks

SYNTAX: SPACES(<numeric expression>)

DESCRIPTION: The value of the <numeric expression> must be an integer between 0 and 255. If <numeric expression> has the value 0, then the null string is generated.

EXAMPLES:

```
X = SPACES(5)
```

will create a new string with the name X, which contains five blanks

```
? SPACES(10), [CHCHECKNO]
```

SQRT–compute the square root of a number

SYNTAX: SQRT(<numeric expression>)

DESCRIPTION: The value of <numeric expression> must be non-negative.

EXAMPLE:

```
SQRT(25)
```

returns the value 5

STRVAL–convert any type of object to a character string

SYNTAX: STRVAL(<any type of expression>)

DESCRIPTION: This function will convert any type of data object to a character string. The following table shows how each conversion is accomplished.

ORIGINAL TYPE	HOW CONVERTED
CHARACTER STRING	Unchanged
DATE	Into the form MM/DD/YY
NUMBER	Into a numeric string, including the sign
LOGICAL	Into True or False

EXAMPLES:

STRVAL("ABC")

returns the value **ABC**

STRVAL(1/01/87)

returns the value **1/01/87**

STRVAL(1/1/87)

returns the value **1/01/87**

STRVAL(-5.1)

returns the value **–5.1**

STRVAL(5.25)

returns the value **5.25**

X = TRUE
STRVAL(X)

returns the value **True**

NOTES: When a number is converted to a character string, the result is left justified. There are no leading and no trailing blanks in the result. Note also that most Paradox functions that require character string arguments automatically convert the argument to a character string for you.

SUBSTR–extract a substring

SYNTAX: SUBSTR(<character string>, <starting position>, <length>)

DESCRIPTION: This function will return the substring found in the given <character string>, starting at the position given by <starting position>, and having a length of <length>. The starting position must be an integer between 1 and LEN(<character string>). In addition, <length> must be an integer such that the resultant substring does not extend beyond the righthand boundary of the original character string. Therefore, if S is the starting position and L is the length of the desired substring, then S+L–1 must be less than or equal to LEN(<character string>).

EXAMPLES:

SUBSTR("ABC",2,3)

produces an error

SUBSTR("ABC",4,1)

produces an error

SUBSTR("ABC",2,2)

returns the value **BC**

SYSMODE–determine the current Paradox mode

SYNTAX: SYSMODE( )

DESCRIPTION: Determine the current Paradox mode and return the mode as a character string. The possible modes are Create,

DataEntry, Edit, Form, Main, Report, Restructure, Sort, and Script.

EXAMPLE:

```
SYSMODE( )
```

TABLE–determine the name of the current table

SYNTAX: TABLE( )

DESCRIPTION: This function returns the name of the current table as a character string. If there is no table on the screen, then an error occurs.

EXAMPLE:

```
TABLE( )
```

TAN–compute the tangent of an angle

SYNTAX: TAN(<angle>)

DESCRIPTION: The angular measurement must be in radians.

EXAMPLES:

```
TAN(PI( )/4)
```

returns the value 1

```
TAN(0)
```

returns the value 0

```
TAN(PI( ))
```

returns a negative value close to 0

```
TAN(PI( )/2)
```

returns a large positive number

TIME–obtains the current time from the system clock

SYNTAX: TIME( )

DESCRIPTION: The current time is returned as a character string in the standard MS/DOS format "HH:MM:SS".

EXAMPLE:

```
TIME( )
```

NOTE: You may find this function handy if you wish to include a time within a report.

TODAY–obtain today's date from the system clock

SYNTAX: TODAY( )

DESCRIPTION: This function returns an object of type date.

EXAMPLE:

```
TODAY( )
```

TYPE–determine the data type of an expression

SYNTAX: TYPE(<expression>)

DESCRIPTION: The type of the argument is returned as a character string, as given by the following table.

DATA TYPE	VALUE RETURNED
CHARACTER STRING	A, followed by the length of the string
DATE	D
LOGICAL	L
NUMERIC	N

EXAMPLES:

TYPE("Paradox")

returns **A7**

TYPE([])

returns the type of the current field. It is important to note that the value returned is completely dependent on the actual content of the field. For example, even if the current field has been defined as a character string of length 10, then the value returned depends only on the actual content of the field. If the field is empty, then the value returned is **A0.** If the field contains five characters, then the value returned is **A5.**

TYPE(01/01/87)

returns D

TYPE(5.1)

returns N

UPPER–convert all characters to uppercase

SYNTAX: UPPER(<expression>)

DESCRIPTION: The value of the expression is first converted to a character string and all the letters in the resultant string are then converted to uppercase.

EXAMPLE:

```
X = "aBc"
@ 1,1 ?? UPPER(CODE)
```

displays the result "ABC"

WINDOW–return the current window message

SYNTAX: WINDOW()

DESCRIPTION: The content of the current message window is returned as a character string. If no window is currently displayed, then a blank string is returned. This function cannot access messages displayed through the use of the MESSAGE command. It accesses only system-generated messages in the workspace.

YEAR–return the year as a four-digit number

SYNTAX: YEAR(<date>)

DESCRIPTION: The default century for the year is 1900.

EXAMPLES:

YEAR(01/01/2001)

returns the value 2001

YEAR(01/01/87)

returns the value 1987

2.1.4 Mathematical and Logical Operators

The arithmetic operators are:

+	Addition
–	Subtraction
*	Multiplication
/	Division
POW	Exponentiation (actually a function)
( )	Parentheses

The relational operators are:

>	Greater than
>=	Greater than or equal to
=	Equal to
<=	Less than or equal to

<	Less than
<>	Not equal to

The logical operators are:

AND	and
OR	or
NOT	not

Most of the operators to manipulate character strings are found earlier in the section in this chapter that lists the Paradox functions. In addition to these functions, the + operator can also be used for string concatenation.

Arithmetic expressions are scanned from left to right, and the precedence of the operators is

1. *, /
2. +, -
3. relational operators
4. NOT
5. AND
6. OR

2.2 SOME PRELIMINARY REMARKS ON THE PAL LANGUAGE ELEMENTS

The Paradox Application Language (PAL) is rich in both functions and commands (programming language statements). In addition to the commands in the language, you can also use special keystroke names in PAL programs. The use of the keystroke names in a program accomplishes approximately the same function as if the actual keystrokes had been entered interactively. In some instances, a PAL command is equivalent to several interactive keystrokes. One major difference between entering keystrokes interactively and using them by name in a PAL program is that interactive usage often requires user confirmation for the desired action, while use in a program does not require this confirmation.

2.2.1 PICTURE Clause to Format Input

A PICTURE clause, in conjunction with an ACCEPT statement, allows you to specify the format to be used for input. The formatting characters are given in the following table.

CHARACTER	USE
#	Digit
?	Uppercase or lowercase letter
@	Any character
&	Uppercase letter (convert if necessary)
!	Any character, converting letters to uppercase
;	Take the next character literally
*	Repeat the following character(s) as indicated
[]	Optional characters
{}	Specify a group of characters
,	Alternative choices

When a PICTURE clause is used in an ACCEPT statement, it appears in the form

PICTURE "format characters"

SOME EXAMPLE PICTURES

1. ###-##-####
   For social security number. When the third digit has been entered, the hyphen automatically appears.
2. *3#-*2#-*4#
   Again for social security number. The asterisk indicates repetition.
3. [(###)]###-####
   May be used for a telephone number. If the first character entered by the user is a left parenthesis, then the next three digits are taken as the area code. After these three digits have been entered, the right parenthesis appears on the screen. If the first character is a digit, then the optional group is skipped. You must use the brackets with care, since Paradox must be able to distinguish whether or not to use the optional

group. You must provide a means for Paradox to distinguish one type of input from another. In this case, the entry of a left parenthesis "triggers" the use of the optional group.

4. ???;@;#
May be used to input three letters, and then place the characters @# immediately to the right of these letters.

WARNING: The use of the semicolon (;) to indicate the literal use of a character in a PICTURE clause does not appear to work correctly when placed at the left of the PICTURE.

2.2.2 Procedures

PAL supports procedures with parameter passing. The parameters are called by value, and you may not pass the name of an array as a parameter. Because all parameters are called by value, there are no problems with side effects associated with parameter passing. Since each element of an array is treated by Paradox as an independent variable, you can pass an array element as a parameter. Global variables are available with a procedure unless you hide them through the use of the PRIVATE statement. If you do not use the PRIVATE statement, you can manage parameter passing more easily, but you run the risk of undesired side effects (the undesired changing of values of global variables). If you use the PRIVATE statement in the procedure, you can often control these side effects. See the primer of PAL statements in section 2.3 later in this chapter for a detailed explanation of the PRIVATE statement. You can use the RETURN statement to pass a value back from a procedure, effectively allowing you to create user-defined functions, or you can use a procedure in the ordinary manner, i.e., as a stand-alone statement.

Programs (.SC files) are paged into memory as needed, while procedures remain memory-resident once they have been entered into memory. The procedures are stored in memory in a form that speeds up their execution, so you may wish to place frequently used code in a procedure rather than a script file (ordinary program). You can control the retention of procedures through the use of the RELEASE PROCS command to clear out procedures that are no longer needed. If you don't manage procedures in a careful manner, you may find that you run out of memory.

2.2.3 Macros

Paradox provides for macros through the use of the EXECUTE statement. Merely construct a character string expression containing a valid Paradox statement and place it after the word EXECUTE in the statement. The command will then be executed in the normal manner. The macro facility in a language usually offers the programmer a high degree of flexibility by allowing the programmer to create features or functions not currently available through the standard statements in the language.

2.2.4 System Initialization

When you first invoke Paradox, the current directory is searched for a file with the name INIT.SC. If this file is found by Paradox, then the statements in the file are executed before any other action is taken. This allows you to customize your application. In particular, you can reconfigure the keyboard, initialize macros, and invoke the application system.

2.2.5 A Help in Constructing Programs

If you would like to see how Paradox performs certain operations and possibly include these operations in a program, you can use the instant script recording feature of Paradox. At any point in the use of Paradox, enter the keystroke ALT-F3 to initiate this facility. A new file called INSTANT.SC will be created for you. As you enter keystrokes, they will then be recorded for you in this file. At any point, you can use the Edit function in the main menu of Paradox to terminate the recording. As usual, you can access the contents of this file and edit it as appropriate. Examination of this file can be most enlightening. Once a program with the name INSTANT.SC has been constructed, you can execute it in a number of places in Paradox by entering the keystroke ALT-F4. In addition, you can construct a file of this name just as you would any other program (not using the instant recording feature, but the editor) and still invoke it through the use of the ALT-F4 keystroke.

2.3 THE LANGUAGE ELEMENTS

Table 2.3 A TABLE OF PAL STATEMENTS

TYPE	NAME	DESCRIPTION
ARRAYS	ARRAY	Define an array
	COPYFROMARRAY	Copy from an array to a database
	COPYTOARRAY	Copy from a database to an array
	RELEASE	Deallocate arrays, variables, or procedures
	SAVEVARS	Save values in a file
DATABASE OPERATIONS	[]	Field reference
	CREATE	Create a new database table
	DELETE	Delete a table and its indexes
	EMPTY	Delete all records from a table
	LOCATE	Find a record in a table
	MOVETO	Change currency of field/record
	RENAME	Change the name of a table
	SORT	Sort the records in a table
	SUBTRACT	Delete records from a table
DATA DISPLAY	?	Write on the screen below the cursor
	??	Write on the screen at the cursor
	@	Position the cursor on the screen
	BEEP	Emit a sound at the terminal
	CLEAR	Clear the screen
	ECHO	Show execution of a program
	MESSAGE	Display string in the message area of the screen
	PICKFORM	Select a form for output
	PRINT	Output to file or printer
	PRINTER	Echo screen output to the printer
	QUERY	Place a query on the screen
	REPORT	Print a report
	STYLE	Set screen attributes
	TEXT	Display text on the screen
	VIEW	Display a table on the screen
	WAIT	Wait for a keystroke
DATA INPUT	ACCEPT	Get input from the keyboard
	WAIT	Wait for a keystroke
DEBUGGING	DEBUG	Enter Debug mode
EDITING OF DATABASE RECORDS	CANCELEDIT	Abort editing
	EDIT	Enter Editing mode
INDEXES	INDEX	Create a secondary index for a database table
KEYSTROKES	KEYPRESS	Get a character from the keyboard and pass it to Paradox

Table 2.3 A TABLE OF PAL STATEMENTS (*continued*)

TYPE	NAME	DESCRIPTION
KEYSTROKES	SETKEY	Redefine the keyboard
	TYPEIN	Pass a string to Paradox
MACROS	EXECUTE	Execute a macro
MENUS	SELECT	Select a function from a Paradox menu
	SHOWMENU	Display a user menu on the screen as a Paradox-style menu
PROCEDURE LIBRARIES	CREATELIB	Create a new procedure library
	INFOLIB	List the names of the procedures in the library
	READLIB	Load the procedure from the library
	WRITELIB	Add a procedure to the library
PROGRAMMING	=	The assignment operator
	EXIT	Exit from Paradox
	IF	The IF-THEN-ELSE
	LOOP	Immediately advance to the next ENDWHILE; skip the remainder of the statements in the loop
	PLAY	Execute a program
	PROC	Start a procedure
	QUIT	End a program
	QUITLOOP	Immediately go to the statement following the loop
	RETURN	Pass a value to a calling routine
	SCAN	Sequentially scan through a table and apply a group of commands to selected records
	SLEEP	Delay the program for a preset time
	SWITCH	Start a CASE structure
	WHILE	Start a loop
RECORD INSERTION	ADD	Copy records from one table to another
	COPY	Copy records to a new table
SECURITY	PASSWORD	Enter one or more passwords
	PROTECT	Assign a password to a table
	UNPASSWORD	Cancel the entry of a password
SYSTEM	DOS	Suspend Paradox and invoke DOS
	RESET	Cancel the current activity and return to Paradox Main mode
	RUN	Execute a DOS command without leaving Paradox
	SETDIR	Change the current directory
VARIABLES	=	The assignment operator
	RELEASE	Deallocate variables, arrays, or procedures
	SAVEVARS	Save values in a file

The following syntax is used in this section:

<object>	Means that an object of the appropriate type should be substituted. The object may be a variable, array elements, reference, field reference, etc.
[ ]	May be a field reference or be used in conjunction with an array
<< >>	Designates an optional part of a statement
{ }	Indicates a Paradox keystroke

<variable> = <expression>

Assign a value to a variable. The expression may evaluate to any data type. The variable is dynamically given the type of the expression.

EXAMPLE:

```
X = "ABC"
X = 1
```

In the first assignment, the character string "ABC" is stored in the variable named X. At this point, X is a character string of length 3. After the second assignment, X is now a number with the value 1.

<array element> = <expression>

Assign a value to an element of an array. The expression may evaluate to any data type. The array element is dynamically given the type of the expression. The elements of an array do not need to have the same type. For example, A[1] might be a number, while A[2] is a character string, and A[3] is a date.

EXAMPLE 1:

```
A[1] = 25
```

EXAMPLE 2:

```
A[LASTNAME] = "SMITH"
```

In this example, instead of a numeric subscript, the name of the field in the database record is used. You may use this technique if the data in the array was placed there with a COPYTOARRAY command.

<field specifier> = <expression>

Assign a value to a field in a table. The type of the expression must match the type of the field. See section 2.1.2 for a discussion of the various forms for a <field specifier>.

EXAMPLE:

```
[DUEDATE] = 5/1/87
```

assigns the date to the field named DUEDATE in the current record of the current image

```
[] = "Smith"
```

assigns the name Smith to the current field of the current record in the current image

? <expression list>

Display the value of each expression on the screen, left to right, starting at the beginning of the line immediately following the current cursor position. The values are displayed without spaces between them. The display statement <expression list> is a list of expressions, and the members of the list are separated by commas. If the expression list is empty, i.e., there are no expressions following the ?, then the cursor is simply advanced to the next line. If necessary, nonstring values are automatically converted to strings for display purposes. If the output will not fit on the line, then the display is continued on the next line (wrapped around).

EXAMPLE:

```
? "Today's date is :", TODAY( )
```

?? <expression list>

Display the value of each expression on the screen, left to right, starting at the current cursor position. The values are displayed without spaces between them. The display statement <expression list> is a list of expressions, and the members of the list are separated by commas. If necessary, nonstring values are automatically converted to strings for display purposes. If the output will not fit on the line, then the display is continued on the next line (wrapped around).

EXAMPLE:

```
@ 0,0 ?? "Today's date is :", TODAY( )
```

displays the output starting at row 0 and column 0

@ <row number>, <column number>

Position the cursor on the screen in the indicated position. The home position for the screen is in the upper lefthand corner, where row = 0 and column = 0. There are 25 lines on the screen (numbered 0 through 24) and 80 columns (numbered 0 through 79). Reference to a row or column outside these limits causes an error.

EXAMPLES:

```
@ 0,0 ?? "This is the home position"
R = 1
C = 2
@ R,C ?? "This is position 1,2"
@ ROW( )+1, COL( )+1 ?? "This is one position down and to the right"
```

ACCEPT <"data type"> <<PICTURE <"edit string">>> <<MIN <minimum value>>> <<MAX <maximum value>>> <<LOOKUP <"lookup table name">>> <<DEFAULT <default value>>> <<REQUIRED>> TO <variable name>

Get a value from the keyboard and store it in a variable. The data type must be one of the values that can be returned by the TYPE function: N (numeric), D (date), L (logical), S (short integer), and A<length> (character string). Input is allowed until the user presses RETURN. During entry, BACKSPACE can be used to delete the previous character, and CTRL-BACKSPACE can be used to delete the entire entry. If fewer keystrokes have been entered than is indicated by the data type or the edit string, then the user is so notified, a beep sounds, and entry continues.

PICTURE, MAX, MIN, and LOOKUP can be used to provide validity checking. The edit string in the PICTURE option specifies the format of the input, MAX specifies the upper bound, MIN specifies the lower bound, and LOOKUP specifies the table of allowable entries.

DEFAULT can be used to initialize the data area to facilitate entry of the expected input.

WARNING: The purpose of the <"data type"> in this statement is to define the type (and size) of the receiving field as it is displayed on the screen. The actual size of the variable is determined by the data itself. For example, if the data type is **A5** and if the entry area is displayed on the screen in reverse video, then five positions will be displayed in reverse video on the screen. The purpose of the PICTURE is to control the format for the input of the data, not the size of the display area. For example, if the edit string is **???**, then only three letters will be accepted. Unfortunately, it is possible to enter a data type and an edit string that are in conflict. For example, if the data type is **A2** and the edit string is ???, then you will only be able to enter two letters. Since the edit string specifies three characters, you will be informed by Paradox that the input is incomplete (INCOMPLETE FIELD) when you press RETURN. If you find yourself in such a situation, enter CTRL-BREAK to interrupt the execution of the program.

EXAMPLES:

```
STYLE ATTRIBUTE 7
                ; set normal video (gray on black)
@ 0,0 ?? "string a3:"
                ; display a prompt
STYLE ATTRIBUTE 112
                ; set reverse video
accept "a3" PICTURE "???" default "ABC" to a3
                ; get input
STYLE ATTRIBUTE 7
                ; set normal video
```

```
@ 1,0 ?? "short integer:"
                  ; display prompt
STYLE ATTRIBUTE 112
                  ; set reverse video
accept "s" picture "###" to s
                  ; get input
STYLE ATTRIBUTE 7
                  ; set normal video
@ 5,0 ?? a3
                  ; display value
@ 6,0 ?? s
                  ; display value
X=GETCHAR( )
                  ; freeze the screen
```

ADD <"source table name"> <"destination table name">

Use this statement to copy all the records from the source table to the destination table. You must be in Main mode to use this statement.

EXAMPLE:

```
ADD "FROMTABLE" "TOTABLE"
```

NOTE: The example is equivalent to the following sequence of Paradox keystrokes

```
Menu {Tools} {More} {add} {FROMTABLE}
    {TOTABLE}
```

ARRAY <array name> [<dimension>]

The name of the array may be any valid variable name. The dimension is a numeric expression that must evaluate to an integer between 1 and 15,000. You must assign a value to an array element before you reference that element. Different elements in an array can have different types, since each element of an array is treated by Paradox as a separate variable. An array cannot be passed as a parameter to a procedure, but can be declared PRIVATE within a procedure.

WARNING: You cannot have an array and a variable with the same name. For example, the code

```
ARRAY A[2]
A = 1
@ 1,1 ?? A[1]
```

will produce an error indicating that A is not an array at the time that the @ statement is executed. The first line of the code defines A as an array, but the second line of the code redefines A as an ordinary variable.

EXAMPLE 1:

```
ARRAY A[5]
```

EXAMPLE 2:

```
D = 100
ARRAY K[D + 3]
```

BEEP

Sound a tone at the terminal.

EXAMPLE:

```
BEEP
MESSAGE "Your entry is incorrect"
```

CANCELEDIT

This statement ends the current editing session without saving any changes. It is equivalent to the following sequence of Paradox keystrokes

```
Menu {Cancel} {Yes}
```

EXAMPLE:

```
IF <condition>
    THEN
            CANCELEDIT
ENDIF
```

CLEAR

Erase the screen. It is a wise idea to erase the screen at the beginning of each program and at appropriate times within each program. Any image on the screen before the CLEAR is not erased.

EXAMPLE:

```
CLEAR
```

CLEAR EOL

Erase from the current cursor position to the end of the current line. Any image on the screen before the CLEAR is not erased.

EXAMPLE:

```
CLEAR EOL
```

CLEAR EOS

Erase a rectangle from the current cursor position to the end of the screen. Any image on the screen before the CLEAR is not erased.

EXAMPLE:

```
CLEAR EOS
```

CLEARALL

Remove all images from the work area. An error will occur if Paradox is in Edit mode.

COPY <"source table name"> <"new table name 2">

Make a copy of a table and all its associated files (e.g., the index files) and assign a new name to the copy. Paradox must be in Main mode to use this statement. This statement can only be used to copy a Paradox database table, since you are not allowed to enter an extension (the extension .SC is assumed). If a table with the new name already exists, it is simply replaced with the new table.

EXAMPLE:

```
COPY "MYTABLE" "NEWTABLE"
```

NOTE: The example is equivalent to the following sequence of keystrokes

```
Menu {Tools} {Copy} {MYTABLE} {NEWTABLE}
    {Replace}
```

COPYFROMARRAY <array name>

Copy the contents of the named array to the fields in the current record of the current display image. Note that Paradox must be in Edit mode to use this statement. The array in use must have been created previously as a result of a COPYTOARRAY statement. It appears that one of the major uses of the COPYTOARRAY/COPYFROMARRAY statements is to transfer data easily from a database record to variables, edit or examine the contents of the variables, and then replace the contents of the record with a copy of the contents of the array (update the database record).

EXAMPLE:

```
EDIT "MYTABLE"
MOVETO RECORD 5
COPYTOARRAY MEMORY
        <manipulate the contents of the array>
COPYFROMARRAY MEMORY
```

COPYTOARRAY <array name>

An array of the given name is created and the contents of the current record of the current display image is copied into the array. If A is such an array and the image contains a column named X, then the corresponding element in the array is accessed by a reference of the form

```
A["X"]
```

The newly created array has a dimension one greater than the number of fields in the image, since both the field names and the field contents are stored in the array. If a field obtains its value as a result of a calculation rather than an assignment, then the content of the field is not copied to the array.

EXAMPLE:

See the previous section, COPYFROMARRAY.

CREATE <"new table name"> LIKE <"existing table name">

Create a new database table with the given name. If a table with this name already exists, it is replaced with the new one. The structure for the new table will match the structure for the existing table. The new table contains no data records.

EXAMPLE:

```
CREATE "NEWTABLE" LIKE "MYTABLE"
```

CREATE <"new table name"> <field list>, where each of the elements in the <field list> have the form <"field name"> : <"field type">

Create a new database table with the given name. Use the information in the field list to determine the fields in the table. If a table with this name already exists, it is replaced with the new one. The new table contains no data records. Use a designator of <"field type*"> to indicate a key field.

EXAMPLE:

```
CREATE "NEWTABLE" "SSN":"A9*", "NAME":"A25", "DATE":"D"
```

The new table will have three fields in it. The first field is a character string of length 9, the second field is a character string of length 25, and the third field is a date. The asterisk in the first field indicates that this field will be the key field.

CREATELIB <"library name">

This statement is available in Version 1.1 or higher and is used to create a new procedure library. The name of the library must start with a letter and must be between one and eight characters long. The library must exist on the disk before you can store a procedure using the WRITELIB statement. If you create a library with the same name as an existing one, the existing library, and all of its associated procedures, will be erased from the disk and replaced with the new (empty) library.

EXAMPLE:

```
CREATELIB "TESTLIB"
```

DEBUG

Use this statement to suspend execution of your program and enter Debug mode. The actual debugging starts at the statement immediately following the DEBUG statement. Once this statement has been executed, your program will be in the ordinary Debug mode, and all of the special CTRL key combinations will be in effect. In order to resume normal execution of your program (leave Debug mode and resume execution), enter CTRL-G (Go), or display the debug menu on the screen and select the Go function from the menu.

EXAMPLE:

```
<the debugged portion of your program>
DEBUG
<the code to be debugged>
```

DELETE <"table name">

This statement deletes the named table and all the associated files, such as indexes, forms, and reports. Paradox must be in Main mode at the time that this statement is used.

EXAMPLE:

```
DELETE "MYTABLE"
```

NOTE: The above example is equivalent to the following sequence of keystrokes

```
MENU {TOOLS} {DELETE} {TABLE} {MYTABLE} {OK}
```

DOS

This statement is available in Version 1.1 or higher and is used to suspend Paradox and invoke DOS. After you have completed your DOS work, enter the command EXIT to return to Paradox at the point of interruption. You must not run memory resident programs or use DOS commands like PRINT and MODE after using the DOS statement and before reentering Paradox, or Paradox will not be able to continue correctly. Note that this statement is equivalent to the following sequence of keystrokes: MENU {TOOLS} {MORE} {TODOS} and to the keystrokes CTRL-0.

EXAMPLE:

```
DOS
```

ECHO <option>, where <option> is FAST, SLOW, or OFF

The purpose of the ECHO statement is to enable or to disable the display of the actions of an executing program. FAST causes a smaller delay between the execution of the actions (and the subsequent display) than does SLOW. You can selectively turn the display on with either the ECHO FAST or the ECHO SLOW statements, and you can turn the display off with the ECHO OFF statement. It is recommended that you place the ECHO OFF statement in the beginning of the main driver for your application system.

EDIT <"table name">

The EDIT statement is used to edit the contents of a table. When this statement is executed, an image of the table is brought to the screen and Paradox changes to Edit mode.

EXAMPLE:

```
EDIT "MYTABLE"
```

NOTE: The example is equivalent to the following sequence of keystrokes

```
MENU {MODIFY} {EDIT} {MYTABLE}
```

EMPTY <“table name”>

Physically delete all of the records from the named table.

EXAMPLE:

```
EMPTY "MYTABLE"
```

NOTE: The example is equivalent to the following sequence of keystrokes

```
Menu {Tools} {More} {Empty} {MYTABLE} {Ok}
```

EXECUTE <“command”>

The EXECUTE statement provides a macro facility by allowing you to store a Paradox command in a character string and then execute the command. The <“command”> may actually be a sequence of PAL commands. When an EXECUTE statement is executed, Paradox creates a temporary program (named Execute). If the RETURN statement appears in the program named Execute, execution of this statement passes control of execution back to the program containing the original EXECUTE statement.

EXAMPLE:

```
MYTABLE = "MYTABLE"
COMSTRING = "VIEW  "
TABLENAME = "MYTABLE"
EXECUTE COMSTRING+TABLENAME
```

In this example, when the EXECUTE statement is executed, the command to be executed is

```
VIEW MYTABLE
```

Since there are no quotation marks around MYTABLE, it is interpreted as a variable name—hence the inclusion of the first line of the example to give a value to this variable. Equivalent code that uses embedded quotation marks is given next.

```
COMSTRING = "VIEW  "
TABLENAME = "\"MYTABLE\""
EXECUTE COMSTRING+TABLENAME
```

In this version, the backslash (\) indicates to Paradox that the next character (the quote) should be taken literally, i.e., it should be included as part of the character string and not be used as a delimiter. As a result, then the EXECUTE statement is executed, the command to be executed is

```
VIEW "MYTABLE"
```

which is in the correct format to be executed.

NOTE: The maximum length of the <"command"> is 255 characters.

EXIT

Use this statement to exit from Paradox and return to MS/DOS. You will want to use this statement when you wish to exit from your application system.

NOTE: This statement is equivalent to the following sequence of keystrokes

```
Menu {Exit} {Yes}
```

IF <condition>
THEN <then clause>
ELSE <else clause>
ENDIF

This is the Paradox IF-THEN-ELSE. The <then clause> and the <else clause> may be any sequence of valid paradox statements. Note that the ELSE and its clause are optional. There must be one ENDIF for every IF in your program.

INFOLIB <"library name">

This statement is available in Version 1.1 or higher and is used to list the names of the procedures stored in the library. When the statement is executed, a temporary list table is created and the names of the procedures are stored in this table. In addition to the name of each procedure, the space used to store each procedure is given. This statement corresponds to the DIR command in DOS.

EXAMPLE:

```
INFOLIB "TESTLIB"
```

INDEX <"table name"> ON <"field name">

Use this statement to create a secondary index for the table based on the given field. Whenever you access a table, either in the form of a query or through the use of a LOCATE statement, then Paradox examines the indexes to see if one can be used. If one can be used, it is automatically selected for use by Paradox. When you create a secondary index, two files are used to store the index information. If the name of the table is MYTABLE, then the two new files are MYTABLE.Xnn and MYTABLE.Ynn, where nn is the number of the field on which the index is based, in hexadecimal notation. A secondary index is automatically updated when you add, delete, or modify records in the table. The actual update takes place when you subsequently access the table, not when it is modified. Since the first field of a table-keyed table is always used in the primary index, you should avoid creating a secondary index just for this field. Do not attempt to create (or recreate) a secondary index when the table is being edited.

EXAMPLE:

```
INDEX "MYTABLE" ON "SSN"
```

KEYPRESS <keystroke>, where <keystroke> is a non-negative integer or a single character string for an ASCII code, a negative integer for an extended IBM code, and a character string that names a special key name

When this statement is used, the keystroke identified by <keystroke> is passed to Paradox just as if it had been entered at the keyboard. This statement allows your program to intercept responses from the user and convert them to instructions to Paradox.

EXAMPLES:

```
KEYPRESS 65
```

passes the letter A to Paradox

```
KEYPRESS "A"
```

also passes the letter A to Paradox

```
KEYPRESS "F1"
```

passes the keystroke for F1 to Paradox

```
KEYPRESS "MENU"
```

is equivalent to passing F10 to Paradox

```
IF RESPONSE = "Y"
    THEN
          KEYPRESS "F1"
ENDIF
```

intercepts a user response and passes a different keystroke to Paradox

LOCATE << NEXT >> <expression>

Use this command to find a record in the current column of the current table (display image) that contains the value of the expression. Use the MOVETO statement to position the currency pointer to the desired column in the table. If the NEXT option is used, then the search starts with the current record; otherwise the search starts at the beginning of the table. If the search was successful, then the system variable RETVAL is set to True, otherwise it is set to False. Paradox automatically uses any appropriate primary or secondary indexes for the search process. As a result, this statement is the one to be used for direct access to a record in a table.

EXAMPLES:

```
VIEW "MYTABLE"
MOVETO [SSN]
LOCATE "123-45-6789"
```

is an example of a direct access to a specific record

```
EDIT "SALES"
MOVETO [ACCOUNT_NUMBER]
LOCATE 125
WHILE RETVAL
        <process the record here>
        DOWN
        LOCATE NEXT 125
ENDWHILE
```

is an example of a direct access to the first record in the table with the desired value, followed by a loop that accesses all remaining records in the table with the same field value. The access in the loop automatically uses the index on the field [ACCOUNT_NUMBER], if there is one. Note the use of the DOWN command, which makes the next record the current record. Since the LOCATE statement starts the search with the current record, if you neglect to include the DOWN command in this manner in your loop, your program will be caught at the first record found and an infinite loop will occur.

LOCATE << NEXT >> <list of n expressions>

This form of the LOCATE statement must have at least two expressions in the list (n must be > = 2). Paradox searches the first n columns in the table for a match of all the given expression values. When you use this form of the LOCATE statement, the first n columns of the table are used, so no MOVETO statement is required to position the search at a specific column. A record is selected (located) if the value in the record in column 1 matches the value in the first expression, the value in the record in the second column matches the value in the second expression, and so on. This form of the LOCATE can be used both for direct access to a single record and for sequential access to a number of records (with the desired values).

EXAMPLE 1:

```
EDIT "MYTABLE"
LOCATE "123-45-6789", 100
```

is an example of direct access to a specific record in the table, using two values

EXAMPLE 2:

```
EDIT "SALES"
LOCATE "Smith", 125
WHILE RETVAL
        <process the record here>
        DOWN
        LOCATE NEXT "Smith", 125
ENDWHILE
```

is an example of a direct access to the first record in the table with the desired values, followed by a loop that accesses all remaining records in the table with the same field values. The access in the loop automatically uses the appropriate indexes, if there are any. Note the use of the DOWN command, which makes the next record the current record. Since the LOCATE statement starts the search with the current record, if you neglect to include the DOWN command in this manner in your loop, your program will be caught at the first record found and an infinite loop will occur.

WARNING: Paradox must be in Edit mode in order for the LOCATE NEXT to work correctly, i.e., in order for Paradox to be able to find a record if it is last in the table. Note also that Paradox must be in Table view, not Forms view, for the LOCATE NEXT to work correctly.

LOOP

When this statement is executed inside of a WHILE or SCAN loop, control is immediately passed to the nearest ENDWHILE or ENDSCAN (the nearest end-of-loop marker). This causes all the remainder of the statements in the loop to be skipped, but, except for the skipping of these statements, the loop continues to execute in the normal manner.

EXAMPLE:

```
EDIT "SALES"
MOVETO [LAST NAME]
LOCATE "Smith"
WHILE RETVAL
        IF <this is not one of the desired records>
                THEN
                        DOWN
                        LOCATE NEXT "Smith"
                        LOOP
        ENDIF
        <process the record here>
        DOWN
        LOCATE NEXT "Smith"
ENDWHILE
```

MESSAGE <expression list>, where the members of the list are separated by commas and the type of each expression is arbitrary

The values in the expression list are converted, if necessary, to character strings and are all displayed at once in the Paradox message area. The message area appears at the lower righthand corner of the screen either in reverse video or with a color background. The message remains on the screen either until the user presses a key (enters a keystroke) or until the program clears the screen. The size of the message areas is automatically adjusted by Paradox to accommodate the length of your message.

EXAMPLES:

```
MESSAGE "The value in record number ", RECNO( ), "is ",X
```

might display the message

```
The value in record number 1 is 10
```

in the message area.

```
MESSAGE "The record will be deleted"
```

MOVETO <field specifier>

This statement is used to make the named field the current field in the current record of the current table image. This statement is often used before a LOCATE statement to specify the column to be used for the scan. One of the major uses of this statement is to specify which of the images in the workspace is to become the current image.

EXAMPLE 1:

```
VIEW "MYTABLE"
MOVETO [SSN]
```

See also the example for the LOCATE statement.

EXAMPLE 2:

```
VIEW "X"
VIEW "Y"
EDIT "Z"
MOVETO [X —> SOMEFIELD]
```

MOVETO RECORD <record number>

This statement is used to make a specific record the current record in the current table image. The record number must be an integer between one and the number of records in the table (NRECORDS("table name")).

EXAMPLES:

```
VIEW "MYTABLE"
MOVETO RECORD 10
MOVETO RECORD NRECORDS("MYTABLE")
```

PASSWORD <password list>, where each password is a character string

When this statement is executed, the entire list of passwords is given to Paradox. Paradox stores these passwords for later reference. Then, whenever access is made to a password-protected table, Paradox looks in the list of passwords for a match. If the desired password is in the list, then Paradox allows access to the table without challenge.

EXAMPLE:

```
PASSWORD "TABLE", "ASC123", "MYFILE"
```

PICKFORM <"form name"> or PICKFORM <form number>

Use this statement to select a custom form for viewing the current display image. If the parameter is not a character string, then it is automatically converted to one. The parameter can be the letter F or any one of the digits between 1 and 9.

EXAMPLES:

```
PICKFORM "F"
PICKFORM "2"
PICKFORM 2
```

NOTE: The last example is equivalent to the following sequence of keystrokes

```
MENU {IMAGE} {PICKFORM} {2}
```

WARNING: It is a good idea to select a form just before it is used and then to revert to Table view after the form is used (KEYPRESS "F7"). When the PICKFORM statement is used, Paradox expects that specific form number to have been defined for each table (image) accessed from that point on, until you either select another form number or until you change back to Table mode. If there is no such form for an image, then Paradox can act in an unexpected manner—for example, Paradox can freeze up.

PLAY <"program name">

This statement is used to execute a program or subroutine. The name of the program is the name of the file in which it is stored. If the name of the program is X, then the name of the file must be X.SC, i.e., the extension of the file name must be SC.

EXAMPLE:

```
PLAY "MYPROG"
```

WARNING: The name of the program must not exceed eight characters, the maximum file name allowed in MS/DOS. For example, if you create a file named COMPANIE.SC and try to refer to it as COMPANIES in a PLAY statement (PLAY "COMPANIES"), then there will be an error when the PLAY statement is executed.

PRINT <expression list>, where each expression is of arbitrary type. This statement automatically converts each value to a character string before output

Output the value of each expression to the printer. The values are printed in sequence, on one line, without any separating spaces. The inclusion of certain characters preceded by the backslash character (\) can be used to send special control characters to the printer.

CHARACTERS	ACTION	KEYSTROKE
\f	Form feed	(CTRL-L)
\n	Line feed	(CTRL-J)
\0	Null character	
\r	Carriage return	(CTRL-M)
\t	Tab	(CTRL-I)

You must include your own control characters, or output will be performed as one long line, even with multiple executions of the PRINT statement.

EXAMPLES:

```
PRINT "First line.\r\n", "Second line."
PRINT "\f"
```

can be used to cause a form feed

PRINT FILE <"file name">, <expression list>

This statement is basically similar to the previous PRINT statement, except that the output is appended to the end of the names file. If the names file does not exist, a file of that name is first created, and then the values of the expressions are appended to the file.

EXAMPLE:

```
PRINT FILE "MYREPORT", "Date :", TODAY( )
```

PRINTER ON/OFF

Use this statement to enable or disable output to the printer through the use of the ?, the ??, and the TEXT statements. When the PRINTER is ON, output to the screen through these statements is also echoed to the printer. You may find this statement useful for debugging purposes.

EXAMPLE:

```
<part of the program here>
PRINTER ON
<more of the program here>
PRINTER OFF
<the remainder of the program here>
```

PRIVATE <variable list>

This statement is used to make variables local to a procedure, and should appear immediately after the PROC statement. If a global variable, say X, is used in a program, you can create a new variable (also called X) for use within the procedure. When execution of the procedure starts, X is a new name for a new variable and does not refer to the global variable X. When execution of the procedure terminates, the original value of X is restored. You can use the PRIVATE statement to guarantee that variables that are used only within the procedure do not accidentally change any global variables.

EXAMPLE:

```
PROC MYPROC()
        PRIVATE X,Y,Z
        <sequence of commands>
ENDPROC
```

PROC <procedure name> (<parameter list>)

This statement starts a procedure. The procedure name and each of the parameters are unquoted names (are not enclosed in quotation marks). The list of formal parameters may be empty. In this case, you must follow the name of the procedure with empty parentheses. Once a procedure has been defined, a procedure of the same name encountered in a program is ignored, so that the quick code is generated only once, not each time the procedure is encountered. If procedures are released (RELEASE PROCS), then encountering a procedure with the same name causes the procedure to be defined as if it were a new procedure.

EXAMPLE:

```
PROC MYPROC(A,B,C)
        .
        .
        .
        RETURN Z
ENDPROC
```

NOTE: The physically last statement in a procedure should be ENDPROC. In order to terminate execution of a procedure, use the RETURN statement. Note also that the RETURN can be used to pass a value back to the calling routine, effectively allowing you to use a procedure as a user-defined function.

PROTECT <"table name"> <"password">

Encrypt a table and assign an access password to it. This statement is equivalent to protecting a table through the use of a sequence of Paradox keystrokes. This statement cannot be used to protect a script, only a table. To protect a table, use the usual menu selections.

EXAMPLE:

```
PROTECT "MYTABLE" "MYPASSWORD"
```

NOTE: The example is equivalent to the following sequence of Paradox keystrokes

```
MENU {TOOLS} {MORE} {PROTECT} {PASSWORD}
    {TABLE} {MYTABLE} {MYPASSWORD}
    {MYPASSWORD}
```

QUERY <query forms> ENDQUERY

Place a query on the screen. To execute the query, select the Do_it! function from the menu. A query form can be constructed interactively and then saved using the QuerySave function in the scripts menu. This technique appears to be the only viable method to construct such a query. You can then use the Paradox to copy this saved query program into your PAL program, as needed. References to PAL variables appear in such a query as a name preceded by a tilde (~). You will need to insert the tilde yourself, after the query has been saved.

QUIT <message>, where the type of the message is arbitrary

Terminate the execution of the current program, display a message at the lower righthand corner of the screen, and pass control to Paradox (not to DOS). See also the EXIT statement.

EXAMPLE:

```
QUIT "Emergency abort."
```

QUITLOOP

Exit from the current loop and go directly to the statement that immediately follows the end-of-loop marker. If the current loop is a WHILE loop, then go to the statement immediately following the ENDWHILE. If the current loop is a SCAN loop, then go to the statement immediately following the ENDSCAN. You may wish to use this statement rather than use a RETURN statement within a loop. In a number of situations, I found that a RETURN statement within a WHILE loop caused an internal Paradox error in version 1.0.

EXAMPLE:

```
WHILE <condition 1>
        .
        .
        .
        IF <condition 2>
              THEN
                    QUITLOOP
        ENDIF
        .
        .
        .
ENDWHILE
```

READLIB <"library name"> <procedure name 1>, <procedure name 2>, . . . , <procedure name n>

This statement is available in Version 1.1 or higher and is used to load procedures stored in a procedure library. Once a procedure has been loaded using this statement, it is available for immediate execution. You can use this statement to retrieve procedures from a library and prepare them for execution.

EXAMPLE:

```
READLIB "TESTLIB" MAIN, FIRST, SECOND
```

RELEASE PROCS

Deallocate all procedures and release the space occupied by the procedures. You cannot release just one procedure at a time. Releasing procedures can be a good technique to regain main memory when the procedures have been used and are no longer needed.

RELEASE VARS ALL

Deallocate all the variables and arrays and release the space occupied by the variables and arrays. It is a good idea to release all the variables and arrays on a periodic basis to gain control over global variables.

EXAMPLE:

```
WHILE TRUE
        SHOWMENU
                "A": "EXIT"
                "B": "PROCESS B"
                "C": "PROCESS C"
        TO CODE
        SWITCH
                CASE CODE = "A"
                        EXIT
                CASE CODE = "B"
                        PLAY "PROGB"
                CASE CODE = "C"
                        PLAY "PROGC"
                OTHERWISE: MESSAGE "Illegal entry. Please
                    re-enter."
        ENDSWITCH
        RELEASE ALL
ENDWHILE
```

RELEASE VARS <variable list>

Deallocate selected variables and/or arrays and release the space occupied by the variables and arrays. If you reference a variable or array that has not been defined yet, the reference is ignored.

EXAMPLE:

```
RELEASE VARS A, B, C, UPPERL
```

RENAME <“current table name”> <“new table name”>

Change the name of a table and also the name of all the associated files, such as indexes and forms. Do not include the extension in either table name.

EXAMPLE:

```
RENAME "MYTABLE" "NEWNAME"
```

NOTE: The example is equivalent to the following sequence of keystrokes

```
MENU {TOOLS} {RENAME} {TABLE} {MYTABLE}
    {NEWTABLE}
```

REPORT <“table name”> <report designator>, where <report designator> is “R”, a single-digit numeric character, or a digit, with the digits between one and nine

This statement invokes the report writer using the indicated report form for the given table. When the report is produced, it goes to the printer. This statement can be used only when Paradox is in Main mode.

EXAMPLE:

```
REPORT "MYTABLE" 1
```

NOTE: The example is equivalent to the following sequence of keystrokes

```
MENU {REPORTS} {OUTPUT} {MYTABLE} {1}
    {PRINTER}
```

RESET

If Paradox is not in Main mode, cancel the current activity, clear the workspace, and go to Main mode. You can use this statement to reinitialize Paradox before a program is run. This statement does not affect variables, arrays, or procedures.

RETURN << expression >>

This statement is used to pass control back to a calling program. You can also optionally pass a value back to the calling program. Both procedures and programs (scripts) may return values. If a procedure is used within an expression, it must return a value. See the following for an example. If a procedure is used in a stand-alone manner, then any value returned is ignored by Paradox. If a program returns a value, it is displayed in the message area at the lower righthand corner of the screen, a feature that you may find useful for debugging purposes. As an unusual side effect of the use of the RETURN statement, the value returned is also stored in the system variable named RETVAL.

EXAMPLE 1: A procedure within an expression

```
X = MYPROC(A) * OTHERPROC(B)
```

In this example, the two procedures are expected to pass back (return) values. The procedure MYPROC might have the following form

```
PROC MYPROC(FA)
        .
        .
        .
        RETURN <value>
ENDPROC
```

EXAMPLE 2: Using a procedure in a stand-alone manner

```
MYPROC(A)
```

In this case, the procedure is not expected to return a value, so any value returned is simply ignored.

WARNING: In version 1.0, the RETURN statement may cause an internal Paradox error if it appears within a WHILE loop. If you encounter this type of error, merely replace the RETURN statement with a QUITLOOP statement and then place the RETURN statement immediately after the loop. See Chapter 8 for several examples.

RUN <<SLEEP <milliseconds> >> <"DOS command">

This statement is available in Version 1.1 or higher and is used to execute a DOS command from within Paradox. You can use the SLEEP option to cause a pause to take place. The value of <milliseconds> can be from 0 to 30,000, effectively causing a pause of up to 30 seconds. In addition to DOS commands, you can run COM, EXE, or BAT files. When the DOS operation has been completed, Paradox automatically resumes at the point of interruption. If you are using a dual floppy system, make sure that COMMAND.COM is located on the disk in drive A.

EXAMPLE 1:

```
RUN SLEEP 3000 "DIR A:"
```

This example shows how to list the directory of drive A and then pause for 3 seconds before returning to Paradox.

EXAMPLE 2:

```
RUN "WS"
```

This example shows how to call the WordStar editor to change a script.

EXAMPLE 3:

Since commands of this type are really statements in a program (script), there are two ways to invoke such a command: you can place the

```
RUN "WS"
```

statement in a script and invoke it each time that you wish to use your own editor, or you can use the SETKEY command to associate your RUN command with a single keystroke, making the use of your editor much more practical. The desired SETKEY command is

```
SETKEY "F1" RUN "WS"
```

SAVEVARS ALL
SAVEVARS <variable list>, where the variable list is a list of names of variables and/or arrays

Both forms of the SAVEVARS statement create a program named SAVEVARS.SC that contains sufficient information to restore the variable and array names and their contents. If a variable or array has no value at the time that the statement is executed, then no reference to it will appear in SAVEVARS.SC. SAVEVARS.SC will contain the assignment statements necessary to restore the variables and values at a later time. The value used is the current value at the time of the creation of the SAVEVARS program. The first form saves all variables and arrays, including RETVAL, a variable used by the Paradox system. The second form saves only the variables and arrays that you select.

SCAN

```
SCAN << FOR <condition> >>
        .
        . <commands go here>
        .
```

ENDSCAN

Starting with the first record in the table, visit each record in a table, optionally select records, and apply a collection of statements to the selected records. If a FOR clause does not appear in the statement, all the records are selected. When a record is selected, the commands are executed. In this manner, you can apply a sequence of commands to each record in the table. Since the SCAN is a type of loop, you can use the LOOP and the QUITLOOP statements within it. Use the LOOP to skip statements within the body of the SCAN and use QUITLOOP to exit from the SCAN. If the QUITLOOP statement does not appear in the body of the SCAN, then, when the SCAN has been completed, the last record in the table will be the current record.

EXAMPLE 1:

```
EDIT "MYTABLE"
MOVETO [LAST NAME]
SCAN FOR NOT ISBLANK([])
        IF NOT PRINTERSTATUS()
            THEN
                MESSAGE "The printer is not ready yet."
                X = GETCHAR()
        ENDIF
        PRINT [LAST NAME], " ", [AMOUNT_OWED], "\r\n"
ENDSCAN
PRINT "\f"
```

EXAMPLE 2:

```
EDIT "MYTABLE"
MOVETO [LAST NAME]
SCAN
        IF ISBLANK([])
           THEN
               LOOP
        ENDIF
        PRINT [LAST NAME], " ", [AMOUNT_OWED], "\r\n"
ENDSCAN
PRINT "\f"
```

This rather contrived example illustrates the use of the LOOP statement within the body of the SCAN.

WARNING: You will probably want to be in Edit mode when the SCAN statement is used; otherwise the SCAN can cause an infinite loop by leaving the currency pointer at the last record of the image.

SELECT <Paradox menu item>

This statement allows you to select items from a Paradox system menu, one item at a time. The <Paradox menu item> can be a character string constant or variable, allowing a considerable amount of flexibility.

EXAMPLE:

```
SELECT "VIEW"
CODE = "MYTABLE"
SELECT CODE
```

NOTE: The example is equivalent to the following sequence of keystrokes

```
MENU {VIEW} {MYTABLE}
```

SETDIR <"directory name">

This statement is available in Version 1.1 or higher and is used to change the name of the current directory. Paradox must be in MAIN MODE when this statement is executed, or an error occurs. When this statement is used, the workspace is cleared and all temporary files are deleted from memory before the change is made. If a backslash appears in the directory name, then it must appear twice (it must be doubled) each time that it is used. This statement is equivalent to the following sequence of keystrokes

```
MENU {TOOLS} {MORE} {DIRECTORY} {"directory name"} {OK}
```

EXAMPLE:

```
SETDIR "A:\\ALTREFLE"
```

SETKEY <key name> <statement list>

This statement is used to associate a sequence of statements with a keystroke. If the statement list is empty, then any statements previously associated with the keystroke are disassociated and the keystroke returns to its original function. All three elements of this statement must appear on one line. If you have too many statements in the list to fit on one line, use a single statement that calls a program. A collection of statements associated with a keystroke is called a keyboard macro. The choices for <key name> include each of the following:

1. Single character strings
2. Integers between 0 and 255 (ASCII codes)
3. Negative integers (IBM extended codes)
4. Function key designators
5. PAL key names

EXAMPLES:

SETKEY "F1" MENU {VIEW} "MYTABLE"

will assign to F1 the statements that start the process for placing an image of MYTABLE on the screen, but the user will still need to press RETURN to complete the selection and display

SETKEY "F1" MENU

change the meaning associated with F1

SETKEY "F1"

will return F1 to its original meaning, the help function

SETKEY " ^ " PLAY "MYPROG"
SETKEY "HOME" PLAY "MYPROG"

WARNING: When a keyboard macro is used, it does not always work as expected. For example, when the statement SETKEY "F1" MENU {SCRIPTS} {EDITOR} {EDIT} "MYFILE" is used, it fails. When the {SCRIPTS} function is selected from the Paradox menu in this manner (when F1 is pressed) the menu that is displayed in the screen does not contain EDITOR as a selection. As a result, you will need to thoroughly test each keyboard macro before use.

SHOWMENU

```
        <"menu item 1"> : <"prompt 1">
                          .
                          .
                          .
        <"menu item n"> : <"prompt n">
        << DEFAULT <"menu item i"> >>
    TO <variable name>
```

Use this statement to display a Paradox-style menu at the top of the screen and capture the user response. The user can select an item from the menu either by moving the highlight to the desired function and pressing RETURN, or by entering the first letter of the function name. When a menu item is selected, then the value to the left of the colon (:) is captured in the named variable. If the user presses the ESCAPE key, then the string "Esc" is placed in the variable, and control returns to the program. You can use the DEFAULT option to initially position the highlight when the menu is first entered and when control returns to a calling program that displays a menu. Alternatively, you may create your own menus using a sequence of @ . . . ?? statements, followed by an ACCEPT statement to capture the user response.

EXAMPLE:

```
SHOWMENU
        "Exit":         "Exit from the system"
        "Invoices"    : "Invoice subsystem"
        "Companies":    "Company subsystem"
        "Reports"     : "Print reports"
        DEFAULT "Exit"
TO ACTION
SWITCH
    CASE ACTION = "Exit"        : QUIT
    CASE ACTION = "Invoices"    : PLAY "INVOICES"
    CASE ACTION = "Companies":    PLAY "COMPANIE"
    CASE ACTION = "Reports"     : PLAY "REPORTS"
ENDSWITCH
```

SLEEP <number of milliseconds>

Use this statement to cause your program to pause for the specified number of milliseconds. The number that you select must be between 0 and 30,000, allowing a delay of up to 30 seconds. You can use this feature to freeze the screen for a specified number of seconds so that the user can see any message that you choose to display.

EXAMPLE:

```
MESSAGE "Illegal entry. Please Re-enter."
SLEEP 1000
```

SORT <"table name"> << ON <field name list> << D >> >> << TO <"new table name"> >>, where each field name is a character string constant or variable

Use this statement to sort the records in a table. If the ON option is not used, then the sort is based on all the fields in the table. If the ON option is used, then only the named fields are used to perform the sort. In this case, there is one sort for each named field, and the sorting takes place for the named fields in the order in which the names appear in the list. The default sort order is ascending. Use the D option (available only if you have also chosen the ON option) to sort in descending order. If the TO option is not selected, then the original table will be sorted and no new table will be created. If the TO option is used, then the sorted records will be placed in a new table and the original table will remain unchanged. If the source table is keyed, then the TO option *must* be used.

EXAMPLES:

```
SORT "MYTABLE" ON "LAST NAME", "FIRST NAME" TO
    "NEWFILE"
SORT "MYTABLE"
```

STYLE << <option list> >>

Use the STYLE statement to set certain attributes for screen output produced by ?, ??, or TEXT. The STYLE statement used without any options clears all the previously selected style options and the display reverts to the default (normal) display. The style options are as follows.

OPTION	MONOCHROME	COLOR
REVERSE	Reverse video	Cyan background
BLINK	Flashing characters	Flashing characters
INTENSE	High intensity	High-intensity green

EXAMPLE:

```
STYLE REVERSE, INTENSE
@ 23,0 ?? "Error."
STYLE
```

now the screen has been reset to normal display

STYLE ATTRIBUTE <integer>

This statement is similar to the previous form of the STYLE statement, except that you can choose from any of the style attributes offered by your particular color graphics board. For a complete listing of the attributes available for both the IBM monochrome and color graphics monitor, see Appendix A in the PAL User's Guide. Once an attribute has been set, it stays in effect until it is reset.

EXAMPLES:

```
STYLE ATTRIBUTE 41
```

displays light blue characters on a green background if you are using a color monitor, or high intensity with underlining if you are using a monochrome monitor

SUBTRACT <"source file name"> <"destination file name">

This statement is one of the standard relational database operators. Each record of the source file is compared one at a time with each record of the destination file. If an exact match is found, the record in the destination file is deleted. Paradox must be in Main mode to use this statement.

EXAMPLE:

```
SUBTRACT "MYFILE1" "MYFILE2"
```

NOTE: The example is equivalent to the following sequence of keystrokes

```
MENU {TOOLS} {MORE} {SUBTRACT} {MYFILE1}
    {MYFILE2}
```

SWITCH

```
CASE <condition 1> : <statement list 1>
                   .
                   .
                   .
CASE <condition n> : <statement list n>
<< OTHERWISE       : <statement list> >>
```

ENDSWITCH

This is the CASE statement in PAL. I recommend that you use the SWITCH statement instead of deeply nested IFs. Each of the conditions must evaluate either to True or to False. When the statement is executed, only the list of statements associated with the first True condition will be executed. If none of the conditions are True, and the optional OTHERWISE clause is used, then the statements associated with the OTHERWISE will be executed. If none of the conditions are TRUE and the OTHERWISE clause has not been included, then the SWITCH statement has no effect.

EXAMPLE:

```
SHOWMENU
        "Exit":        "Exit from the system"
        "Invoices"   : "Invoice subsystem"
        "Companies": "Company subsystem"
        "Reports"    : "Print reports"
        DEFAULT "Exit"
```

```
TO ACTION
SWITCH
        CASE ACTION = "Exit"          : QUIT
        CASE ACTION = "Invoices"      : PLAY "INVOICES"
        CASE ACTION = "Companies": PLAY "COMPANIE"
        CASE ACTION = "Reports"       : PLAY "REPORTS"
ENDSWITCH
```

TEXT

<one or more lines of text>

ENDTEXT

Use this statement to display one or more lines of text on the screen. The display starts at the current cursor position. Everything between the TEXT and the ENDTEXT statements is taken literally.

EXAMPLE:

```
TEXT
       This system has been especially designed for the
             SUPERIOR MANUFACTURING COMPANY.
ENDTEXT
SLEEP 5000
```

TYPEIN <keystrokes>

Use this statement to pass one or more keystrokes to Paradox as if they had been entered at the keyboard.

EXAMPLE:

```
ACCEPT "N" TO IDNO
VIEW "EMPLOYEE"
EDITKEY
MOVETO [ID #]
LOCATE 537
IF RETVAL
      THEN
              TYPEIN IDNO
```

```
ENDIF
DO_IT!
```

This code will obtain a number from the user, place the table EMPLOYEE on the screen in Edit mode, locate the record in which the ID # has the value of 537, and then append the user-entered number to the right of the current number. If the number entered by the user is 111, then the new ID # is 537111. To replace the curreent ID # with a new value, use the following code

```
ACCEPT "N" TO IDNO
VIEW "EMPLOYEE"
EDITKEY
MOVETO [ID #]
LOCATE 537
IF RETVAL
      THEN
              [] = IDNO
ENDIF
DO_IT!
```

UNPASSWORD <password list>, where each password is either a character string constant or variable

This statement reverses the effect of the PASSWORD statement. Once a password has been given to Paradox through the use of the PASSWORD statement, it is used by Paradox, as necessary, to verify access privilege to password-protected tables. The UNPASSWORD statement informs Paradox that you wish to remove one or more passwords from active use. At this point, you no longer have automatic access privilege to a table that requires the password that you have just removed. The passwords are removed from the list of passwords associated with the current session, not from tables.

EXAMPLE:

```
PASSWORD "FREE"
EDIT "MYTABLE"
```

.
.
.

```
UNPASSWORD "FREE"
```

Access to the table MYTABLE at this point would require you to enter the appropriate password.

VIEW <"table name">

Use this statement to place a new display image of the table on the screen. This image becomes the current image, and the first record in the table becomes the current record. The field containing the record numbers (the leftmost field) becomes the current field.

EXAMPLE:

```
@ 1,0 ?? "Enter the name of the table:"
ACCEPT "A8" TABLENAME      ; The user enters MYTABLE
VIEW TABLENAME
```

NOTE: This example is equivalent to the following sequence of keystrokes

```
MENU {VIEW} {MYTABLE}
```

WAIT <object type>
<<PROMPT <"prompt1"> <<, <"prompt2"> >> >>
<<MESSAGE <"msg1"> <<, <"msg2"> >> >>
UNTIL <keystroke list>

where each keystroke is a non-negative integer or a single character string for an ASCII code, a negative integer for an extended IBM code, or a character string that names a special key name. The object type is FIELD, RECORD, or TABLE.

Use this statement to temporarily halt a program, display a persistent prompt and a transient message, allow the user to manipulate the named object (a field, record, or table), and then, upon entry of one or more keystrokes, resume execution of the program. Ordinarily, when a VIEW statement is executed by a program, it is placed in the user's workspace but does not appear on the screen. When the WAIT statement is executed, the image of the table becomes visible on the screen, the prompt (up to two lines) is displayed at the top of the screen, and the message appears in the message area at the lower righthand corner of the screen. If you wish to allow the user to edit a field, record, or table, the EDIT statement should be executed before the WAIT statement is executed. If the object type is FIELD, then only the current field is available. If the object type is RECORD, then only the current record is available. If the object type is available, then the entire table is available, but the actions of the F7 and the F10 function keys are suppressed. The WAIT statement controls the user activity until one of the keystrokes in the list is entered.

The syntax and definition given above apply to Version 1.1 and higher. In Version 1.0, the PROMPT option is not allowed. In addition, in Version 1.0, only one message is allowed.

EXAMPLE:

```
@ 1,0 ?? "Enter an ID number:"
ACCEPT "N" TO IDNO
VIEW "EMPLOYEE"
MOVETO [ID #]
LOCATE IDNO
IF RETVAL
  THEN
      EDITKEY
      WAIT RECORD
          PROMPT "Press ESC when editing has been
               completed."
      UNTIL "Esc"
      DO_IT!
  ELSE
      @ 3,0 ?? "Cannot find the desired record."
      @ 5,0 ?? "Press any key to continue."
      X = GETCHAR()
ENDIF
```

WHILE <condition>
<statements>
ENDWHILE

This is the major type of loop. The WHILE loop is used both for counter- and condition-controlled loops. There must be one ENDWHILE statement in your program for every WHILE statement.

EXAMPLE 1: (Counter-controlled loop)

```
I = 1
WHILE I <= 10
        <statements>
        I = I + 1
ENDWHILE
```

EXAMPLE 2: (Condition-controlled loop)

```
EDIT "SALES"
MOVETO [LAST NAME]
LOCATE "Smith"
WHILE RETVAL
        IF <this is not one of the desired records>
              THEN
                      DOWN
                      LOCATE NEXT "Smith"
                      LOOP
        ENDIF
        <process the record here>
        DOWN
        LOCATE NEXT "Smith"
ENDWHILE
```

WRITELIB <"library name"> <procedure name 1>, <procedure name 2>, . . . , <procedure name n>

This statement is available in Version 1.1 or higher and is used to add one or more procedures to a procedure library. When a procedure is stored in a library, it is first examined for correctness and then stored in a form that insures rapid execution. Before you attempt to store a procedure in a library, the library must already have been created using the CREATELIB statement. You can store up to 50 procedures in one library. You can add a new procedure to a library at any time, and the addition of a procedure with a name that matches a procedure already in the library replaces the current version. At the time that this book was written, there was no way to delete a (just one) procedure from a library and leave the library intact. I expect that such a function will be available in the future.

When a procedure is added to a library, it must currently exist in memory, i.e., it must be defined in a program and must be in memory. Sample code to add a procedure to a library follows.

EXAMPLE:

```
PROC TESTPROC( )
        <body of procedure goes here>
ENDPROC

WRITELIB "TESTLIB" TESTPROC
```

2.4 THE EDITOR

Call the editor from the main Paradox menu. Select Script, Edit, and then Write to create a new program or Edit (again) to modify an existing program. A line may have up to 132 characters. While editing, you can press F1 to receive help with the various keystrokes and editing functions. The Paradox editor is quite simple in nature—for example, it does not allow you to search and replace. If you wish, you may use your usual editor (like WordStar). Just make sure that you use the .SC extension for each program. Nevertheless, you may find it convenient to use the Paradox editor rather than another editor, since it can be called from within Paradox, especially in the case when an error is encountered within your program. The result of the Paradox editor is a simple ASCII file. You cannot accidentally include special characters in your program that might cause a Paradox script error. The editor keystrokes and menu selections are given in the following table.

KEYSTROKE OR MENU SELECTION	ACTION
←	Go left one character
→	Go right one character
↑ (up arrow)	Go up one line
↓ (down arrow)	Go down one line
BACKSPACE	Delete the previous character
CANCEL	Terminate editing and discard the changes—called from the edit menu
CTRL-←	Scroll left
CTRL-→	Scroll right
CTRL-END	Go to the last character on the line
CTRL-HOME	Go to the first position on the line
CTRL-V	Toggle the vertical ruler on and off
CTRL-Y	Delete from cursor to end of the line
DEL	Delete the current character
END	Go to the last line
ENTER	Go to the next line—insert a blank line if in Insert mode
F1	Help
F2	Save the file
F10	Display the Paradox edit menu
GO	Save the file and execute the program—called from the edit menu
HOME	Go to the first line
INS	Toggle the Insert mode on and off
READ	Copy a file to current cursor position—called from the edit menu
RETURN	Go to the next line—insert a blank line if in Insert mode

2.5 DEBUGGING

When Paradox encounters an error in a program, the execution of the program stops and you will be asked whether you wish to cancel the execution or debug the program. If you decide to debug the program, you can select a number of different functions that will aid in the debugging process. In addition, you can halt the execution of a program by entering CTRL-BREAK and then select the debug menu by entering ALT-F10. The debugger can also be invoked from the main menu by entering the keystroke ALT-F10. The functions allowed in Debug mode are given in the following table.

KEYSTROKE	ACTION
CTRL-E	Go directly to the editor. After the changes have been made in the program, enter CTRL-G to directly execute the edited program.
CTRL-G	Execute the program directly.
CTRL-N	Skip to the next command.
CTRL-P	Immediately return to the next higher calling level.
CTRL-Q	Exit the debugger and cancel program execution.
CTRL-S	Execute one command at a time. This command is particularly helpful when you wish to see the individual statement actions. If your program seems to "die", then use the debugger and the CTRL-S key to see which statement in the program fails.
CTRL-W	Examine nesting of programs and procedures.

When you are debugging a program, and the program has halted, you may find it useful to interrogate Paradox for the current value of a variable or array element. Enter ALT-F10, select VALUE from the menu, and then enter the name of the variable. The value of the variable will be displayed in the lower righthand corner of the screen. Enter ALT-F10 and select VALUE for the current value of each variable or array element. If your program halts as a result of a QUIT, Paradox will return to the main menu but the current values of the variables are still available from Paradox. Simply enter ALT-F10 and then select VALUE in the usual manner.

CHAPTER

3 FUNDAMENTAL PAL PROGRAMMING CONCEPTS

3.1 INTRODUCTION

In every programming language, there are a small number of language elements that form the nucleus of the language. These are the statements that perform the following operations:

1. Input
2. Output
3. Assignment
4. Decision
5. Looping

Although the statements that perform these operations are explained elsewhere in this book, I have included them here because, when I learn a new language, I like to see how each of the above five operations are performed in the language. It is one thing to read a primer on the language, and quite another to start to build a structure for understanding the language.

3.2 OBTAINING INPUT FROM THE USER

In PAL there are two basic methods to obtain input from the user. Use the ACCEPT statement to get individual values from the user and use the DataEntry function available under the Modify entry in the Paradox main menu to enter new records. The ACCEPT statement is powerful, in that it allows you to specify each of the following:

1. The name, type, and size of the variable to receive the input
2. A PICTURE clause to specify the format for the input
3. Bounds for minimum and maximum values
4. A table for a list of acceptable input values
5. A suggested (default) input value

The DataEntry function allows the user to enter records interactively into a temporary database table with the same structure as the target table. Once the records have been entered into the temporary table, selection of the Do_it! function causes the newly added records to be transferred to the target database table.

3.3 PRODUCING OUTPUT

Output may be sent either to the screen or to the printer. The ? will send output to the next available line of the screen. If the screen is full, it will scroll. The ?? will send output to the current cursor position. The @ is used to position the cursor on the screen. The PRINTER ON/OFF statement is used to direct output from the ?, the ??, and the TEXT statements, either to the screen or to the printer. The default is to send output to the screen. An alternative technique for producing output is to use the REPORT statement, which invokes the Paradox report writer.

3.4 ASSIGNMENT

It is possible to assign values to variables or to fields in database tables (either the current table or some other named table). A variable is any storage location that is not a field in a database record. The operator for assignment to a variable or to a field is the equal sign (=). Paradox distinguishes between variables and fields in database records through the use of brackets ([ ]). When a name is enclosed in [ ]'s, it always refers to the name of a field. Note that [ ]'s are also used to denote subscripts in an array.

3.5 DECISION: THE IF-THEN-ELSE

The IF-THEN-ELSE construct is provided in the following form

```
IF expression
  THEN
      <statements>
  ELSE
      <statements>
ENDIF
```

and the IF–THEN is provided in the form

```
IF <condition>
  THEN
       <statements>
ENDIF
```

All the parts of the IF–THEN–ELSE may be on one line, but I recommend that you program as shown above, in order to increase the clarity of your code. Note that there must be a separate ENDIF for each IF.

3.6 LOOPING

There is only one type of loop. It is of the form

```
WHILE <condition>
       <statements>
ENDWHILE
```

All the parts of the WHILE loop may be on one line, but I recommend that you code as shown above to increase the clarity of your code. This statement satisfies the need for both a condition-controlled loop and a counter-controlled loop. To create counter-controlled loops, use the following type of construct

```
LOOPINDEX = 1
WHILE LOOPINDEX <= <value>
       <statements>
       LOOPINDEX = loopindex + 1
ENDWHILE
```

To skip all the statements in a loop from some point on, execute the statement LOOP. For example, if an error condition occurs in a loop and you wish to skip the remainder of the statements in the loop, use the following construct

```
WHILE <condition>
       <statements group a>
       IF ERROR
         THEN
```

```
            LOOP
        ENDIF
        <statements group b>
ENDWHILE
```

In this case, if ERROR is True, then <statements group b> will not be executed, but the execution of the loop continues if the expression is True. To leave a loop immediately, use the QUITLOOP statement. When this statement is executed, control passes to the statement immediately following the next ENDWHILE statement.

```
WHILE <condition>
        <statements group a>
        IF ERROR
          THEN
            QUITLOOP
        ENDIF
        <statements group b>
ENDWHILE
<next statement>
```

During the execution of this loop, if ERROR is True, then control passes to <next statement> when the QUITLOOP statement is executed.

PAL has an additional type of loop, the SCAN loop. The purpose of this type of loop is to select records from a database table and then apply a group of code to each of the records that has been selected. Both the LOOP and the QUITLOOP statements can be used in this type of loop.

CHAPTER

4 WORKING WITH DATABASE FILES

4.1 THE STRATEGY

Paradox contains a wide variety of features. Some of them are useful and others are not. Before you do any significant programming in PAL, it is a good idea to be able to answer each of the following:

1. What kind of file and program design works best for Paradox?
2. Which of the features of Paradox work correctly and which don't?
3. Which features of Paradox are fast and which are slow?
4. What programming aids are provided by the Paradox system?
5. How should the error message be interpreted?

Each of these questions will be addressed in this book.

4.2 GOALS FOR APPLICATION DEVELOPMENT

If you are a professional, you know that users often understand their own systems better than analysts do, at least at the start, and the analyst often has a considerable amount to learn about the current system before being able to construct a successful application system. Even if you are a user yourself and you plan to build a system for your own use, you will find that your understanding of the system will evolve over a period of time. In order for the analyst to be able to incorporate his or her improved understanding of the actual and the desired system into the design of the new system, the design must be as general as the analyst can make it.

> **GOAL NUMBER 1:** The design of the application system must be flexible enough to accommodate practically any kind of changes.

Because of the relatively slow speed of microcomputers, it is necessary to avoid any practices that will cause application programs to run slowly. Operations that take several seconds should be avoided, whenever possible, by substituting faster techniques.

GOAL NUMBER 2:	Features of Paradox that take several seconds to execute should be avoided when possible.

The application system should be as easy to use as you can make it. The user should be able to select appropriate functions from a menu rather than be forced to use an instruction manual. All the user instructions should be given in nontechnical terms. This does not mean that there should not be any documentation for the system, but rather that the first line of documentation should be the first menu itself. In addition, complex operations should be nested so that a complex function selected from one menu should display another menu on the screen.

GOAL NUMBER 3:	Make the application system as easy to use as possible. In particular, use menus that allow the selection of functions.

The application system should work correctly. Use modern analysis, design, and programming techniques when you build your system. Avoid the features of Paradox that are known to work incorrectly.

GOAL NUMBER 4:	The application system should work correctly. Use good analysis, design, and programming techniques and avoid the features of Paradox that don't work correctly.

An excellent source of modern analysis and design techniques that lead to a flexible design is a book by Tom DeMarco, titled *Structured Analysis and System Specifications* (Prentice-Hall, 1979). The following is a sketch of the techniques recommended in DeMarco's book, specially modified and simplified for use with Paradox.

4.3 USEFUL ANALYSIS AND DESIGN TECHNIQUES

The most fundamental aspect of analysis technique is to treat the data as the most important item under observation and to treat processes (programs) as data transformations. Start with an examination of the input and output documents. Determine the objects being described on these documents. For example, an employee time card contains information about two distinct objects: the employee and the work hours. In general, each object about which you gather data will appear (eventually) in the system as a record type. Each instance of an object type (in this case, each employee and each work time) will appear as a distinct record in a file, where all the records in one file have the same structure. There will be a file for employees and each record in this file will contain information for one employee. In addition, all the records in the employee file will have the same structure. There will also be a file for the work times (time cards). Since this is repeated information (there is one start and one stop time for each work period), this data should be stored in a time card file in the following manner.

> Each time card record will contain at least two fields. One field will link it to the appropriate employee record (probably through the employee number) and the other field will contain elapsed-time information. This record, depending on the requirements of the system, may contain more than two fields. For example, if start and stop dates and times are required, then the record will contain at least five fields: one field for the employee number, one for each of the start and stop dates, and one for each of the start and stop times.

After the files have been determined in this manner, consider the objects being described in each file (remember that each file should describe exactly one object). If the same object is being described in more than one file, consider combining these into a single file. Then determine the processes necessary to produce the desired outputs. To make the most flexible possible application system, try to make the processes as simple as possible (DeMarco calls such processes *functional primitives*). Then if processes have to be changed, the scope of effect of such changes is usually limited to the processes to be changed and any process for which it provides data. Examine the data needed by each process. If the data is already in a file, fine. If not, consider whether a file already in existence describes the same object (the missing data may be descriptive of an object already in a file). If so, simply add the new field to the appropriate existing record type. If there is no appropriate file in existence, you will need to create a new file containing the field(s) for the missing data.

The data file construction techniques described above lend themselves very well to programming in Paradox, since you can modify the structure of an existing file at any time and you can add indexes to a file at any time.

Example of File Construction

A client wants to produce a report indicating the number of hours employees spend on assigned projects. As you analyze the situation, you discover that there are three object types: employees, projects, and time cards. You decide to create three files, one for each object type. Let us call the files EMPLOYEE, PROJECTS, and TIMECARD. Further analysis indicates that the records in these files will need at least the following fields.

```
EMPLOYEE : EMPLOYEE_NO, NAME, HOURLY_RATE
PROJECTS : PROJECT_ID, MAX_BUDGET
TIMECARD: EMPLOYEE_NO, PROJECT_ID, DATE,
          ELAPSED_HOURS
```

After further discussions with the client you discover that the firm also desires to keep track of the employee costs associated with each project. For this purpose, you may add a new field to each PROJECTS record. The records in this file will then contain the fields:

```
PROJECTS : PROJECT_ID, MAX_BUDGET,
           EMPLOYEE_COSTS
```

You then discover that the client desires to give awards for the most productive employees. Since an employee may receive more than one award and since the client wishes to record each award for future reference, you decide to create a new file for the awards with the record structure:

```
AWARDS : EMPLOYEE_NO, AWARD_TYPE,
         DOLLAR_AMOUNT, DATE_OF_AWARD
```

These four files will represent the state of the analyst's understanding up to a particular point in time. Since they each describe one object, they each consist of a unique identifier for the object and descriptive information for the object. For example, the EMPLOYEE record has EMPLOYEE_NO as the unique identifier and NAME and HOURLY_RATE describe the employee. The object described by the TIMECARD file is the hours worked by an employee on a particular project on a particular date, so the unique identifier consists of the three fields EMPLOYEE_NO, PROJECT_ID, and DATE. Files (or more precisely, records in files) are logically related to each other in the following manner: If an employee with an EMPLOYEE_NO of 1 has worked on a project with a PROJECT_ID of P1, then the EMPLOYEE record with an EMPLOYEE_NO of 1 provides the employee's name and hourly salary, the PROJECTS record with a PROJECT_ID of P1 provides the budget information, and the TIMECARD records with an EMPLOYEE_NO of 1 and a PROJECT_ID of P1 provide the time that this employee has worked on this project. If the specific start and stop times for work performed by employees are recorded in the TIMECARD file and if the client desires the time worked on a specific day by this employee on this project, then this information is available.

The example given above illustrates a number of points.

1. In a number of simple systems, the construction of the files can start with an examination of the input documents.
2. As the understanding of the analyst grows, the files that have been constructed from the input documents can be modified to match more closely what is desired by the client.
3. A good choice of file structure will make it easy to change the system when modifications are necessary.

The principles of good analysis and design will be continued in subsequent chapters of this book.

4.4 SPECIFYING THE DATABASE FILE(S)

There may be any number of database files currently in use, but only one of them (the most recently accessed) is considered to be the current file (table). A table is opened through the use of the VIEW statement, which creates an image of the table in the workspace. When a table is opened in this manner, it is not an open file in the DOS sense. Therefore, you are not limited by the FILES statement in CONFIG.SYS. Whenever you access a table for direct access to a record in the table, Paradox automatically examines the primary and secondary indexes. If an index exists that will speed up the access, then it is used. The programmer has no responsibility to inform Paradox of which indexes should be used. The programmer merely creates the indexes once and Paradox uses them as needed.

4.5 CREATING DATABASE FILES

Database tables are created through the use of the CREATE command. The user is prompted in graphic form for the name, type, and size of each field. You may create a primary index on any contiguous collection of fields as long as you start with the first field in the table. You may also create a secondary index on any (one) field in the table. You may create an index on any type of field in a database table. Nevertheless, as a general principle, I have found it to be a good idea to make a field numeric only if I expect that I might need to perform arithmetic operations with it.

> **HINT:** When creating a database table, make those fields numeric only when you actually expect to use them in arithmetic operations.

There are six data types in Paradox, but only five of them can be used to type a field in a table. They are given in the following table.

DATA TYPE	DESCRIPTION
A	Character string
D	Date
N	Numeric (real number)
S	Short number
$	Dollar

The other data type, logical, is used only with variables and constants. When you specify a character string, you must also specify the length of the string. For example, to specify a character string of length 25, use the type specification of A25. You can specify a length (field width) only for a character string.

When you specify the name of a database table, never enter more than 8 characters. The length of a field name is limited to 25 characters. Note that this is different from the length of a variable name, which is 132 characters. Always enter the name of a database table without an extension. Paradox will append the correct extension to the name for you.

4.6 STORING DATA IN A DATABASE FILE

There are two major techniques for adding a new record to an existing file. The first is to use the DataEntry function in the Modify menu, and the second is to use the Edit function in the Modify menu. Use DataEntry when you wish to enter new records in Interactive mode. You can select the specific form to be used for the entry of the new records (including the system default form) simply by using the PICKFORM statement. Use Edit when you wish to enter a new record under program control. Typical code for the second technique using the Edit function is

```
ECHO OFF              ; do not show unnecessary Paradox activity
EDIT "EMPLOYEE"       ; select the table to be edited
END                   ; go to the last record in the table
DOWN                  ; append a blank record to the end
PICKFORM "F"          ; select the form to be use for the input
WHILE TRUE            ; start the input loop
        WAIT RECORD ; transfer control to user for entry of record
            MESSAGE "PRESS F2 WHEN ENTRY HAS BEEN COMPLETED"
        UNTIL "F2"
        IF ISBLANK( [ID #] ) ; if this field is empty after record has been entered,
                      ; assume that user has no more records to enter
             THEN
                     DEL ; delete this empty record
                     QUITLOOP ; exit from the loop
        ENDIF
```

```
[15]        MOVETO [ID #]; makes ID # the current field
[16]        LOCATE [ID #] ; see if there already is a record in the table with this ID # value
[17]        IF NOT ATLAST() ; if there already is a record in the table with this ID #
                            ; value, then skip the entry of this record
[18]            THEN
[19]                  MESSAGE "a record is already on file for this ID #"
[20]                  BEEP          ; make a sound
[21]                  SLEEP 2000    ; pause
[22]                  END           ; go to the end
[23]                  DOWN          ; skip entry of the last record
[24]            ELSE                ; otherwise
[25]                  END           ; go to the end
[26]                  PGDN          ; enter the last record and append a new blank
                                    ; record
[27]        ENDIF
[28] ENDWHILE                     ; end of entry of new records
[29] DO_IT!                       ; update table
[30] KEYPRESS "F7"                ; change to Table view
[31] KEYPRESS "HOME"              ; go to the first record
[32] KEYPRESS "CTRLHOME"          ; go to the first field
```

Note that comments can be included in code merely by inserting a semicolon (;). Everything to the right of and on the same line as a semicolon is a comment. Line numbers have been included in this code for explanatory purposes only. They do not appear in the text of a PAL program. The explanations of some of the more obscure parts of the code follow.

[3–4] Create the first empty record in anticipation of entry of a new record.

[10] Test to see if any data was entered in this field. This field is examined to determine whether the user has entered another record or wishes to conclude entry of records.

[15] Make [ID #] the current field, in order for the LOCATE statement to work correctly.

[16] Notice that the LOCATE statement uses the current value of [ID #] to see if there already is a record in the table with this value. The record being entered is not actually a part of the

table yet, so the LOCATE statement cannot find the record currently being entered. The LOCATE can only find a record already in the table. This is precisely the desired operation. If you attempt to enter a record with the same ID # value after the processing of the current record has been completed, then the LOCATE statement does correctly find the record with the same ID # value that was previously entered during the current entry session.

[17] When a LOCATE is performed in this manner, the value of RETVAL is always True. Use the function ATLAST to determine if the LOCATE was successful or not. If the value of ATLAST is False, then the LOCATE was successful, and another record with the same ID # value already was in the table.

[22–23] Place a new blank record right over the top of the previously entered record. This will effectively delete the record that was last entered.

[25–26] Add a new blank record to the end of the table. This will preserve the record that was last entered and allow the entry of an additional new record.

4.7 INDEXES, DIRECT ACCESS, AND THE LOCATE STATEMENT

An index is actually an additional file that you create and that is maintained for you by Paradox. To create an index you use the INDEX statement. For example, assume that you wish to index the database file named EMPLOYEE on the field named EMPNO. In order to accomplish this, use the following code:

```
INDEX EMPLOYEE ON EMPNO
```

Whenever you use a field in conjunction with the LOCATE statement, Paradox determines whether there is an index that would speed up the process. If there is such an index, it is automatically used. Therefore, once you create an index, its use is automatic and you do not have to worry about it again.

Whenever you enter a new record into a table or modify a record already in the table, you need not be concerned with the names of the index files. At the time that records are entered or changed, only the primary index is updated. When you attempt to access a table and the access should use a secondary index, Paradox can tell that the file does not match the index (the file and index date/time markers are examined) and the desired index is automatically rebuilt. This approach tends to speed up all three of the following operations: data entry, data modification, and direct access to a record.

The most fundamental use of an index is to perform direct access to a record. For example, suppose we wish to directly access the employee record with the value of EMPNO = "ABCDE". Remember that direct access is possible only on a field that has been indexed. If the field has not been indexed, then a sequential search of the table is performed by Paradox.

To perform the act of direct access, we use the MOVETO and the LOCATE statements, as follows.

EXAMPLE:

```
VIEW "EMPLOYEE"
MOVETO [EMPNO]
LOCATE "ABCDE"
```

When a LOCATE statement is executed using a constant or variable, the result of the LOCATE is reflected in the value of the variable RETVAL. The value of RETVAL is True if the LOCATE was successful. If the LOCATE was unsuccessful, then the value of RETVAL is False. In addition, the record in the user buffer (the current record) is available for use if the LOCATE was successful.

To use the LOCATE statement with a character string variable rather than with a character string constant (such as "ABCDE"), use the following technique.

```
CLEAR
@ 1,0 ?? "ENTER THE EMPLOYEE NUMBER:" ACCEPT "A5" TO MEMEMPNO
EDIT "EMPLOYEE"
MOVETO [EMPNO]
LOCATE MEMEMPNO
```

```
IF NOT RETVAL
      THEN
            @ 3,0 ?? "NO RECORD ON FILE FOR THIS EMPLOYEE NUMBER."
            @ 5,0 ?? "Type any key to continue."
            CONTINUE = GETCHAR( )
      ELSE
            <other code goes here>
ENDIF
```

The purpose of the GETCHAR in the above code is to freeze the screen. The user must type a key to get the program to continue. This insures that the information displayed on the screen does not disappear before it is read.

Whenever a LOCATE statement is executed, a record is found only if there is an exact match. For example, if the records all contain six-character employee numbers (EMPNO) and a five-character string is used for the search, then the search will fail. In addition, there must be an exact match in case. If the EMPNO is "ABCDEF" and the string used in the LOCATE statement is "abcdef", then the search will fail. As a result, you might wish to automatically convert any character strings entered by the users to uppercase before the data is stored.

If you desire a partial match on a character string, you might try the query facility using the LIKE option.

4.8 SEQUENTIAL ACCESS

Sequential access to a database file may be started either at the beginning of the file or may follow a previous direct access. The first method allows sequential access to the entire file and the second allows sequential access from a point other than the beginning of the file. Both of these methods are of value in appropriate circumstances. In order to move sequentially through a file visiting every record in order, obtain the number of the record where the search is to start, and then use the MOVETO statement with appropriate incrementation of the associated record number. In order to move sequentially through a file, but visiting only those records with a specific value or set of values in specified fields, use the LOCATE NEXT statement. If you wish to start the scan at the first record of the file, you may alternatively use the SCAN statement. Note that the SCAN always starts at the beginning of the file and so cannot be used for sequential access starting at a specific record after a direct access. Examples of the various techniques follow.

EXAMPLE USING A SCAN:

```
EDIT "EMPLOYEE"
SCAN
    MESSAGE [LAST NAME]
    SLEEP 1000
ENDSCAN
```

EXAMPLE USING A MOVETO:

```
COUNT = NRECORDS("EMPLOYEE")
VIEW "EMPLOYEE"
LINDEX = 1
WHILE LINDEX <= COUNT
    MOVETO RECORD LINDEX
    MESSAGE [LAST NAME]
    SLEEP 1000
    LINDEX = LINDEX + 1
ENDWHILE
```

EXAMPLE USING A LOCATE:

```
EDIT "EMPLOYEE"
MOVETO [LAST NAME]
LOCATE "SMITH"
WHILE RETVAL
    MESSAGE [ID #]
    SLEEP 10
    DOWN
    MOVETO [LAST NAME]
    LOCATE NEXT "SMITH"
ENDWHILE
CANCELEDIT
```

NOTES ON USING A LOCATE: When I performed a sequential pass through the file using VIEW instead of EDIT, there seemed to be a problem with an infinite loop. If the last record in the file satisfied the selection criteria, then the DOWN followed by the LOCATE NEXT stayed at the last record in the file. When I changed VIEW to EDIT, the process worked correctly, but it was necessary to have a MOVETO before the LOCATE NEXT. When a DOWN is performed while the cursor is positioned within the last record of the file, a new blank record is (temporarily) appended to the file and the cursor moves to the first data field in the file. The MOVETO [LAST NAME] within the above loop forces the cursor to the correct field before the final LOCATE NEXT. Note that a blank record is never permanently appended to the file.

If the EMPLOYEE file contains the field EMPNO, EMPNO is the first field in the file, and the file has a primary index, then the records will be displayed and accessed in order by EMPNO value. Since secondary keys are used only for access purposes (to speed up queries), they never affect the order in which the records are presented to the user. As a result, if EMPNO is not the first field in the primary index, the only way to access the records in order by EMPNO is to sort the file first.

CHAPTER 5

PROGRAMMING HINTS AND NOTES ON STYLE AND PROBLEMS

5.1 STYLE

Constructing Menus

It is strongly suggested that all application systems be menu driven, i.e., that the user be presented with a menu from which he or she may select operations appropriate to his or her needs. This reduces the amount of documentation necessary and makes the system easier to use. The use of a menu entails four distinct functions: the display of the menu itself, the obtaining of the code for the selected function from the user, the execution of the function itself, and the return to the menu. I prefer to embed all these functions in a loop that will be executed until the user decides to exit from the module in which the menu is contained. Exit implies a return to the calling routine or an exit from the application system, as appropriate. The sequence of operations is as follows:

1. Display the menu.
2. Obtain the code for the selected function.
3. Perform the operation indicated by the selection code.
4. Loop to display the menu again.

Two versions of code to accomplish this follow.

```
; SALES.SC - WITH A CONVENTIONAL TYPE OF MENU
; THIS IS THE MAIN DRIVER FOR THE SALES SYSTEM
ECHO OFF
WHILE TRUE
    PRINTER OFF
    CLEAR
    CLEARALL
    @  5, 5 ?? "SALES REPORTING SYSTEM"
    @  6, 5 ?? "————————————————"
    @  7,10 ?? "A. EXIT FROM THE SYSTEM"
    @  8,10 ?? "B. SALESMAN RECORD, ENTER"
    @  9,10 ?? "C. SALESMAN RECORD, CHANGE"
    @ 10,10 ?? "D. ACCOUNT RECORD, ENTER"
    @ 11,10 ?? "E. ACCOUNT RECORD, CHANGE"
    @ 12,10 ?? "F. SALES RECORD, ENTER"
```

```
    @ 13,10 ?? "G. SALES RECORD, CHANGE"
    @ 14,10 ?? "H. SALES REPORT, PRINT"
    @ 15, 0
    MESSAGE "ENTER A SELECTION CODE"
    CODE = CHR(GETCHAR( ))
    SWITCH
        CASE CODE = "A":
            MESSAGE "NORMAL TERMINATION OF SALES SYSTEM"
            SLEEP 1000
            EXIT
        CASE CODE = "B":
            PLAY "SMANENTE"
        CASE CODE = "C":
            PLAY "SMANCHAN"
        CASE CODE = "D":
            PLAY "ACCRECEN"
        CASE CODE = "E":
            PLAY "ACCRECCH"
        CASE CODE = "F":
            PLAY "SRECENTE"
        CASE CODE = "G":
            PLAY "SRECCHAN"
        CASE CODE = "H":
            PLAY "SREPPRIN"
        OTHERWISE:
            MESSAGE "ILLEGAL SELECTION CODE"
            BEEP
            SLEEP 2000
    ENDSWITCH
    RELEASE VARS ALL
ENDWHILE

; SALES.SC - WITH A PARADOX TYPE OF MENU
; THIS IS THE MAIN DRIVER FOR THE SALES SYSTEM
ECHO OFF
WHILE TRUE
    PRINTER OFF
    MESSAGE "MAKE A SELECTION"
```

```
    SHOWMENU
        "EXIT"             : "EXIT FROM THE SYSTEM",
        "SALESMAN-ENTER"   : " ENTER A RECORD FOR A SALESMAN",
        "SALESMAN-CHANGE"  : " CHANGE A RECORD FOR A SALESMAN",
        "ACCOUNT-ENTER"    : " ENTER AN ACCOUNT RECORD",
        "ACCOUNT-CHANGE"   : " CHANGE AN ACCOUNT RECORD",
        "SALES-ENTER"      : " ENTER A SALES RECORD",
        "SALES-CHANGE"     : " CHANGE A SALES RECORD",
        "SALES-REPORT"     : " PRINT THE SALES REPORT"
    TO CODE
    SWITCH
        CASE CODE = "EXIT":
            MESSAGE "NORMAL TERMINATION OF SALES SYSTEM"
            SLEEP 1000
            EXIT
        CASE CODE = "SALESMAN-ENTER":
            PLAY "SMANENTE"
        CASE CODE = "SALESMAN-CHANGE":
            PLAY "SMANCHAN"
        CASE CODE = "ACCOUNT-ENTER":
            PLAY "ACCRECEN"
        CASE CODE = "ACCOUNT-CHANGE":
            PLAY "ACCRECCH"
        CASE CODE = "SALES-ENTER":
            PLAY "SRECENTE"
        CASE CODE = "SALES-CHANGE":
            PLAY "SRECCHAN"
        CASE CODE = "SALES-REPORT":
            PLAY "SREPPRIN"
    ENDSWITCH
    RELEASE VARS ALL
    CLEAR
ENDWHILE
```

An explanation of some of the features in the above code is as follows:

ECHO OFF	Inhibit display on the screen of results of program operations

EXIT	Exit from Paradox and return to the operating system
PLAY "X"	Obtain the PAL program located in the MS/PC DOS file with name = X.SC and execute it
CLEAR	Clear the screen
RELEASE VARS ALL	Deallocate all of the variables

The following do not appear in this program, but are used in the associated application system:

CLEARALL	A statement that can be placed either at the end of the loop or at the end of a called program to delete images in View mode from the work area
DO_IT!	Terminate Edit mode and save the changes

Name Selection

The choice of names for procedures, files, fields in a record, and variables is, of course, up to the individual programmer. Nevertheless, a reasonable and uniform technique for naming may save the programmer considerable debugging time. I recommend the following:

1. Name files so that the contents of the file are clear. For example, name the file for employees EMPLOYEE, not something like X27A4. Restrict the names of files to no more than eight characters. Paradox examines each name and returns an error if the name is longer than eight characters.
2. The names of variables are limited to 132 characters and the names of fields in database records are limited to 25 characters. Again, I recommend that you always choose meaningful names. Since reference to a field in a record always uses square brackets ([ ]), it is not really necessary to distinguish between the name of a variable and the name of a field in a program.

3. Use the default-naming convention. A program might have the name CASHPURC.SC at the level of the operating system, but when you wish to invoke the program do not include the **.SC**. For example, invoke the program with the statement

```
PLAY "CASHPURC"
```

When referring to the name of a database file, use EMPLOYEE rather than EMPLOYEE.DB.

4. When using more than one database file, it may be necessary to prefix the name of the field with the name of the file. For example, if there are two images in the workspace for two different files and if records from both files each contain a field named X, then the reference [X] refers to the field named X in the current record of the current image. If the name of the noncurrent image is Y, then you can refer to the field named X in the current record of the noncurrent image as [Y —> X].

5.2 PROGRAMMING TIPS

Programming for Speed

Because of the speed limitations associated with microcomputers, it is always important to avoid use of operations that might cause a program to run too slowly. Some principles to be applied are the following:

1. Avoid use of statements that unnecessarily access the disks or that create new files. In particular, each time you execute a VIEW or an EDIT statement, the system obtains the definition of the data file from the disk. The MOVETO statement allows you to use definitions obtained through the VIEW or EDIT statements that appear in the program previous to the loop.
2. Avoid the use of statements that sequentially scan files when direct access will do. In particular, use the LOCATE statement with appropriate indexes when possible.

Testing for End of File

You will want to test for the end of the file (table) whenever you perform a sequential search of the database, otherwise you will get caught in an infinite loop. The end of file test works correctly, whether the database is empty or not. In Version 1.0, test for the end of file condition using the ATLAST function. In Version 1.1 and higher, you can choose between the ATLAST and the EOT functions. In Version 1.1 and higher, you can also scan backwards toward the front of the file and use the function BOT to determine when you have reached the beginning of the file (table). The functions ATLAST and EOT return the value True when the end of the file is encountered, otherwise they return the value False. Similarly, the function BOT returns the value True when the beginning of the file is encountered, otherwise it returns the value False. In this book, the ATLAST function is used exclusively in all of the programs and examples, but you may choose to use either the ATLAST or the EOT in your programs.

Several Statements on One Line

PAL allows you to place several statements on one line, without any intervening punctuation. For example, the @, the ??, and ACCEPT statements often appear on one line, since, in a logical sense, they belong together. An example is

```
@ 1,0 ?? "Enter the salesman number:" ACCEPT "A10" TO MEMNO
```

If you desire, you can place an entire module on one line. An example is

```
IF ISBLANK(MEMNO) THEN QUITLOOP ENDIF
```

Using the Case Statement to Simplify Nested IFs

It is not unusual to have nested IFs, even if you carefully adhere to the techniques of modern structured programming. For example, if you have the following code:

```
IF X = "A"
  THEN
      PLAY "A"
ELSE IF X = "B"
  THEN
      PLAY "B"
ELSE IF X = "C"
  THEN
      PLAY "C"
  ELSE
      PLAY "E"
ENDIF
ENDIF
ENDIF
```

you may wish to use the CASE statement, which has the form

```
SWITCH
        CASE X = "A":
                PLAY "A"
        CASE X = "B":
                PLAY "B"
        CASE X = "C":
                PLAY "C"
        CASE X = "D":
                PLAY "D"
        OTHERWISE:
                PLAY "E"
ENDSWITCH
```

HINT: Use the CASE (SWITCH) statement instead of nested IFs, where appropriate.

Note that you may physically nest CASE (SWITCH) statements in a single program and you may also logically nest CASE (SWITCH) statements. For example, in the above code, the program A may contain a CASE (SWITCH) statement.

Auto Generation of Unique IDs

As a matter of style, I prefer to have the application system generate unique IDs rather than require the user to input them. Clearly, this does not apply to IDs such as social security numbers, but does apply to IDs arbitrarily assigned by the organization. This certainly applies to all the situations in which the user assigns a unique ID only for the purpose of distinguishing between records in a database file and the user is free to assign any ID that he or she chooses. In this case, I recommend storing either the last-used ID or the ID to be used next (choose which is more convenient for you) in a database file. In addition, if you make this field a number, then it is easy to increment. In PAL, there is no restriction of the type of field that can participate in the primary key of a file or on which you can create a secondary index.

If you elect to store system-generated IDs as character strings, you will probably store the ID last used (or to be used next) as a number in one database and store the actual ID value as a character string. This implies that the number stored in one database file must then be converted to a character string using the STRVAL function. There is no problem with the use of the LOCATE when the character string is created using the STRVAL function. Just make sure that the data in the table does not have any leading blanks. When STRVAL converts a number to a character string, it does it intelligently. The size of the resultant character string is determined by the size of the original number, so no leading or trailing blanks are possible.

Emergency Exit from a Program

To effect a quick exit from a program, enter the keystroke CTRL-BREAK. This is useful when caught in an infinite loop or if you observe that a program is behaving improperly. Since you have interrupted the updating of database and index files, there is a (remote) possibility of file problems. I have not noted any errors caused by the use of the CTRL-BREAK keystroke, but you might find some. You may need to reindex the database files to guarantee that the index files match the associated database files. There may also be records in a buffer that have not been transferred to the database file. In addition, the number of records in the database file may not match the count of records in the header for the database file, so you may need to apply an appropriate technique to make the count in the header agree with the actual number of records in the database file. A DO_IT! statement may be helpful in this case.

Adding a Blank Record to the End of a Database File

In order to add a new record to a file, make sure that the file is in Edit mode. The statement END will position the currency pointer to the end of the file. If Paradox is in Table view, use the statement DOWN to add the new blank record. If Paradox is in Forms view, use PgDn to add the new blank record.

A Problem with Sequential Searching

If Paradox is not currently in Edit mode, then the LOCATE NEXT statement does not work properly. The LOCATE NEXT statement can never find a record in View mode if the record is the last one in the file.

Conflict Between View and Edit

I have observed that a VIEW statement following an EDIT statement can cause a runtime error. Simply place the VIEW statement before the EDIT statement in your program. For example, replace

```
EDIT "X"
VIEW "Y"
```

with

```
VIEW "Y"
EDIT "X"
```

Changing to Edit Mode

Once you have used a statement of the type EDIT "NAME", Paradox goes into Edit mode. Once in Edit mode, you can edit any image in the workspace, i.e., you are in Edit mode for all images currently in the workspace, not just the one associated with the EDIT statement. When you subsequently execute a DO_IT! statement, all modified tables are updated and you will return to Main mode. Once you are in Edit mode, you cannot execute a VIEW statement, so VIEW all the necessary tables (images) before you enter Edit mode. See also the preceding section Conflict Between View and Edit.

If you are in Main mode, you can immediately change to Edit mode with the statement EDITKEY. If you wish to change back to Main mode, for example if you need to use the EMPTY statement, then use the CANCELEDIT or the DO_IT! statement, depending on whether you wish to abort or save any changes.

A Small Problem with the NRECORDS Function

When you enter an image in Edit mode, the function NRECORDS never returns the value 0. This happens because Paradox automatically adds a new blank record to the image at entry if it is currently empty. When you wish to determine if a file is empty, use the NRECORDS function before the image is placed in the workspace (before any VIEW or EDIT statement).

Designation of Forms

When you select a form, for example with a PICKFORM statement, the form that you choose becomes the designated form for all the images in the workspace, not just the current image. Therefore, it is suggested that you select the form in your program immediately before it is needed and that you release or change the form when you are done with it. For example, if you are using form F, then there is no trouble, because form F is the default form and is defined for every image. But, if you are using (for example) form 1, then form 1 must exist for each image encountered in the program either until you change the form selection or until you change to Table view.

Placement of the Return Statement

I have found that a RETURN statement does not always work correctly if included within a WHILE loop (I get an internal system error). Rather than include a RETURN within a loop, use a QUITLOOP to exit from the loop and place the RETURN after the ENDWHILE statement.

Using the View . . Do_It! Combination

When a transfer from Display mode to Edit mode is performed using the EDITKEY statement, a subsequent DO_IT! statement appears to cause Paradox to lose a pointer to the image. For example, if you are editing a file with code similar to the following

```
VIEW "MYTABLE"
WHILE TRUE
          .
          .
          .
     MOVETO [MYFIELD]
     EDITKEY
        <perform the editing here>
     DO_IT!
ENDWHILE
```

then the MOVETO statement does not appear to work properly the second time through the loop. To solve this problem, include the name of the table (image) in the MOVETO statement. The MOVETO statement now has the form

```
MOVETO [MYTABLE —> MYFIELD]
```

5.3 INPUT AND OUTPUT

Freezing the Screen

It is occasionally necessary to display messages on the screen for consumption by the user. In the case of prompts for input, the message will stay on the screen at least until input is accomplished. In the case where no input is expected from the user, but the programmer wishes to present the user with a message, it is advisable to force the user to enter some kind of input. The technique that I recommend is demonstrated by the following code

```
? "NO RECORD ON FILE FOR THE GIVEN ID."
? "PRESS ANY KEY TO CONTINUE."
X = GETCHAR()
```

or

```
MESSAGE "NO RECORD ON FILE FOR THE GIVEN ID—"
        "PRESS ANY KEY TO CONTINUE."
X = GETCHAR()
```

The message NO RECORD ON FILE FOR THE GIVEN ID remains on the screen until one of the keys on the keyboard is depressed.

Input Character Strings without Quotation Marks

The two major techniques for the entry of data from the keyboard is through the use of the ACCEPT statement or through the use of a form. In either case, quotation marks should not be used with character string data. One of the added advantages of the use of a form is the full-screen editing feature. If you make a mistake in the current field or in a previous field, you can make the desired corrections by moving to the desired location using the arrow keys.

Interfacing with the Outside World

It is often important to either input data produced by or to output data for use by other software systems. This facility is offered through the Tools/ExportImport function. You can import data from or export data to files of the following types: Lotus 1-2-3, Symphony, dBASE II, dBASE III, pfs:file, VisiCalc, and ASCII. When you work with ASCII files, you may choose to work with delimited or text files. Delimited files have character strings enclosed in quotation marks ("), the data values are separated by commas, and one line of the ASCII file corresponds to one record in a Paradox table (database file). Importing data from or exporting data to a text file requires that you work with a table that has just one (character string) field. In Version 1.0, if you export data to an ASCII text file, the table must have just one field. If you import data from an ASCII text file, then each line of the file becomes a single field value in the table. In Version 1.1 and higher, you can ask Paradox to scan the ASCII table and build a new Paradox table to receive your data. The structure of the Paradox table created in this manner will be determined by Paradox and will be based upon the structure of your ASCII file.

Sending a Form Feed Character to the Printer to Initialize the Print Head

When you print the last line of a report on the printer, the print head usually remains in the column just to the right of the last character printed. On some printers, even if you perform a manual form feed, the print head will remain in the same position, forcing you to shut the printer power off and then turn it back on again in order to position the print head at column 1 for the next report. To avoid this problem, always insert the ? "\f" or the ?? "\f" statement after the last output statement in the program but before any PRINTER OFF statement in the program.

> **HINT:** Always end a report with a ? "\f" or ?? "\f" statement.

Sending Special Characters to the Printer

Some printers may be reconfigured by special codes sent to it from the microcomputer. For example, when you power up your printer, it is often initialized to a standard print font, 6 lines per inch vertical and 10 characters per inch horizontal. You may wish to dynamically reconfigure your printer to an alternate print font, 8 lines per inch, and/or 12 characters per inch. The ? or the ?? statement with PRINTER ON is used for this purpose. To change the printer configuration at the beginning of a report, I recommend that you use code of the type

```
PRINTER ON
?? "\<ascii code>"
```

or

```
PRINTER ON
? "\<ascii code>"
```

For example, to switch to 17 characters per inch (compressed printing on the IBM compatible printers, use the following

```
PRINTER ON
? "\015"
```

To change the printer configuration at the end of a report, I recommend that you use code of the type

```
@ 51,0 ?? "\<some decimal number>"
```

where it is assumed that you are printing a maximum of 50 lines per page of the report. The choice of "some decimal number" and the number of special characters is dependent on the type of printer. To send a string containing more than one code to the printer, use something like the following

```
@ 0,0 ?? "\027"+"A6"
```

Document Display and Full-Screen Editing

Although it is possible to enter and edit records in Forms view using the default form (F), it is recommended that you use a form that you have designed yourself. The major reason is that the names used for the fields in the database records will probably not be meaningful to the end user. In addition, entry and editing in Forms view invariably works better than entry and editing in Table view.

In order to enter a new empty (blank) record under program control, enter the table in Edit mode, select an appropriate form, and then execute the two statements END and DOWN. For each subsequent record, use the END and PgDn statements to add a new blank record to the end of the table. In order to enter the data into the new blank record, use the WAIT . . UNTIL statement. When the user exits from the entry of the data, you may either continue with the entry or immediately update the database file with the DO_IT! statement. Similar statements apply to the editing of existing records.

In order to edit a record already in a file, use an appropriate technique to make the desired record the current record (for example, you can use the SCAN or LOCATE statements) and then display it on the screen for editing with the WAIT . . UNTIL statement. Make sure that Paradox is in Edit mode when the form is placed on the screen.

WARNING: Make sure that no forms have been selected when the LOCATE statement is to be used. If you need to LOCATE a record and then present it on the screen using a form, use code similar to the following

```
LOCATE ...
PICKFORM ...
        <perform editing here>
KEYPRESS "F7"
```

See the program INVPAY.SC in Chapter 8 for an example.

Printer Not Ready

On occasion, when I do output to the printer with ? statements and PRINTER ON, Paradox erroneously aborts my program with the error message PRINTER NOT READY. There seems to be a buffering problem between my printer and my micro, since the problem disappears when I use a cache memory program. If you have a similar problem, try the same solution. Alternatively, you can use the PRINT FILE statement and have the output go to a file. Unfortunately, when this statement is used, no output goes to the screen, so you cannot use the COL( ) function to determine the current position of the cursor on the screen. For a discussion of the use of the COL( ) function, see the following section Formatted Output to the Printer.

Formatted Output to the Printer

On occasion, you may find that the Paradox report writer either does not do what you need or that it is too clumsy to use. The solution is to print your own reports. Since the @ statement sends output only to the screen, you will need to use the PRINT statement or one of the following: ?, ??, or TEXT. I have found that I prefer the ? and ?? statements with the printer set on (PRINTER ON) to format output to the printer. The use of these two statements is discussed in the following paragraphs.

When the printer is set on, output to the screen from the ? and ?? statements is echoed to the printer. In addition, since the output is also sent to the screen, the COL( ) function can be used to determine the current cursor position. Once the current cursor position has been established, you can then use the SPACES statement to move the cursor to the right in preparation for more printing on the current line. Assume, for example, that you wish to print the value of X in column 1, the value of Y in column 7, and the value of Z in column 33. Since X, Y, and Z have a variable length, and since there is no way that you can directly position the print head in the desired place, it is necessary to determine the current position of the print head and then move the print head yourself. Consider the following statement

```
? X, SPACES(7-COL()-1), Y, SPACES(33-COL()-1), Z
```

When X is printed in column 1 on the paper, a corresponding value is displayed on the screen in position 1 (really column 0 of the screen, but that does not matter here). After X is displayed on the screen, the cursor is in the column immediately to the right of the value. The number of spaces generated by

```
SPACES(7-COL()-1)
```

is precisely the number of spaces necessary to move the cursor and the print head to the right so that Y will be printed in column 7 on the paper. Similarly,

```
SPACES(33-COL()-1)
```

will position the print head in the correct place before Z is printed.

This technique works equally well with lines more than 80 characters long. See, for example, the program INVREPOR.SC in Chapter 8. When a line is longer than 80 characters, it wraps around on the screen and the correct position of the cursor on the screen can be determined by the formula

Position on the screen = MOD(printer position,80)

In most cases, you will have little trouble determining the appropriate number of spaces. See the program INVREPOR.SC in Chapter 8 for an example of the use of the SPACES statement when the line is longer than 80 characters.

Similar Forms and Reports

If you have created a form or a report and then find that you wish to have another one that is almost the same as the first one, go to the level of the operating system and copy the original form or report to another file. For example, if form F1 for the table INVOICE is the form that you wish to modify (but you wish to keep the original form), copy the file INVOICE.F1 to INVOICE.F2 and then modify form F2 in the usual manner using the Paradox FORMS/CHANGE function. In Chapter 8, form F1 for table INVOICE is used to enter and modify invoice records, and form F2 is used to mark invoices for later payment.

5.4 DATA TYPES

Arrays

PAL allows the use of a one-dimensional array and the members of the array can be of various data types. For example, an array can hold a character string in the first position, a date in the second, and so on. Use the ARRAY statement to create an array, and access the members of the array with a statement of the type NAME[subscript]. The subscript must evaluate to an integer if the array is of the usual type and to a field name if the data was obtained from a table using the COPYTOARRAY statement. Since an array can contain a variety of data types, you might be able to use a collection of arrays to implement a simple spreadsheet.

Date Variables

Variables and database fields can have type date. When you create a database with a field of type date, then a width is automatically assigned to it by Paradox.

When you wish to display the contents of a date variable on the screen or on the printer, you may choose from eight different display formats. The default form is MM/DD/YY. To print a date in a form other than the default, use the FORMAT function.

A number of functions are available for the direct manipulation of date variables. They are as follows:

BLANKDATE	An empty (blank) date value
DAY	Number of day of month
DOW	Name of day of week
MONTH	Number of month
MOY	Name of the month
TODAY	Today's date
YEAR	Number of year (four-digit number)

In addition to these functions, an arithmetic operation using date variables is possible. When a date variable is used in arithmetic, it is converted by the system to an integer. The arithmetic operation is performed and the result, if possible, is then converted back to a date variable. In the following examples, we will consider each date of the form 01/01/87 to be a variable or a constant of type date.

1. 01/01/87 + 1 produces the date 01/02/87. In this example, the date 01/01/87 is converted to an integer, the number 1 is added to the integer, and then the integer is converted back to a date.

2. 01/30/87 - 01/01/87 produces the integer 29. Each date is converted to an integer and then the integer on the right is subtracted from the integer on the left.
3. 01/31/87 - 1 produces the date of 01/30/87.

If you have a variable of type date, you will not be allowed to enter non-numeric characters. In addition, the day and month fields of the date that you enter are checked for the correct range. If the range is incorrect, you will receive an error message and it will then be necessary for you to reenter the date.

If you need to print the date so that all the digits of the year are displayed, just use the appropriate FORMAT function.

5.5 WORKING WITH DATABASES

Closing Database Files

Each database file has associated with it information that reflects the current number of records in the file. Let's call this information the Header. Data that you append to a file actually is stored in a temporary buffer and then transferred to the database file either when the buffer is full or when you enter a DO_IT! statement. Sometimes the Header is updated when you enter the data, sometimes when the data is transferred, and sometimes when the database file is closed. If you exit from Paradox without properly closing the database file, then you may cause two distinct types of problems.

PROBLEM 1: There may be data (records) in the temporary buffer not yet transferred to the database file.

PROBLEM 2: The Header may not have been updated and the number of records actually in the database file is greater than the count of data records reflected in the header.

These problems might occur from abnormal program termination due, for example, to static electricity, to removal of the disks from the drives without execution of the EXIT statement, etc. One way to insure that database files are handled properly (the records in the buffer are transferred to the database file and the Header is properly updated) is to execute the DO_IT! statement when the image in question is the current image and before you exit from Paradox. If you execute a CANCELEDIT before a DO_IT! statement, you will lose changes and additions to the file.

It is sometimes possible to recover from problem 1. If you remove the disks from the system but do not power off and you have not disturbed the contents of main memory, then simply reinsert the disks into their proper places and resume processing. If you power off or in any other way disturb the contents of main memory, you will not be able to recover the records in buffer that have not yet been transferred to the database file.

In Paradox, if you have problem 2 and a DO_IT! statement does not help, you will simply have to enter the data again.

Modifying the Structure of a Database File

During the analysis, design, and construction of an application system, one often discovers data elements that have not yet been included. As previously mentioned in section 4.3, Useful Analysis and Design Techniques, it is helpful to organize the various files so that each file describes exactly one type of object and each record in a file describes exactly one instance (occurrence) of the object. For example, the EMPLOYEE file used in previous examples has these properties. In addition, note that all the fields in a record in the EMPLOYEE file have the property that they directly describe attributes of a specific employee. If you discover that you need to include an employee attribute not yet contained in the records in the EMPLOYEE file, you may add a new field to the existing record (file) definition at any time. You may either insert the new field before an existing field definition or you may append it to the end of the record definition. It is recommended that you perform all modifications in the Interactive mode so that you can take advantage of any warnings that Paradox tries to give to you. Modifications are accomplished using the Modify/Restructure function.

When you modify the structure of an existing database file, Paradox assumes the responsibility to preserve your data for you. If any data will be lost during the restructure process, Paradox will warn you and allow you to decide what action to take.

Primary Index

Each table may have a primary index associated with it. When data is stored in a table with a primary index (when the DO_IT! statement is executed), the records are logically arranged in order by primary index values. Whenever you access records in a table with a primary key, access is always made in primary key order. The use of the primary index by Paradox is always automatic. Some problems associated with a primary index are:

1. The fields that participate in the primary index must come first in the table definition.
2. No two records in the table may have the same primary key value.

A primary index is created when the table definition is created or changed. Place an asterisk (*) after the field type for each field that will participate in the primary index.

Secondary Indexes

A secondary index, like the primary index, is used to speed up access to records in the database files. Unlike the primary index, the secondary index never affects the order in which the records are accessed (the logical record order). A secondary index can be added or deleted at any time. To add a new index, use the PAL INDEX statement. In order to delete an index, use the Tools/Delete function to delete all the secondary indexes associated with a table. You will then need to recreate the desired indexes for the table. See Chapter 6 for an example of a program to create indexes for you (INDEXES.SC). The deletion of secondary indexes does not affect the primary index.

Compound Indexes (Concatenating Fields)

Paradox allows you to create secondary indexes based only on a single field. In order to simulate an index on two or more fields (while using a LOCATE statement), you may either add a new field to the table that is a concatenation of the desired fields or you may use the multiple field form of the LOCATE statement. The multiple field form is preferred.

5.6 DEBUGGING

Control of Overlays and Modularity

Consider the following sequence of statements in PAL

```
PLAY "A"
PLAY "B"
PLAY "C"
```

When each of these statements is executed, the code from the files A.SC, B.SC, and C.SC, respectively, is brought into main memory and executed. The variables retain their values, except for those referenced in RELEASE statements, and form a type of common data area. In this manner, values may be "passed" from A to B to C. This technique may lead to problems. One possible problem is that the program overlays may destroy the integrity of the variables. Another problem is that you may lose control of the meaning and use of the variables; you might be using a variable to mean one thing in one module and another thing in another module. To overcome this problem, I recommend that you design your code so that it is not necessary to pass values from A to B, from B to C, etc. You may then replace the above code with the following

```
PLAY "A"
RELEASE VARS ALL
```

```
PLAY "B"
RELEASE VARS ALL
PLAY "C"
RELEASE VARS ALL
```

There should be no problems with overlays when this technique is used. In addition, this technique tends to limit the effect of global variables ("the" variables) and so promotes modularity.

Special Notes on Debugging

Every programmer eventually encounters the situation where a program should work but doesn't, and the programmer cannot figure out why. PAL has features for debugging such programs. The way that I prefer to use them is as follows. For the program to be debugged, use your editor to remove any TALK OFF statements. From the Paradox main menu, press ALT-F10 and then select the Debug function. After you enter the name of the program to be debugged, you can step through the program one line at a time by pressing CTRL-S for each line. The statement about to be executed appears in the highlighted area at the bottom of the screen and the main part of the screen reflects the activity of your PAL program. You may also wish to change from Forms view to Table view in your program to see more of what is happening with respect to the images on the screen. When you find an error in your code, press CTRL-E to change directly from Debug mode to Program Edit mode. If you wish to see the values of variables and database fields as the program is being executed, you will need to include your own instrumentation (MESSAGE or ? statements).

5.7 USEFUL UTILITIES

A Reindexing Program

During the operation of a system, situations sometimes occur that cause a secondary index file to disagree with the corresponding database file. An example is one in which records have been appended to a database file and static electricity has caused system failure before the appropriate files have been properly updated. In this case, it is advisable to reindex the file in question. One technique to accomplish this is to have a procedure that will recreate all the secondary indexes used in the system. In addition, reindexing a large file might decrease processing time after a large number of records have been appended to the file. An example of such a program is

```
; REINDEX.SX
INDEX "SRECORDS" ON "SRSALESNO"
INDEX "SRECORDS" ON "SRACCTNO"
INDEX "SRECORDS" ON "SRDATE"
RETURN
```

A File Empty Program

After you finish debugging an application system, you will want to empty out all the database files and will want to initialize some of them before delivery to a client. In addition, you may wish to empty out files and initialize some of them before addition of a new module. It is recommended that you create a program that will perform these operations for you. An example of such a program follows.

```
; FILEEMPT.SC
EMPTY "SALESMEN"
EMPTY "ACCOUNTS"
EMPTY "SRECORDS"
EMPTY "MISC"
EDIT "SRECORDS"
DOWN
[LASTNUMBER] = 0
DO_IT!
RETURN
```

CHAPTER

6 AN ILLUSTRATIVE EXAMPLE IN PAL

6.1 INTRODUCTION

A relatively simple example will now be used to illustrate many of the points previously raised. The example is used to illustrate both system development and the use of PAL.

6.2 THE ORIGINAL PROBLEM

A sales manager wishes to record information for each of her salesmen and she intends to produce a report that will allow her to determine the relative success of each salesman. The report is to contain, for each salesman, the name of the salesman, a list of account names, sales for each account during the specified period, and the total sales amount. In addition, the total sales for all salesmen is to be printed at the end of the report.

6.3 THE ANALYSIS AND DESIGN

We originally start with two database files, one for the salesmen and one for the accounts, since we have these two types of data objects. Based on the information given to us by the sales manager, we construct the following file definitions:

The Salesmen table

STRUCT	Field Name	Field Type
1	SASALESNO	A10*
2	SALNAME	A15
3	SAFNAME	A15
4	SAMNAME	A10
5	SATELNO	A13

The Accounts table

STRUCT	Field Name	Field Type
1	ACACCTNO	A10*
2	ACCOMPANY	A20
3	ACSTREET	A15
4	ACCITY	A15
5	ACSTATE	A2
6	ACZIP	A9

NOTES: The display for each of these tables was produced through the use of the Tools/Info/Structure function in Paradox. The asterisk (*) in the first field of each of the tables indicates use of a primary index. It is anticipated that access to SALESMEN records will be made by salesman number and that access to ACCOUNTS records will be made by account number. The choice of a primary index is, in many cases, an arbitrary one. For example, in the SALESMEN file, the combination of last name, first name, and middle name might have been chosen to be the primary index. In any case, the fields that participate in the primary index must come in a group at the beginning of the record. For this reason, it might be wise to select the primary index at the time that the file is first designed.

In each of the two database files, the first two letters of the file name are used to start the name of each of the fields in the record descriptions. This will help us to remember which database record the fields are in when programming. The names of the fields have been chosen so as to indicate their purpose. The fields have been selected based on our current understanding of the system requirements, and we expect that they will change as our understanding of what is desired of the system evolves. The size of each of the fields was chosen based on current information and may also change later. Each of the fields was chosen to be a character string, since it is not anticipated that any arithmetic will be performed using these fields.

At this stage, it is possible to store sales information for the individual accounts in the account records themselves, if we assume that only current totals are necessary. But, if we desire to store sales information according to date, i.e., we desire to have several sales records for each account, then we will have to create a new database file to store this information. As analysts, we have the suspicion that the sales manager will want to look at old records to evaluate the progress of each salesman, in addition to printing out the required report. Based on our suspicion, we contact the sales manager and try to pin her down concerning the value of storing sales records by date and keeping them over a period of time. She is not sure, but thinks that there might be some use for this kind of data. Based on our experience and the suspicion that the data will be needed in the future, we decide to store the sales data in a separate file. To link salesmen and accounts together, we will need the salesman number and the account number for each sale. Accordingly, we create a new database file for the sales records. The file has the following definition:

The Srecords table

STRUCT	Field Name	Field Type
1	SRSALESNO	A10*
2	SRACCTNO	A10
3	SRDATE	D
4	SRAMOUNT	$

So far, the only field that is numeric (dollar format) is the sales amount (SRAMOUNT). This field is numeric because we expect to perform arithmetic using this field. Note that the salesman number (SRSALESNO) in this record definition is chosen to match exactly the definition of salesman number (SASALESNO) in the database file SALESMEN. Both of them are A10. This will facilitate linking the SALESMEN and SRECORDS files together. Similar comments apply to the account numbers.

> **STEP 1:** Make an initial determination of the files from the system inputs, outputs, and processes. The final files will be the product of modifying and adding to your original guess.

It is now time to make an initial determination of the secondary indexes. We can add or delete secondary indexes at any time without disturbing the file system. Since Paradox automatically makes use of available indexes, any future changes in indexes have no effect on any of our programs. We know that we will need to associate the files in some way and to use this association to determine the indexes. Let's consider the following. In the initial report, we know that we will start with the salesman information and then determine the associated accounts and the sales amounts. If, in addition, we decide to select the actual sales information for sales performed within a specified date range, then we have the following requirements:

1. Starting with the salesman number, find each of the accounts associated with this number.
2. For each of the accounts obtained in the above step, find all the sales records within the specified date range.

In addition, let us assume that we are to print the report in order by salesman number. This leads us to the following candidate indexes:

1. Salesman number in SRECORDS: Through this index we can find the sales records associated with a specific salesman.
2. Account number in ACCOUNTS: Through this index we can find the account information for each sales record.
3. Salesman number in SALESMEN: Through this index we can access the salesman information in order by salesman number.

NOTES: Two of these three candidates for indexes have already been chosen as primary indexes. The indexes for SRECORDS will be considered in depth a little later in this chapter. If we had not selected two of them as our primary indexes, we could now use the Paradox Modify/Restructure function to move the named fields to the beginning of the record definitions, if necessary, and make them the primary keys by placing an asterisk (*) after the desired field types.

Upon reflection, we determine that we still have some questions to answer. We would like to start with the salesman, in order by salesman number. This is no problem, since we can access the SALESMEN database file directly through the primary index on SASALESNO. Next, we desire to obtain the name of each account associated with this salesman and then print out the name and sales amount for each sale made during the specified period. The relationship between salesmen and accounts is provided by the SRECORDS file, so we must go there first. To find the appropriate records in this file, we will need both the salesman number and the date. Now we run into the following problem. How do we print out the sales information for each salesman, so that the account names appear in alphabetical order? If we obtain the account number from the SRECORDS file and then go to the ACCOUNTS file for the company name, then the account names will appear in the order of the sales, not in alphabetical order. The solution that we would like to choose here is to order the records in the SRECORDS file in alphabetical order by company name within salesman. In order to accomplish this, we modify the record definition in the SRECORDS database file to include the company name. This certainly creates a redundancy in the stored data, since the company name appears both in the ACCOUNTS file and in the SRECORDS file. We accept this redundancy as a fact of life (in this particular example) and will construct the appropriate programs to (partially) control this redundancy later. Unfortunately, if we choose the combination of SRSALESNO and SRCOMPANY as the primary index, then we can only put one record for a particular salesman and company in the file, since Paradox does not allow duplicate values in the primary index. It appears that we will have to sort the file in the desired order to obtain the records in order by company within salesman. The new record definition for SRECORDS is:

The Srecords table

STRUCT	Field Name	Field Type
1	SRSALESNO	A10
2	SRCOMPANY	A20
3	SRACCTNO	A10
4	SRDATE	D
5	SRAMOUNT	$

If we later decide to add a primary index or one or more secondary indexes, this is easily accomplished.

> **STEP 2:** The indexes are chosen so as to facilitate the required accesses to files that you have already constructed. Remember that the choice of a primary index is influenced by the enforcement of no duplicate primary index values.

> **STEP 3:** As your understanding of the data requirements of the system grows, you will find yourself adding data elements to existing files and also adding new database files. It may also be necessary to duplicate data so as to facilitate report production. This type of redundancy should always be performed by the system itself, in order to control system integrity.

Up to this point, we have not needed to create secondary indexes, since the anticipated accesses are handled by the primary indexes. As the system grows, we expect that we might use secondary indexes in addition to the primary indexes.

First we create a driver program for our small system. In the beginning it will contain only those functions that we originally envision as part of our application. As more functions are desired, they will be added to the driver. We choose to implement the driver for our system in the form that presents a menu on the screen. One version of the program is:

; SALES.SC - WITH A CONVENTIONAL TYPE OF MENU

```
; THIS IS THE MAIN DRIVER FOR THE SALES SYSTEM

ECHO OFF

WHILE TRUE

   PRINTER OFF

   CLEAR

   CLEARALL

   @  5, 5 ?? "SALES REPORTING SYSTEM"

   @  6, 5 ?? "----------------------"

   @  7,10 ?? "A. EXIT FROM THE SYSTEM"

   @  8,10 ?? "B. SALESMAN RECORD, ENTER"

   @  9,10 ?? "C. SALESMAN RECORD, CHANGE"
```

```
@ 10,10 ?? "D. ACCOUNT RECORD, ENTER"
@ 11,10 ?? "E. ACCOUNT RECORD, CHANGE"
@ 12,10 ?? "F. SALES RECORD, ENTER"
@ 13,10 ?? "G. SALES RECORD, CHANGE"
@ 14,10 ?? "H. SALES REPORT, PRINT"
@ 15, 0
MESSAGE "ENTER A SELECTION CODE"
CODE = CHR(GETCHAR())
SWITCH
   CASE CODE = "A":
      MESSAGE "NORMAL TERMINATION OF SALES SYSTEM"
      SLEEP 1000
      EXIT
   CASE CODE = "B":
      PLAY "SMANENTE"
   CASE CODE = "C":
      PLAY "SMANCHAN"
   CASE CODE = "D":
      PLAY "ACCRECEN"
   CASE CODE = "E":
      PLAY "ACCRECCH"
   CASE CODE = "F":
      PLAY "SRECENTE"
   CASE CODE = "G":
      PLAY "SRECCHAN"
   CASE CODE = "H":
      PLAY "SREPPRIN"
   OTHERWISE:
```

```
        MESSAGE "ILLEGAL SELECTION CODE"
        BEEP
        SLEEP 2000
   ENDSWITCH
   RELEASE VARS ALL
ENDWHILE
```

> **STEP 4:** As your understanding of the required processes evolves, add new process functions to the main menu. It is highly recommended that you construct the main menu before you write any of the other processes.

We are constructing our system in a top-down and modular fashion. We determine what functions our system should perform and then list them in the driver. Then we construct each of the programs required by our driver, using the names listed in the driver.

NOTE: The above version of the SALES program produces a conventional menu on the screen. The next version accomplishes the same task, but uses a Paradox type of menu.

; SALES.SC - WITH A PARADOX TYPE OF MENU

```
; THIS IS THE MAIN DRIVER FOR THE SALES SYSTEM
ECHO OFF
WHILE TRUE
   PRINTER OFF
   MESSAGE "MAKE A SELECTION"
   SHOWMENU
       "EXIT"     : "EXIT FROM THE SYSTEM",
```

```
     "SALESMAN-ENTER"  : " ENTER A RECORD FOR A SALESMAN",
     "SALESMAN-CHANGE" : " CHANGE A RECORD FOR A SALESMAN",
     "ACCOUNT-ENTER"   : " ENTER AN ACCOUNT RECORD",
     "ACCOUNT-CHANGE"  : " CHANGE AN ACCOUNT RECORD",
     "SALES-ENTER"     : " ENTER A SALES RECORD",
     "SALES-CHANGE"    : " CHANGE A SALES RECORD",
     "SALES-REPORT"    : " PRINT THE SALES REPORT"
TO CODE
SWITCH
   CASE CODE = "EXIT":
      MESSAGE "NORMAL TERMINATION OF SALES SYSTEM"
      SLEEP 1000
      EXIT
   CASE CODE = "SALESMAN-ENTER":
      PLAY "SMANENTE"
   CASE CODE = "SALESMAN-CHANGE":
      PLAY "SMANCHAN"
   CASE CODE = "ACCOUNT-ENTER":
      PLAY "ACCRECEN"
   CASE CODE = "ACCOUNT-CHANGE":
      PLAY "ACCRECCH"
   CASE CODE = "SALES-ENTER":
      PLAY "SRECENTE"
   CASE CODE = "SALES-CHANGE":
      PLAY "SRECCHAN"
   CASE CODE = "SALES-REPORT":
      PLAY "SREPPRIN"
ENDSWITCH
```

```
    RELEASE VARS ALL

    CLEAR

ENDWHILE
```

NOTE 1: The version with the Paradox type of menu certainly appears to be a slightly simpler program, but you may use either type.

NOTE 2: Notice that the description of each menu item starts with a space. You will need a leading space for the following reason. When there are more menu items than will fit on one line on the screen, Paradox scrolls the line as you move along it. When you move far enough to the right, Paradox places an arrowhead pointing to the left at the beginning of the second line, covering up the first character of this line. If you leave the first character of each description blank, then you are effectively leaving room for the arrowhead. Another way to control this problem is to construct a main menu that will fit on one line of the screen. At the current time, there are two items in the menu that refer to salesmen functions, two that refer to accounts, and three that refer to sales. You can have one salesman function in the main menu, one for accounts, and one for sales records. Then, when you call one of these functions, a submenu can be displayed on the screen for the further selection of functions. This hierarchical arrangement of menus is quite useful for screen control but may add a small level of complexity for users.

After the construction of the menu program(s), it seems useful to construct, as the next step, the programs that allow entry and modification of records. We do this not because they appear on the menu first, but because we need data in the files for the report. It is generally true that you should write the programs for the entry and the changing of data before any other type of program, except for the main driver itself (and possibly for other menus). The program to enter salesman records is

```
; SMANENTE.SC
EDIT "SALESMEN"
END
DOWN
PICKFORM "F"
WHILE TRUE
   WAIT RECORD
      MESSAGE "PRESS F2 WHEN THIS RECORD HAS BEEN COMPLETED."
   UNTIL "F2"
   IF ISBLANK([SASALESNO])
   THEN
      DEL
      QUITLOOP
   ENDIF
   MOVETO [SASALESNO]
   LOCATE [SASALESNO]
   IF NOT ATLAST()
      THEN
         MESSAGE "A record for this salesman number already on file."
         BEEP
         SLEEP 2000
         END
         DOWN
      ELSE
         END
         PGDN
   ENDIF
```

```
ENDWHILE
DO_IT!
CLEARALL
RETURN
```

NOTES ON SMANENTE.SC: The combination of the LOCATE and the test for NOT ATLAST is used to determine if a record for the given salesman number is already in the SALESMEN file. In the above program, the new (blank) record is presented on the screen for the user to fill in. The default form has been used in this program, but a programmer-designed form could just as easily have been used. Merely change the F in the PICKFORM statement to **1** to select the first custom form, to **2** to select the second form, and so on. When a record is entered that has a blank salesman number, the current (empty) record is deleted, and an exit is performed from this program. Note that DO_IT! is used to save the newly entered records and exit from Edit mode.

> **STEP 5:** After you have written the menu, write the data entry and modification programs next. This will allow you to put test data into the database files for testing of the other programs.

The program to modify the contents of a salesman record is

```
; SMANCHAN.SC
EDIT "SALESMEN"
WHILE TRUE
   CLEAR
   @ 2,0 ?? "ENTER THE SALESMAN NUMBER- RETURN TO QUIT:"
   ACCEPT "A10" TO MEMSALESNO
   IF ISBLANK(MEMSALESNO)
     THEN QUITLOOP
```

```
   ENDIF
   MOVETO [SASALESNO]
   LOCATE MEMSALESNO
   IF NOT RETVAL
     THEN
       MESSAGE "NO RECORD ON FILE FOR GIVEN SALESMAN NUMBER"
       BEEP
       SLEEP 1000
   ELSE
       PICKFORM "2"
       WAIT RECORD
         MESSAGE "PRESS F2 WHEN EDITING HAS BEEN COMPLETED."
       UNTIL "F2"
       KEYPRESS "F7"
   ENDIF
ENDWHILE
DO_IT!
CLEARALL
RETURN
```

The programs to enter and modify account records are similar to the programs to enter and modify salesman records. They are as follows:

```
; ACCRECEN.SC
EDIT "ACCOUNTS"
END
DOWN
```

```
PICKFORM "F"
WHILE TRUE
   WAIT RECORD
      MESSAGE "PRESS F2 WHEN THIS RECORD HAS BEEN COMPLETED."
   UNTIL "F2"
   IF ISBLANK([ACACCTNO])
      THEN
         DEL
         QUITLOOP
   ENDIF
   MOVETO [ACACCTNO]
   LOCATE [ACACCTNO]
   IF NOT ATLAST()
      THEN
         MESSAGE "A record for this account number already on file."
         BEEP
         SLEEP 2000
         END
         DOWN
      ELSE
         END
         PGDN
   ENDIF
ENDWHILE
DO_IT!
CLEARALL
RETURN
```

```
; ACCRECCH.SC
EDIT "ACCOUNTS"
WHILE TRUE
   CLEAR
   @ 2,0 ?? "ENTER THE ACCOUNT NUMBER- RETURN TO QUIT:"
   ACCEPT "A10" TO MEMACCTNO
   IF ISBLANK(MEMACCTNO)
     THEN QUITLOOP
   ENDIF
   MOVETO [ACCOUNTS -> ACACCTNO]
   LOCATE MEMACCTNO
   IF NOT RETVAL
     THEN
      MESSAGE "NO RECORD ON FILE FOR GIVEN ACCOUNT NUMBER"
      BEEP
      SLEEP 1000
   ELSE
      PICKFORM "2"
      WAIT RECORD
        MESSAGE "PRESS F2 WHEN EDITING HAS BEEN COMPLETED."
      UNTIL "F2"
      KEYPRESS "F7"
   ENDIF
ENDWHILE
DO_IT!
CLEARALL
RETURN
```

Programs to enter and modify the sales records are similar to those for salesmen and accounts, but do contain some significant differences. The differences occur because

1. It is necessary to obtain the company name and the salesman name from other files.
2. There may be more than one sales record entered for one salesman/account combination on any one day.

The following programs are used to enter and modify sales records.

```
; SRECENTE.SC
VIEW "SALESMEN"
VIEW "ACCOUNTS"
SRECCOUNT = NRECORDS("SRECORDS")
EDIT "SRECORDS"
IF SRECCOUNT <> 0
   THEN
     END
     DOWN
ENDIF
PICKFORM "1"
WHILE TRUE
   CLEAR
   WAIT RECORD
     MESSAGE "Press F2 when entry of the sales record has been completed."
   UNTIL "F2"
   IF ISBLANK([SRSALESNO]) OR ISBLANK([SRACCTNO])
      THEN
         DEL
         QUITLOOP
```

```
ENDIF
MOVETO [SALESMEN -> SASALESNO]
LOCATE [SRECORDS -> SRSALESNO]
IF NOT RETVAL
  THEN
     MESSAGE "No record on file for salesman number:",
             [SRECORDS -> SRSALESNO]
     BEEP
     SLEEP 2000
     LOOP
  ELSE
     MEMLNAME = [SALNAME]
     MEMFNAME = [SAFNAME]
     MEMMNAME = [SAMNAME]
     MEMNAME  = MEMLNAME+", "+MEMFNAME+" "+MEMMNAME
ENDIF
MOVETO [ACCOUNTS -> ACACCTNO]
LOCATE [SRECORDS -> SRACCTNO]
IF NOT RETVAL
  THEN
     MESSAGE "No record on file for account number:",
             [SRECORDS -> SRACCTNO]
     BEEP
     SLEEP 2000
     LOOP
  ELSE
     MEMCOMPANY = [ACCOMPANY]
ENDIF
```

```
MOVETO [SRECORDS ->]
[SRCOMPANY] = MEMCOMPANY
CLEAR
@ 5,0 ?? "Name of salesman: ", MEMNAME
@ 6,0 ?? "Name of company : ", MEMCOMPANY
@ 8,0 ?? "ENTER THE SALES RECORD FOR THIS SALESMAN AND COMPANY (Y/N): "
ACCEPT "A1" TO ANSWER
IF ANSWER <> "Y" AND ANSWER <> "y"
  THEN
     MESSAGE "WILL NOT ENTER THIS RECORD."
     BEEP
     SLEEP 2000
     END
     DOWN
     LOOP
ENDIF
LOCATE [SRSALESNO], MEMCOMPANY, [SRACCTNO], [SRDATE]
IF NOT ATLAST()
 THEN
   @ 15,0 ?? "A SALES RECORD IS ALREADY ON FILE FOR THIS ",
            "SALESMAN AND ACCOUNT ON THIS DATE."
   @ 17,0 ?? "ENTER ANOTHER ONE (Y/N)?" ACCEPT "A1" TO ANSWER
   IF ANSWER <> "Y" AND ANSWER <> "y"
     THEN
        BEEP
        SLEEP 2000
        END
        DOWN
```

```
            ELSE
               END
               PGDN
          ENDIF
        ELSE
          END
          PGDN
      ENDIF
ENDWHILE
DO_IT!
CLEARALL
RETURN
```

NOTES ON SRECENTE.SC: When an empty table is edited, Paradox automatically adds a new blank record to the table for you. On occasion this can cause trouble for you by erroneously inserting an extra blank record in the table when the statements END and DOWN are subsequently executed. To overcome this problem, count the number of records in the table before you enter the table in Edit mode. If the file is not empty, i.e., the count is not zero, then you will need to add a new data record to the end of the table. In order to add a new record, execute the END and the DOWN statements as soon as you enter the table. The LOCATE statement for the table SRECORDS can be speeded up by creating secondary indexes on the following fields: SRSALESNO, SRCOMPANY, SRACCTNO, and SRDATE. Again, we cannot create a primary index using just these four fields, for, if we did, we would not be able to store more than one sales record in the table for a specific combination of salesman, account, and date.

; SRECCHAN.SC

```
VIEW "ACCOUNTS"
EDIT "SRECORDS"
WHILE TRUE
```

```
CLEAR
@  1,18 ?? "          CHANGE A SALES RECORD"
@  3,18 ?? "LEAVE SALESMAN OR ACCOUNT NUMBER BLANK TO QUIT"
@  7, 0 ?? "Salesman number : " ACCEPT "A10" TO MEMSALESNO
@  9, 0 ?? "Account  number : " ACCEPT "A10" TO MEMACCTNO
@ 11 ,0 ?? "Date of the sale: " ACCEPT "D"   TO MEMDATE
IF ISBLANK(MEMSALESNO) OR ISBLANK(MEMACCTNO)
   THEN
      QUITLOOP
ENDIF
MOVETO [ACCOUNTS -> ACACCTNO]
LOCATE MEMACCTNO
IF RETVAL
  THEN
    MEMCOMPANY = [ACCOMPANY]
  ELSE
    MESSAGE "No record on file for this account number."
    BEEP
    SLEEP 2000
    LOOP
ENDIF
MOVETO [SRECORDS -> ]
LOCATE MEMSALESNO, MEMCOMPANY, MEMACCTNO, MEMDATE
IF NOT RETVAL
  THEN
     MESSAGE "NO SALES RECORD ON FILE FOR THIS ",
             "SALESMAN AND ACCOUNT ON THIS DATE."
     BEEP
```

```
        SLEEP 2000
        LOOP
   ELSE
        CLEAR
        ? "IF THERE IS MORE THAN ONE SALES RECORD FOR THIS DATE,"
        ? "ALL OF THE SALES RECORDS WILL BE DISPLAYED ON THE SCREEN"
        ? "ONE AT A TIME.  IF YOU DO NOT WISH TO CHANGE THE RECORD"
        ? "CURRENTLY DISPLAYED, TYPE F2.  TYPE ANY KEY TO CONTINUE."
        ANSWER = GETCHAR()
        PICKFORM "2"
        WHILE RETVAL
           WAIT RECORD
               MESSAGE "Enter F2 when the changes have been completed."
           UNTIL "F2"
           DOWN
           LOCATE NEXT MEMSALESNO, MEMCOMPANY, MEMACCTNO, MEMDATE
        ENDWHILE
   ENDIF
ENDWHILE
DO_IT!
CLEARALL
RETURN
```

NOTES ON SCRECCHAN.SC: Strangely enough, the program does not run correctly when the PICKFORM statement appears immediately after the EDIT statement, so it was moved to its current position immediately before the editing WHILE loop. The reason for the problem is that a form stays in effect for all tables, until another PICKFORM statement or until a CLEARALL. The form is not just in effect for the correct table, but for all tables currently in the work area. Note also the strange use of the variable MEMCOMPANY in the LOCATE and the LOCATE NEXT statements. When these statements are used in conjunction with more than one field name at a time, the referenced fields must appear at the beginning of the records. In this case, the name of the company appears within the group of fields at the lefthand end of the record, so we must provide a value for this field in each of the two statements, even though we do not logically need it. Perhaps a better choice for the arrangement of the first four fields in the table would have been SRSALESNO, SRACCTNO, SRDATE, and SRCOMPANY rather than the current order. But an important lesson is learned here. The order of the fields in a table definition can be important in Paradox.

STEP 6: The order of the fields in a table is often important in Paradox.

NOTES ON ENTERING AND MODIFYING SALES RECORDS: During the analysis necessary for the design of the program SRECENTE.SC, it is determined that new secondary indexes for the database file SRECORDS are necessary. They are used to help determine if a sales record has already been entered for the given salesman/account/date combination. This requires only that we create the secondary indexes. No programs need be modified as a result of the addition of one or more indexes.

STEP 7: Add additional indexes to database files as it becomes clear that they are helpful.

We are now almost finished with the preliminary version of the application system. All that remains to do for the preliminary version is to write the program to produce the report. The program to accomplish this is as follows:

```
; SREPPRIN.SC

CLEAR

@ 1,0 ?? "DO YOU WISH TO PRODUCE THE SALES REPORT (Y/N)?"
```

```
ACCEPT "A1" TO ANSWER
IF ANSWER <> "Y" AND ANSWER <> "y" THEN
  RETURN
ENDIF
@ 5,5 ?? "ENTER THE STARTING DATE FOR THE PERIOD:"
ACCEPT "D" TO MEMSDATE
@ 6,5 ?? "ENTER THE ENDING   DATE FOR THE PERIOD:"
ACCEPT "D" TO MEMEDATE
MAXLINES = 50
MYPAGENO = 1
PRINTER ON
CLEAR
PLAY "REPHEAD"
MYROW = 5
SORT "SRECORDS" ON "SRSALESNO", "SRCOMPANY", "SRDATE" TO "SORTSREC"
TOTGAMT = 0
EDIT "SALESMEN"
SCAN
   IF MYROW > MAXLINES
      THEN
         ? "\f" ; FORM FEED
         MYPAGENO = MYPAGENO + 1
         PLAY "REPHEAD"
         ?
         MYROW = 6
   ENDIF
   MEMSALESNO = [SASALESNO]
```

```
MEMLNAME = [SALNAME]
MEMFNAME = [SAFNAME]
MEMNAME  = MEMLNAME+", "+MEMFNAME
IF LEN(MEMNAME) > 35
 THEN
   MEMSHORTNAME = SUBSTR(MEMNAME,1,35)
 ELSE
   MEMSHORTNAME = MEMNAME
ENDIF
?
? [SASALESNO], SPACES(10-LEN([SASALESNO])+1), MEMSHORTNAME
MYROW = MYROW+2
TOTAMT = 0
TOTSAMT = 0
MOVETO [SORTSREC -> SRSALESNO]
LOCATE MEMSALESNO
IF NOT RETVAL THEN
   MOVETO [SALESMEN ->]
   LOOP
ENDIF
FIRST = TRUE
MEMACCTNO = [SRACCTNO]
MEMCOMPANY = [SRCOMPANY]
WHILE RETVAL AND [SRDATE] >= MEMSDATE AND [SRDATE] <= MEMEDATE
   IF MEMACCTNO <> [SRACCTNO]
    THEN
      IF FIRST
```

```
         THEN
            FIRST = FALSE
            ?? SPACES(35-LEN(MEMSHORTNAME)+1), MEMCOMPANY,
               SPACES(69-COL()+1), FORMAT("W10.2,EC", TOTAMT)
         ELSE
            ?
            MYROW = MYROW+1
            ?? SPACES(47), MEMCOMPANY, SPACES(69-COL()+1),
               FORMAT("W10.2,EC", TOTAMT)
      ENDIF
      TOTAMT = 0
   ENDIF
   TOTAMT = TOTAMT+[SRAMOUNT]
   TOTSAMT = TOTSAMT+[SRAMOUNT]
   TOTGAMT = TOTGAMT+[SRAMOUNT]
   MEMCOMPANY = [SRCOMPANY]
   DOWN
   LOCATE NEXT MEMSALESNO
ENDWHILE
IF NOT FIRST THEN
  ?
  MYROW = MYROW + 1
ENDIF
?? SPACES(47-COL()), MEMCOMPANY, SPACES(69-COL()+1),
   FORMAT("W10.2,EC",TOTAMT)
TOTAMT = 0
?
?
```

```
   MYROW = MYROW+2
   ?? SPACES(70), FORMAT("W10.2,EC", TOTSAMT)
   MOVETO [SALESMEN ->]
ENDSCAN
MOVETO [SORTSREC ->]
CANCELEDIT
?
?
?? SPACES(70), FORMAT("W10.2,EC", TOTGAMT)
? "\f"
PRINTER OFF
RETURN

; REPHEAD.SC
? SPACES(35), "SALES REPORT"
? SPACES(35), "STARTING DATE:",MEMSDATE
? SPACES(35), "ENDING   DATE:", MEMEDATE
?? SPACES(5), "PAGE NO:", FORMAT("W3", MYPAGENO)
?
?
?? "SALESMAN"
?? SPACES(3), "NAME"
?? SPACES(32), "COMPANY"
?? SPACES(16), "AMOUNT"
?
?? "----------"
?? SPACES(1)
WHILE NOT PRINTERSTATUS()
```

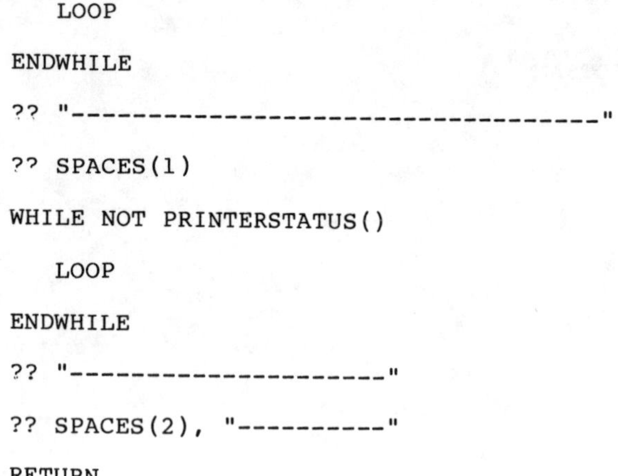

```
    LOOP
ENDWHILE
?? "-----------------------------------"
?? SPACES(1)
WHILE NOT PRINTERSTATUS()
    LOOP
ENDWHILE
?? "---------------------"
?? SPACES(2), "----------"
RETURN
```

NOTES ON REPHEAD.SC: This program is used to print the page header for the report. One unusual feature of the program is the use of the WHILE NOT PRINTERSTATUS( ) loops. In version 1.00 of Paradox, there is a problem with the printer interface. After printing a single space with a statement of the form

? SPACE(1)

the printer is not yet ready to receive the next output. When you insert a loop of the designated type, you will insure that the printer will be ready before the next output is sent. This problem may be printer dependent, so you may not need to include this type of loop in your programs.

Included in the collection of programs for this application system is a program that will empty out all the database files. The purpose of this program is to initialize the system before delivery to the client. Note the simplicity of the program. It contains nothing more than a collection of EMPTY statements. In Paradox, when the records in a table are deleted, all the indexes are automatically updated for you at the appropriate time. The program is

```
; FILEEMPT.SC
EMPTY "SALESMEN"
EMPTY "ACCOUNTS"
EMPTY "SRECORDS"
RETURN
```

STEP 8: Include a program in your system to clear out and initialize all the database files.

The application system is now almost complete. All that remains now is the user documentation and the addition of the programs to delete records from the database files and to include the corresponding functions in the main menu. The user documentation will not be given herein. The new driver for the system and the programs to delete records from the database files follow. The function to recreate the secondary indexes used in the system has not been included in this menu, but you certainly could include it if you wished to. The driver (with the main menu) is

```
; SALES.SC - WITH A PARADOX TYPE OF MENU
; THIS IS THE MAIN DRIVER FOR THE SALES SYSTEM
ECHO OFF
WHILE TRUE
   PRINTER OFF
   MESSAGE "MAKE A SELECTION"
   SHOWMENU
       "EXIT"       : "EXIT FROM THE SYSTEM",
       "SALESMAN-ENTER"   : " ENTER A RECORD FOR A SALESMAN",
       "SALESMAN-CHANGE"  : " CHANGE A RECORD FOR A SALESMAN",
       "SALESMAN-DELETE"  : " DELETE A RECORD FOR A SALESMAN",
       "ACCOUNT-ENTER"    : " ENTER AN ACCOUNT RECORD",
       "ACCOUNT-CHANGE"   : " CHANGE AN ACCOUNT RECORD",
       "ACCOUNT-DELETE"   : " DELETE AN ACCOUNT RECORD",
       "SALES-ENTER"      : " ENTER A SALES RECORD",
       "SALES-CHANGE"     : " CHANGE A SALES RECORD",
       "SALES-DELETE"     : " DELETE A SALES RECORD",
```

```
    "SALES-REPORT"     : " PRINT THE SALES REPORT"
TO CODE
SWITCH
   CASE CODE = "EXIT":
      MESSAGE "NORMAL TERMINATION OF SALES SYSTEM"
      SLEEP 1000
      EXIT
   CASE CODE = "SALESMAN-ENTER":
      PLAY "SMANENTE"
   CASE CODE = "SALESMAN-CHANGE":
      PLAY "SMANCHAN"
   CASE CODE = "SALESMAN-DELETE":
      PLAY "SADELETE"
   CASE CODE = "ACCOUNT-ENTER":
      PLAY "ACCRECEN"
   CASE CODE = "ACCOUNT-CHANGE":
      PLAY "ACCRECCH"
   CASE CODE = "ACCOUNT-DELETE":
      PLAY "ACDELETE"
   CASE CODE = "SALES-ENTER":
      PLAY "SRECENTE"
   CASE CODE = "SALES-CHANGE":
      PLAY "SRECCHAN"
   CASE CODE = "SALES-DELETE":
      PLAY "SRDELETE"
   CASE CODE = "SALES-REPORT":
      PLAY "SREPPRIN"
ENDSWITCH
```

```
   RELEASE VARS ALL
   CLEAR
ENDWHILE
```

Now we show the programs to delete records from the database files:

; SADELETE.SC

```
; DELETE SALESMAN RECORDS
VIEW "SALESMEN"
EDIT "SRECORDS"
WHILE TRUE
   CLEAR
   @ 1,0 ?? "Enter the number of the salesman to be deleted",
            " - RETURN to quit: "
   ACCEPT "A10" TO MEMSALESNO
   IF ISBLANK(MEMSALESNO) THEN
      QUITLOOP
   ENDIF
   MOVETO [SALESMEN -> SASALESNO]
   LOCATE MEMSALESNO
   IF NOT RETVAL THEN
       @ 3,0 ?? "No record on file for salesman number ", MEMSALESNO
       MESSAGE "Press any key to continue."
       X = GETCHAR()
       LOOP
   ENDIF
   PICKFORM "F"
   WAIT RECORD
```

```
      MESSAGE "Press DEL to delete this record, otherwise press ESC."
   UNTIL "Del", "Esc"
   KEYPRESS "F7"
   IF RETVAL = "Del"
     THEN
       DEL
       MESSAGE "The record has been deleted."
       SLEEP 500
       MOVETO [SRECORDS -> SRSALESNO]
       LOCATE MEMSALESNO
       WHILE RETVAL AND NOT ATLAST()
          DEL
          LOCATE NEXT MEMSALESNO
       ENDWHILE
   ELSE
       MESSAGE "The record will not be deleted."
       BEEP
       SLEEP 2000
   ENDIF
ENDWHILE
DO_IT!
CLEARALL
RETURN
```

NOTES ON SADELETE.SC: Notice that the deletion routine also examines the SRECORDS table to delete any associated records. A secondary index on SRSALESNO would clearly be helpful here. Similarly, when we wish to delete records in the SRECORDS table that are associated with specific accounts, we would like to have a secondary index on SRACCTNO.

; ACDELETE.SC

```
; DELETE ACCOUNT RECORDS
VIEW "ACCOUNTS"
EDIT "SRECORDS"
WHILE TRUE
   CLEAR
   @ 1,0 ?? "Enter the number of the account to be deleted",
            " - RETURN to quit: "
   ACCEPT "A10" TO MEMACCTNO
   IF ISBLANK(MEMACCTNO) THEN
      QUITLOOP
   ENDIF
   MOVETO [ACCOUNTS -> ACACCTNO]
   LOCATE MEMACCTNO
   IF NOT RETVAL THEN
       @ 3,0 ?? "No record on file for account number ", MEMACCTNO
       MESSAGE "Press any key to continue."
       X = GETCHAR()
       LOOP
   ENDIF
   PICKFORM "F"
   WAIT RECORD
     MESSAGE "Press DEL to delete this record, otherwise press ESC."
   UNTIL "Del", "Esc"
   KEYPRESS "F7"
   IF RETVAL = "Del"
     THEN
```

```
        DEL
        MESSAGE "The record has been deleted."
        SLEEP 500
        MOVETO [SRECORDS -> SRACCTNO]
        LOCATE MEMACCTNO
        WHILE RETVAL AND NOT ATLAST()
           DEL
           LOCATE NEXT MEMACCTNO
        ENDWHILE
    ELSE
        MESSAGE "The record will not be deleted."
        BEEP
        SLEEP 2000
    ENDIF
ENDWHILE
DO_IT!
CLEARALL
RETURN
```

; **SRDELETE.SC**

```
; DELETE SALES RECORDS
VIEW "SALESMEN"
VIEW "ACCOUNTS"
EDIT "SRECORDS"
WHILE TRUE
   CLEAR
   @ 1,32 ?? "DELETE A SALES RECORD"
   @ 2,32 ?? " LEAVE BLANK TO QUIT"
```

```
@ 5, 1 ?? "Salesman number: " ACCEPT "A10" TO MEMSALESNO
@ 6, 1 ?? "Account  number: " ACCEPT "A10" TO MEMACCTNO
@ 7, 1 ?? "Date of the sale:" ACCEPT "D"   TO MEMDATE
IF ISBLANK(MEMSALESNO) OR ISBLANK(MEMACCTNO) THEN
   QUITLOOP
ENDIF
MOVETO [SALESMEN -> SASALESNO]
LOCATE MEMSALESNO
IF RETVAL
  THEN
    MEMLNAME = [SALNAME]
    MEMFNAME = [SAFNAME]
    MEMMNAME = [SAMNAME]
    MEMNAME = MEMLNAME+", "+MEMFNAME+" "+MEMMNAME
  ELSE
    MESSAGE "No record on file for salesman number: ", MEMSALESNO
    BEEP
    SLEEP 2000
    LOOP
ENDIF
MOVETO [ACCOUNTS -> ACACCTNO]
LOCATE MEMACCTNO
IF RETVAL
  THEN
    MEMCOMPANY = [ACCOMPANY]
  ELSE
    MESSAGE "No record on file for account number: ", MEMACCTNO
```

```
      BEEP
      SLEEP 2000
      LOOP
ENDIF
CLEAR
@ 1,0 ?? "SALESMAN:"
@ 2,3 ?? "NAME:", MEMNAME
@ 3,3 ?? "NUMBER:", MEMSALESNO
@ 5,0 ?? "ACCOUNT:"
@ 6,3 ?? "COMPANY:", MEMCOMPANY
@ 7,3 ?? "NUMBER:", MEMACCTNO
MESSAGE "IS THIS THE CORRECT SALESMAN AND COMPANY (Y/N)?"
@ 10,0 ACCEPT "A1" TO ANSWER
IF ANSWER <> "Y" AND ANSWER <> "y" THEN
   LOOP
ENDIF
MOVETO [SRECORDS -> SRSALESNO]
LOCATE MEMSALESNO, MEMCOMPANY, MEMACCTNO, MEMDATE
IF NOT RETVAL
  THEN
     MESSAGE "NO RECORDS ON FILE FOR THIS SALESMAN, ACCOUNT, AND DATE."
     BEEP
     SLEEP 2000
     LOOP
  ELSE
     MESSAGE "RECORDS WILL BE DISPLAYED ON THE SCREEN, ONE AT A TIME."
     SLEEP 2000
```

```
ENDIF
PICKFORM "1"
WHILE RETVAL
   CLEAR
   WAIT RECORD
      MESSAGE "Press DEL to delete, ESC to skip this record."
   UNTIL "Del", "Esc"
   IF RETVAL = "Del"
     THEN
        DEL
        MESSAGE "Will delete this record."
        SLEEP 1000
     ELSE
        MESSAGE "WILL NOT DELETE THIS RECORD."
        BEEP
        SLEEP 2000
        MOVETO RECORD RECNO()+1
   ENDIF
   LOCATE NEXT MEMSALESNO, MEMCOMPANY, MEMACCTNO, MEMDATE
ENDWHILE
KEYPRESS "F7"
IF [SRSALESNO] = MEMSALESNO AND [SRACCTNO] = MEMACCTNO AND
        [SRDATE] = MEMDATE
   THEN
      CLEAR
      WAIT RECORD
         MESSAGE "Press DEL to delete, ESC to skip this record."
```

```
                UNTIL "Del", "Esc"
                IF RETVAL = "Del"
                  THEN
                     DEL
                     MESSAGE "Will delete this record."
                     SLEEP 1000
                  ELSE
                     MESSAGE "WILL NOT DELETE THIS RECORD."
                     BEEP
                     SLEEP 2000
                     DOWN
               ENDIF
     ENDIF
ENDWHILE
DO_IT!
CLEARALL
RETURN
```

NOTES ON SRDELETE.SC: In some applications, it is desirable to delete records based on dates, i.e., to delete old records. It is certainly possible to include this kind of deletion here also, by deleting the appropriate sales records only if the date of the record is less than the given date. This is relatively easy to do, since you can directly compare one object (variable or field) of type date with another object of type date. Note also that a secondary index on SRDATE seems desirable.

> **STEP 9:** Include a program in your system to delete old or undesirable records.

By this time, you might find it hard to keep track of all the secondary indexes being used in the application system. The following program is not only useful to keep track of the secondary indexes, but can also be used to rebuild these indexes in case of a failure on the part of Paradox to properly maintain one or more of these indexes.

```
; INDEXES.SC

INDEX "SRECORDS" ON "SRSALESNO"

INDEX "SRECORDS" ON "SRACCTNO"

INDEX "SRECORDS" ON "SRDATE"

RETURN
```

> **STEP 10:** Include a program in your system to recreate the secondary indexes.

SOME LAST NOTES ON THE SYSTEM: One problem remains that has not been satisfactorily resolved. If the user changes the company name in the ACCOUNTS file, how does it get changed in the SRECORDS file? This system does not automatically perform this operation. To handle this problem, it would be necessary to modify the program ACCRECCH.SC to find the appropriate records in the SRECORDS file and change them.

Another problem has to do with the use of the ? and ?? statements in the programs. In a number of cases, you might wish to replace the ? statements with PRINT statements, but, if you do, then the COL( ) function cannot be used. In addition, I believe that the ? and ?? statements are more useful than the PRINT statement in debugging the programs.

CHAPTER

7 ADVANCED DESIGN PRINCIPLES

7.1 REASONS FOR DESIGN PRINCIPLES

We are interested in good design principles for three major reasons:

1. To help us to quickly build systems that work efficiently
2. To allow us to modify systems during construction
3. To allow us to modify systems after they have been in use for some time

7.2 THE DESIGN PRINCIPLES

7.2.1 Where To Start

7.2.1.1 Discover the Nature of the Problem to be Solved

Most of the time, when you construct a new system using Paradox you will be converting from a manual (paper work) system to an automated one (one that uses a computer). Even if you are converting from another computerized system, most of the principles are the same. In this section, we will look at some of the more modern design principles and adapt them especially for use with Paradox.

I think of analysis as attempting to determine the nature of the current system (the current method of doing business) and of determining what is wrong with it. Design is the determination of a solution to problems with the current system. If there is no current system, i.e., if the system to be designed will be an entirely new one, then the design question changes from "what do we have to do to fix the problem" to "what do we want to do here." In order to understand what is wrong with the current system, we must understand the nature of the current system. There are two parts to an existing system: the problem to be solved by the system and the manner in which the system attempts to solve the problem.

> In order to understand a system, we must understand both the nature of the problem that the system is attempting to solve and the manner in which it attempts to solve it.

> One task of analysis is to determine how the current system falls short of meeting the needs of the users. In order to do this, you will need to determine both the problem to be solved by having a system in the first place and the manner in which the system attempts to solve that problem. You will then be able to determine the manner in which the current system falls short of what is desired.

7.2.1.2 Examine the Inputs, Outputs, and Processes

The first step in the analysis of an existing system is to examine all the paper work associated with it. Examine both the input documents and the output documents for data elements. Also examine what the people or the computer does with the data. The processing of the raw data, either by people or by the computer, can often give valuable insights into the entire process of converting raw data into information.

We examine how people (or computers) use the data in order to determine the nature of the problem that they are trying to solve. At this point, we are interested in what they wish to do, not how they actually do it. Since people almost always think in terms of how they do their job, it is necessary to convert what they say into a different form. Consider the following:

> A clerk must produce the payroll for all the employees in the company. When you talk to her about her job, she gives the following information:

> "I go to the main office and collect all the time cards for the employees. Then I compute the number of hours worked during the week for each employee. From John, I get a list that has the name of each hourly employee and his or her hourly pay rate. I carefully examine the number of hours for each employee to make sure that only authorized employees have submitted time cards with more than 40 hours per week. Then I fill out the paychecks and record the amount paid."

It is clear from the above that we must be able to separate "what" must be done from "how" it is done. We must also be able to fill in the missing details for the payroll computation. The following is a description of the "what" that must be done to produce a payroll, with many of the missing details filled in.

For each hourly employee

    Verify the number of hours

For each salaried employee

    Determine amount to be paid

Then, for each employee

    Compute the gross earnings

    Compute all deductions

    Compute taxes and withholding

    Compute net pay

    Update quarterly and year-to-date totals

In this manner, we strip the *nature of the problem to be solved* away from *how someone has chosen to solve the problem*. This does not mean that we ignore or discard the manner in which the problem is currently being solved. Rather, we wish to understand the nature of the problem before we attempt to build a system in Paradox to solve it. At each step we ask the question "How do you do your job?" Then we analyze the responses to determine "What is the actual problem that you are trying to solve?"

ANALYSIS RULE 1: Ask people how they do their jobs. Then separate the "how" from the "what," in order to increase your understanding of the real nature of the problem to be solved.

At this point, you have obtained a list of all the input documents, all the reports (output documents), and all the things that people (or machines) do—at least all that you currently know about. There will always be gaps in your knowledge at this stage.

ANALYSIS RULE 2: Your understanding of a system will evolve over a period of time.

7.2.1.3 A First Attempt at Files

The next step in our understanding of the current system is to examine the nature of the stored data, or the files. From discussions with the clients (users), you may discover what data is currently being kept on file. Compare the data items (sometimes called fields) in these records with the data items on the input documents and the output documents. It is clear that all the data used by processes must come either directly or indirectly from the input documents and that all the data used for reports must come from the files. Our task now is to discover the true nature of the data. We now wish to understand "what" the data really is, not just "how" it is currently used and stored.

ANALYSIS RULE 3: Understand what the data is, not just how it is currently stored.

The technique that I prefer, in an attempt to understand the nature of the data, is to start with the input documents. There is great organizational knowledge manifested in the standard working documents of the organization. Consider, as an example, a sales receipt of the following form:

SALES RECEIPT				
RECEIPT NUMBER:		DATE:		
NAME:				
STREET:				
CITY:				
STATE:	ZIP:			
TYPE OF SALE				
CASH:	CHARGE:	ACCOUNT NUMBER:		
ITEMS SOLD				
ITEM NUMBER	DESCRIPTION	QUANTITY	COST	TOTAL

DIAGRAM 7.1

This input document has two main parts, the fields at the top and the tabular arrangement at the bottom. The fields at the top allow the clerk to enter specific information exactly once on the form. There is room at the bottom for each item sold. The major difference between the two parts of the form is that information at the top can (and need) be entered only once. The information at the bottom may be repeated. We will call the information entered in the top part the HEADER and the information entered in the bottom part the ITEMs. The organization has placed each of the indicated fields into the SALES RECEIPT, because it considers it appropriate to do so. Use this kind of information as a starting point in your analysis of the data.

> **ANALYSIS RULE 3:** Look for input documents that have both a HEADER and ITEMs. They will help you understand how the organization views the relationship between certain types of raw data items.

For now, we will think of the SALES RECORDs as being stored in a file in the imaginary collection of files that we are building. We will construct this imaginary collection of files for our own use so that we can better understand the nature of the data that we are working with. We continue in this manner, building data files for each of the input documents that we have encountered so far in our analysis.

Assume that we have discovered the following files: INVENTORY, SALES, and CHARGE ACCOUNTS. The main input document for the SALES file is the SALES RECEIPT. The organization uses this document to update the INVENTORY file and, if the sale is a charge, to update the CHARGE ACCOUNT file. We are not specifically interested here in precisely how the organization currently stores this data. We are interested in constructing an imaginary collection of files in order to better understand the data that we are working with. The major rule that we now impose is that HEADERs and ITEMs will always be separated into different files and that each file will contain exactly one type of record. For example, there will be a file for all SALES HEADERs, and there will be another file for all SALES ITEMs, no matter which SALES RECEIPT they originally came from. In fact, whenever we find a document that has both HEADER and ITEMs (the items are the repeating information), we will separate the document and store it in two files. In each case, we will need to record which ITEMs are associated with which HEADERs in order to make the stored data useful. A record in the SALES HEADER file (at this point in our analysis) will have the fields

RECEIPT NUMBER
DATE
NAME
STREET
CITY
STATE
ZIP
TYPE OF SALE
ACCOUNT NUMBER

and a record in the SALES ITEM file will have the fields

RECEIPT NUMBER
ITEM NUMBER
DESCRIPTION
QUANTITY
COST
TOTAL

ANALYSIS RULE 5: Every file will contain exactly one type of record, i.e., each of the records in any one file will look just like any other record in that file, except for the actual data that it contains.

ANALYSIS RULE 6: Whenever we have input documents that contain a HEADER and ITEMs, or any type of repeating information, we will store the HEADER in one file and store the ITEMs in another file.

Further investigation reveals that the INVENTORY file contains the following fields

ITEM NUMBER
DESCRIPTION
COST TO ORGANIZATION
RETAIL COST
QUANTITY ON HAND
REORDER POINT
REORDER AMOUNT

and that the CHARGE file contains the following fields

ACCOUNT NUMBER
NAME
STREET
CITY
STATE
ZIP
TOTAL AMOUNT DUE
CURRENT AMOUNT DUE
AMOUNT DUE OVER 30 DAYS
AMOUNT DUE OVER 60 DAYS
AMOUNT DUE OVER 90 DAYS

We observe that some of the data appears in more than one file. In particular, the fields NAME, STREET, CITY, STATE, ZIP, and ACCOUNT NUMBER appear both in the SALES HEADER file and in the CHARGE file.

ACCOUNT NUMBER appears in the CHARGE file because it identifies the specific account (it is the key of the CHARGE file). The ACCOUNT NUMBER appears in the SALES HEADER file in order to identify the associated CHARGE ACCOUNT record. It is clear that we cannot remove it from either file. Note the role that the ACCOUNT NUMBER plays in each of the files. In the CHARGE file, ACCOUNT NUMBER is the key or major identifier. In the SALES HEADER file, it provides information for us to link the SALES RECEIPT to the correct CHARGE ACCOUNT record. It is necessary that it appears in both of these files. But what about the fields NAME, STREET, CITY, STATE, and ZIP? Must they appear in *both* files? The answer is no. We can remove these fields from the SALES HEADER file records, and obtain them when we need them from the CHARGE ACCOUNT record. Remember that we are now performing analysis. We are trying to understand the data that we are working with, so we remove any extraneous fields from our files.

> **ANALYSIS RULE 7:** Group fields into records so that each record describes just one type of object (like a charge account record, a sale, or a sales item).

> **ANALYSIS RULE 8:** If the same field appears in more than one file (type of record), determine where it most appropriately belongs. Make sure that it appears in that file. In all other files where it appears, determine if it must appear there for linking purposes. If so, leave it there. If it does not *have* to appear there, entirely remove it from that file.

7.2.1.4 A Refinement of the Files

Applying analysis rule 8, we remove the fields NAME, STREET, CITY, STATE, and ZIP from the SALES HEADER file records and the new SALES HEADER file records will contain only the fields

RECEIPT NUMBER
DATE
TYPE OF SALE
ACCOUNT NUMBER

We apply this rule to the SALES ITEM file records and remove the DESCRIPTION and COST field since they are available in the corresponding INVENTORY file record

RECEIPT NUMBER
ITEM NUMBER
QUANTITY
TOTAL

At this point, we might examine the SALES ITEM file to see if there are any more fields that should be removed. Since TOTAL can always be computed from the COST (available from the INVENTORY file) and the QUANTITY, it is not absolutely necessary that we retain this field in the SALES ITEM record. The TOTAL field in the SALES ITEM records may, in the end, not even be something that we wish to store. At this point we just don't know, so we remove it from the SALES ITEM file records. The new SALES ITEM file has the fields

RECEIPT NUMBER
ITEM NUMBER
QUANTITY

> **ANALYSIS RULE 9:** If a field can be computed from other fields already in the collection of files, then remove it. (It can always be put back in later, if we decide that we really do want it.)

We are now close to a bare-bones collection of files. We have a minimal number of files and a minimal number of fields in each file. This helps us to understand the data itself.

7.2.1.5 Indicating Linkages

The next step is to indicate how the data will be used. In our system, we may wish to perform the following operations:

1. Enter records
2. Change records

3. Delete (remove) records
4. Produce bills for the customers

Therefore, we will need to directly access ACCOUNT records by account number, INVENTORY records by ITEM NUMBER, SALES HEADERs by receipt number, and SALES ITEMs by a combination of receipt number and item number. In addition, we will need to link SALES HEADERs to the corresponding SALES ITEMs and SALES ITEMs to the appropriate INVENTORY records. We will see later that all these accesses and linkages will determine what indexes are necessary in our final files, so it is important to record them as we discover them.

> **ANALYSIS RULE 10:** As you discover the need for accesses to your files, record this information.

I personally like to record the necessary accesses with the following type of diagram:

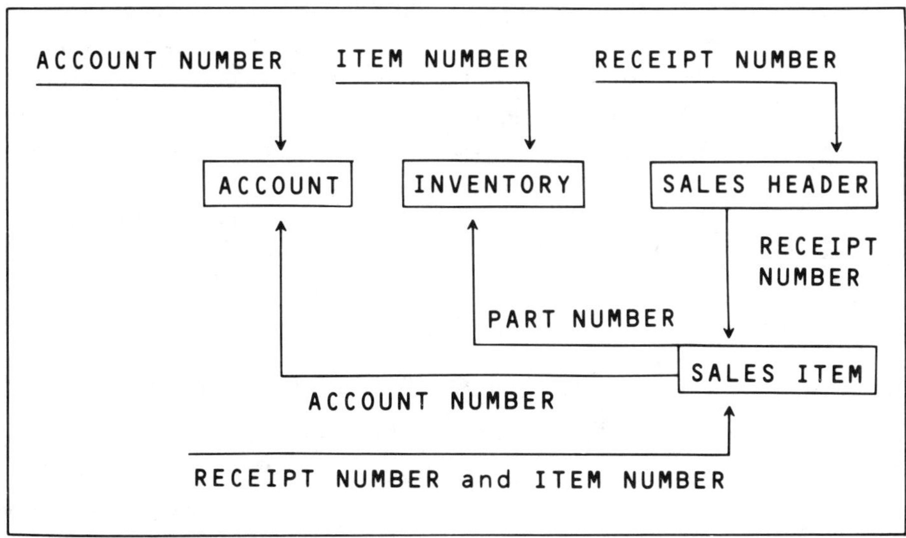

In the above diagram, rectangular boxes represent the files that we have constructed so far and each arrow represents a type of access to a file. Each arrow is labeled with the name of a field. If we wish to access the INVENTORY file and obtain a record with a specific ITEM NUMBER, then we show this in the following manner:

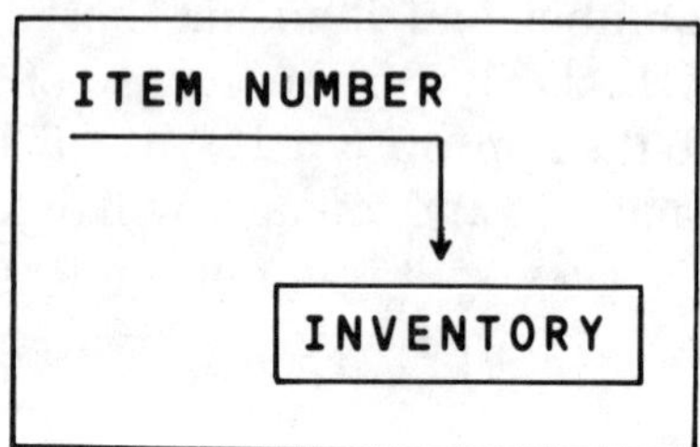

In a later place, we will see that this means that it will be necessary to index the INVENTORY file on the field ITEM NUMBER.

7.2.1.6 Additions to the Current Files

As our knowledge of the system evolves, and it most assuredly will, we may discover more input documents. This may lead to the need for more files or for more fields in existing files. It may also lead to the need for more accesses, as represented by the access arrows. Even an examination of output documents (reports) could tell us that we need more files, fields, and/or access arrows. But we must be careful here. No matter what we add to our (imaginary) file structure (the files together with the arrows), we must make sure that our files are as clean and as simple as possible. We wish to increase our understanding of the data items and how they are related to each other, not confuse things with a messy diagram.

Whenever we wish to add new fields to our collection of files, we follow these simple rules:

1. Determine the type of object that the field describes.
2. See if there is a file that describes that same object.
3. If the field in question is already in the file, no further action is necessary.

4. If the field is not already in the file, add it to the file.
5. If there is no file that describes the same object, add a new file and put the field in it (with any necessary key).
6. Add new linkages as necessary.

Consider our simple SALES/INVENTORY system as developed in this chapter. Suppose that we discover the need to have a credit limit for each of our accounts. Surely this is account information, so we try to add it to the ACCOUNT file records. It does not already exist in the file, so we add it to each of the records in that file. In the case where we wish to record individual payments for each account, we first determine that this is account information. But, since there may be a number of payments for each account, this is really repeating account information. As demonstrated above, we do not add this information directly to the ACCOUNT file. Rather, we create a new file for the payments and link it to the ACCOUNT file. If we wish to find all payments associated with a specific account, we will need the linkage shown by the following diagram:

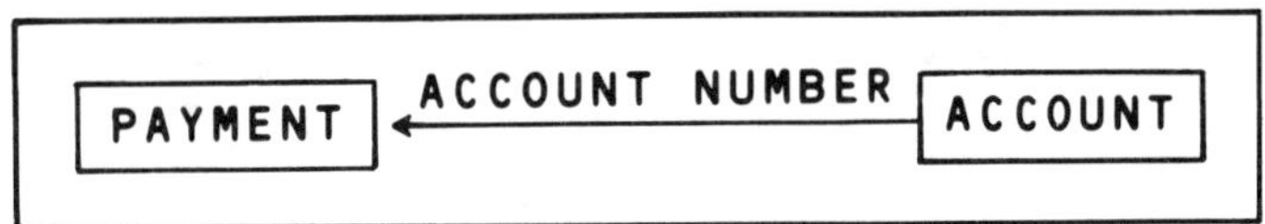

and the fields in the PAYMENT file will be

ACCOUNT NUMBER
AMOUNT PAID
DATE PAID
CHECK NUMBER

7.2.2 Examination of the Files for Other Problems

7.2.2.1 Problems Caused by Data Redundancy

Redundancy, or the duplication of data, might be useful or might cause trouble. Most of the trouble caused by redundancy shows up in maintenance of the files. In particular, it may be difficult to add, delete, or modify records in files if there is data redundancy. We will examine some of the problems caused by data redundancy in this section. Let us examine a relatively simple situation first.

> A company wishes to maintain a record for each employee. The specific information to be stored is: last name, first name, current address, name of spouse, date hired, the department where employed, and the name of the manager of the department. If the data for each employee is placed all in one record, i.e., there is one record for each employee and there are no other records in the system, then the record will contain the following fields
>
> **EMPLOYEE FILE FIELD NAMES**
>
> EMPNO (EMPLOYEE NUMBER)
> LAST NAME
> FIRST NAME
> ADDRESS
> SPOUSE
> DATE
> DEPARTMENT
> MANAGER
>
> and will have the following structure:

EMPLOYEE FILE

EMPNO	LAST NAME	FIRST NAME	ADDRESS	SPOUSE	DATE	DEPARTMENT	MANAGER
25	Able	Mary	Elm	John	1984	Research	A. Jones
37	Green	Tom	Maple	Jane	1985	Accounting	S. Smith
15	Black	John	Main	Sally	1982	Research	A. Jones
20	Brown	Nancy	Oak	Bill	1983	Research	A. Jones
	. . .	. . .	. . .	. . .	. . .	. . .	. . .

DIAGRAM 7.2

This file has problems with maintenance. If you wish to record the name of a manager for a new department, you will have to wait until there is at least one employee in the department. If there is only one employee in a department and that employee leaves that department, then the name of the manager of the department will also be removed from the file. If the manager of the department is changed, then every occurrence of the name in the MANAGER field must be changed. Finally, we must always be concerned that all the occurrences of a MANAGER name in a file are spelled the same.

All the problems mentioned above are directly related to the inclusion of the MANAGER field in the EMPLOYEE file. In fact, the EMPLOYEE file, as it is currently structured, contains information about two different types of objects: employees and managers. If we separate the two types of information into two different files, we obtain the following:

NEW EMPLOYEE FILE	DEPARTMENT FILE
EMPNO	DEPARTMENT
LAST NAME	MANAGER
FIRST NAME	
ADDRESS	
SPOUSE	
DATE	
DEPARTMENT	

and the data now looks like this:

NEW EMPLOYEE FILE

EMPNO	LAST NAME	FIRST NAME	ADDRESS	SPOUSE	DATE	DEPARTMENT
25	Able	Mary	Elm	John	1984	Research
37	Green	Tom	Maple	Jane	1985	Accounting
15	Black	John	Main	Sally	1982	Research
20	Brown	Nancy	Oak	Bill	1983	Research
	.	.	.	.	.	.
	.	.	.	.	.	.
	.	.	.	.	.	.

DIAGRAM 7.3

DEPARTMENT FILE

DEPARTMENT	MANAGER
Research	A. Jones
Accounting	S. Smith

DIAGRAM 7.4

Now the only duplicated data is in the DEPARTMENT field (Diagram 7.4). This kind of duplication is normally considered to be acceptable, since it is necessary to link employees to the departments in which they work. The kind of problems with file maintenance that we encounter in this example are not unusual. Since file maintenance is always important, we need some general techniques both to determine problems and to fix the problems.

One method to determine problems is through the use of *dependency diagrams.* A dependency diagram shows which fields in a file (or collection of files) are determined by which other fields. We say that a field named B is determined by a field namedA, if A and B are fields in the same record and, knowing the value of A, you can then uniquely determine the value of B. In this case, we also say that B is dependent on A. In the example given in Diagram 7.2, each of the following is dependent on or determined by EMPNO: LAST NAME, FIRST NAME, ADDRESS, SPOUSE, DATE, DEPARTMENT, and MANAGER. In addition, MANAGER is determined by DEPARTMENT, since, if you know the department, then you can determine the manager. In the example in Diagram 7.2, if you know that the DEPARTMENT is Research, then you can search through the file for a record with the value Research in the DEPARTMENT field. Once such a record is obtained, the MANAGER field in the same record gives you the name of the manager of the Research department. A dependency diagram for the original EMPLOYEE file is shown in Diagram 7.5.

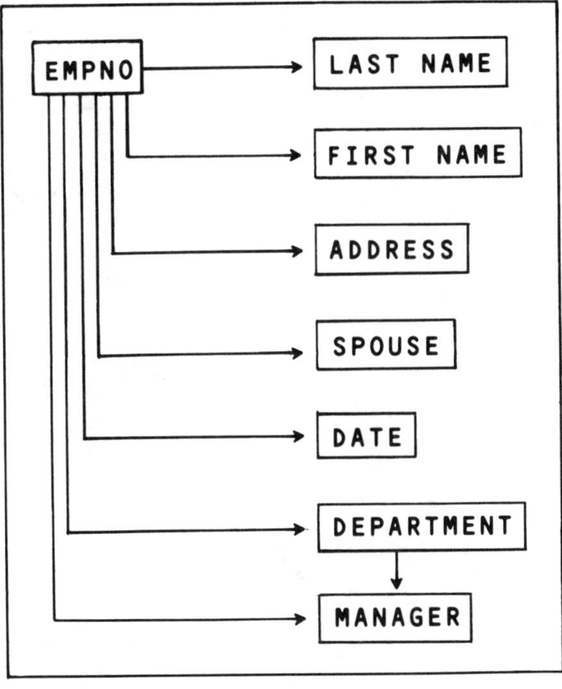

DIAGRAM 7.5

After the decomposition, the two dependency diagrams are:

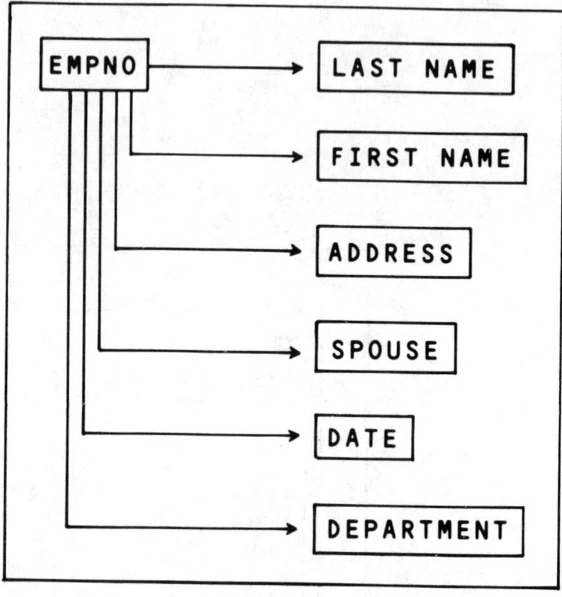

DIAGRAM 7.6

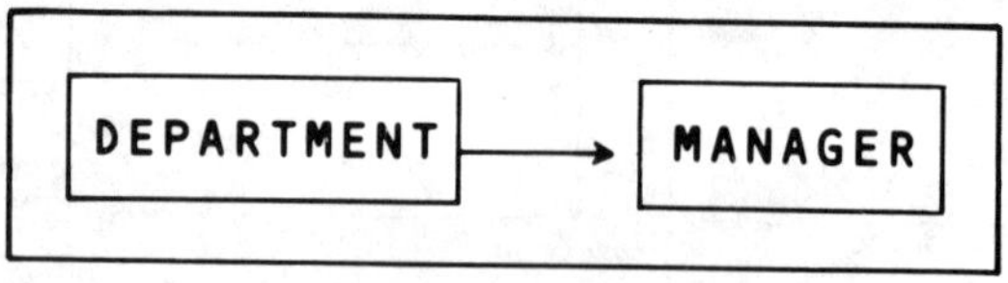

DEPARTMENT

MANAGER

DIAGRAM 7.7

In Diagram 7.5 we can clearly see that all the fields in the record are dependent on the key EMPNO. We can also see that MANAGER is dependent on DEPARTMENT.

In general, there are good dependencies and bad dependencies. In the following, a field or combination of fields is called a *key* if it can be used to uniquely distinguish one record in a file from any other.

1. If a record has only one choice for a key and if that key has exactly one field in it, then a good dependency is when a nonkey field, i.e., one that is not the key, is dependent on the key.
2. If a record has only one choice for a key and if that key has more than one field in it, then a good dependency is when a nonkey field, i.e., one that is not part of the key, is dependent on the entire key, but not dependent on any subpart of the key.
3. If a record has a choice of more than one key, then a good dependency is when a nonkey field, i.e., one that is not part of any choice of key, is dependent on each choice of key, but not dependent on any subpart of any choice of key.

Any other dependency is considered to be a bad dependency. Note that there are two major kinds of bad dependencies: a nonkey field dependent on another nonkey field and a nonkey field dependent on part of a key. There are other kinds of bad dependencies, but they are much more complex and are not easily determined by dependency diagrams.

When we break up a file into two or more files in order to remove any bad dependencies, we call this process *file decomposition*. The following provides examples of bad dependencies and the decompositions that remove these bad dependencies. Remember: bad dependencies will lead to problems with maintenance of files.

EXAMPLE 1: A DEPENDENCY BETWEEN NONKEY FIELDS (ONE KEY)

See the employee record system above.

EXAMPLE 2: A DEPENDENCY BETWEEN NONKEY FIELDS (TWO KEYS)

Let's use the same file as used in Example 1, but let's add a field for the social security number (SSN). In this case, both the employee number (EMPNO) and the social security number (SSN) could be used as keys. The dependency diagram that we start with is

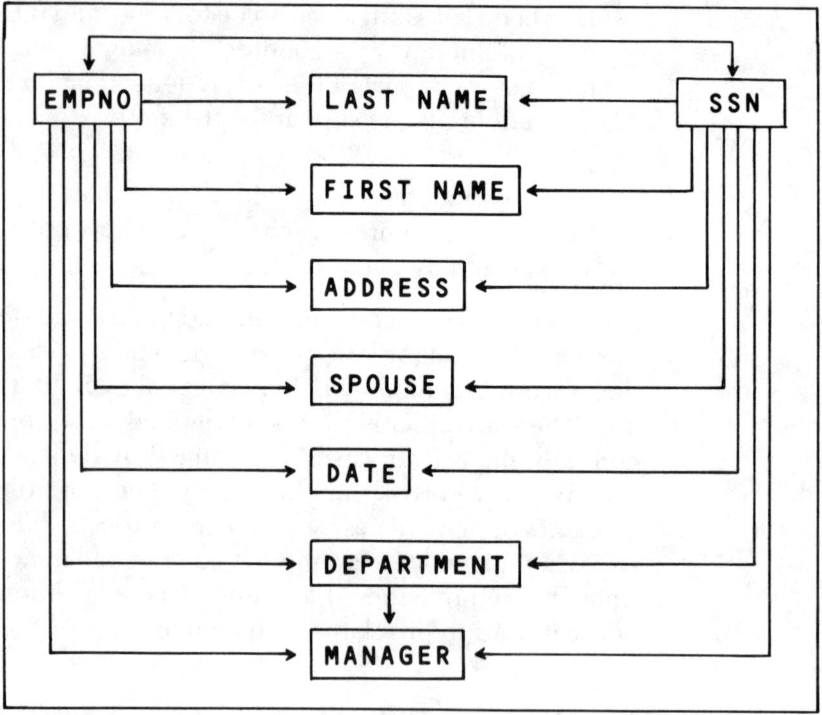

DIAGRAM 7.8

This example is almost the same as Example 1 above, except that there are two keys. Note that *either* EMPNO *or* SSN could be chosen for the key here. We will decompose this diagram in a manner similar to the decomposition used in Example 1 and obtain the following two diagrams:

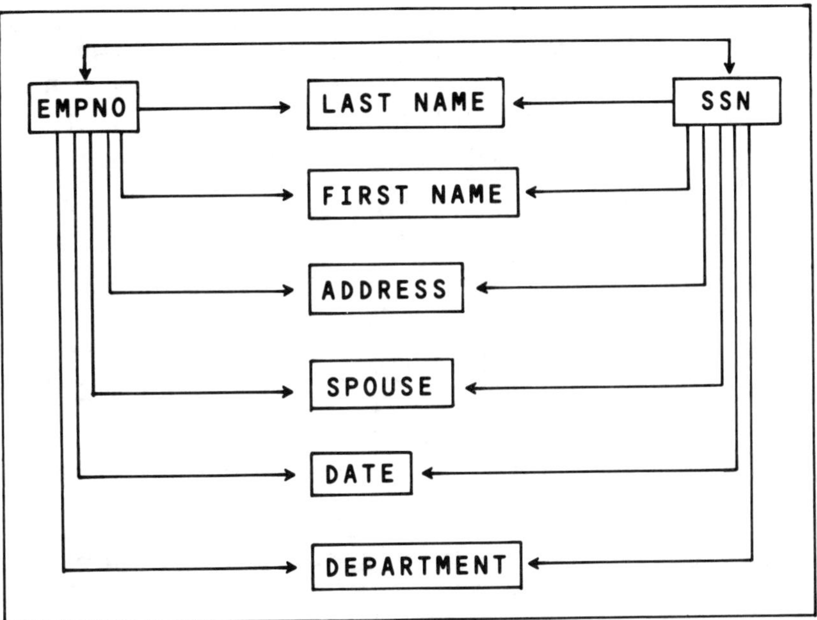

DIAGRAM 7.9

and

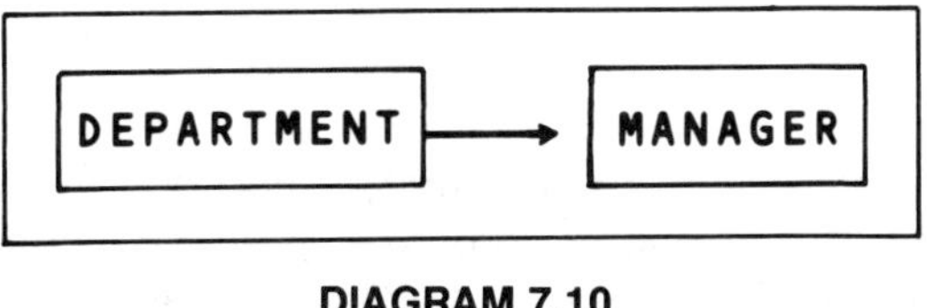

DIAGRAM 7.10

This decomposition would lead to two files. The first file would have the fields: EMPNO, SSN, LAST NAME, FIRST NAME, ADDRESS, SPOUSE, DATE, and DEPARTMENT. The second file would have the fields DEPARTMENT and MANAGER.

EXAMPLE 3: DEPENDENCY UPON PART OF THE KEY

In this example, we consider inventory records. The fields that we wish to store in our records are: PARTNO (part number), DESCRIPTION, ITEM WEIGHT, SUPPLIERNO (supplier number), SUPPLIERNAME, ADDRESS, and QOH (quantity on hand). If we store all these fields in one record, then the dependency diagram is:

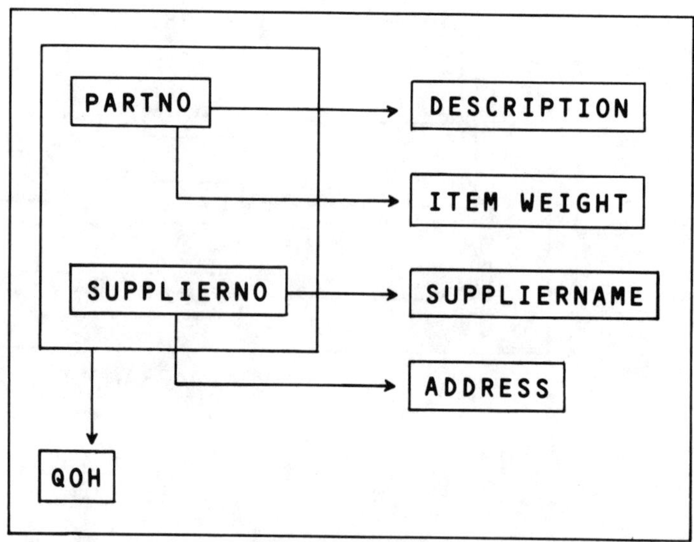

DIAGRAM 7.11

We actually have three types of information in this record: part, supplier, and quantity. The part information consists of: PARTNO, DESCRIPTION, and ITEM WEIGHT. The supplier information consists of: SUPPLIERNO, SUPPLIERNAME, and ADDRESS. The quantity information consists of: PARTNO, SUPPLIERNO, and QOH, where QOH depends, in this example, on both PARTNO and SUPPLIERNO. In this manner, we can keep track of the quantity on hand from each supplier. The key for the whole record is the combination of PARTNO and SUPPLIERNO, since, if we know these two values, we can determine all the other field values. Note that DESCRIPTION and ITEM WEIGHT are each dependent only on PARTNO and that SUPPLIERNAME and ADDRESS are each dependent only on SUPPLIERNO. An example of the duplication that you would obtain with this type of file is shown in the following diagram:

PARTNO	DESCRIPTION	ITEM WEIGHT	SUPPLIERNO	SUPPLIERNAME	ADDRESS	QOH
P1	COMPUTER	55	S1	OFFICE MACH.	NEW YORK	5
P1	COMPUTER	55	S2	BUSINESS SUP.	CHICAGO	3
P2	PRINTER	35	S1	OFFICE MACH.	NEW YORK	2
P2	PRINTER	35	S2	BUSINESS SUP.	CHICAGO	4
.	.	.	.	.	.	.
.	.	.	.	.	.	.
.	.	.	.	.	.	.

DIAGRAM 7.12

In Diagram 7.12 we see that both part and supplier information must be duplicated. In particular, DESCRIPTION and ITEM WEIGHT is the duplicated part information, and SUPPLIERNAME and ADDRESS is the duplicated supplier information. If we wish to remove this unnecessary duplication, we will need to decompose the original file into a number of new files. To accomplish this, we make use of the dependency diagram given in Diagram 7.11. The key for the original record is the combination of PARTNO and SUPPLIERNO. Since DESCRIPTION and ITEM WEIGHT are dependent only on PARTNO, we place PARTNO, DESCRIPTION, and ITEM WEIGHT in one file. Similarly, we place SUPPLIERNO, SUPPLIERNAME, and ADDRESS in another file. Since QOH depends on both PARTNO and SUPPLIERNO, we place PARTNO, SUPPLIERNO, and QOH in a third file. At this point, we have the following (decomposed) dependency diagrams:

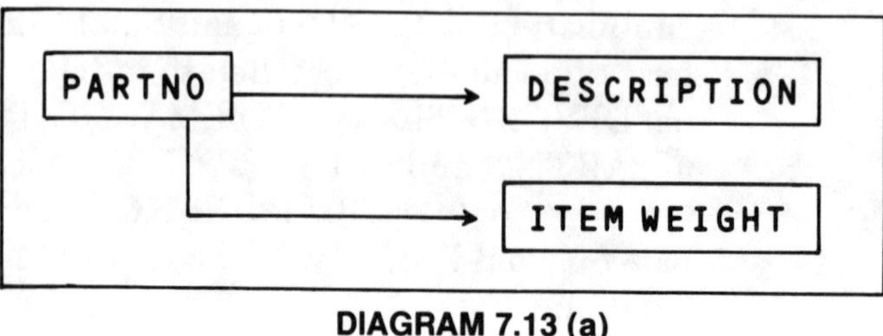

DIAGRAM 7.13 (a)

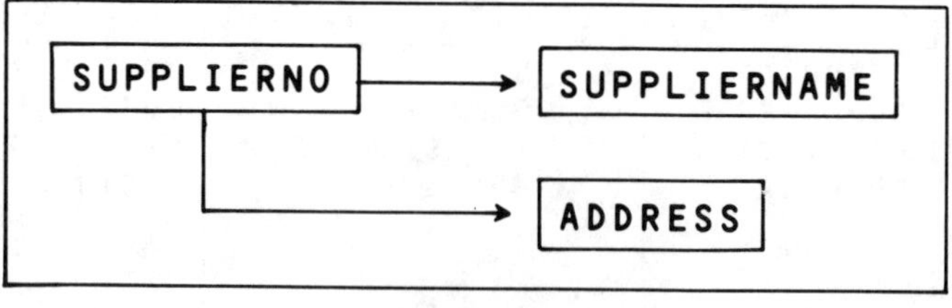

DIAGRAM 7.13 (b)

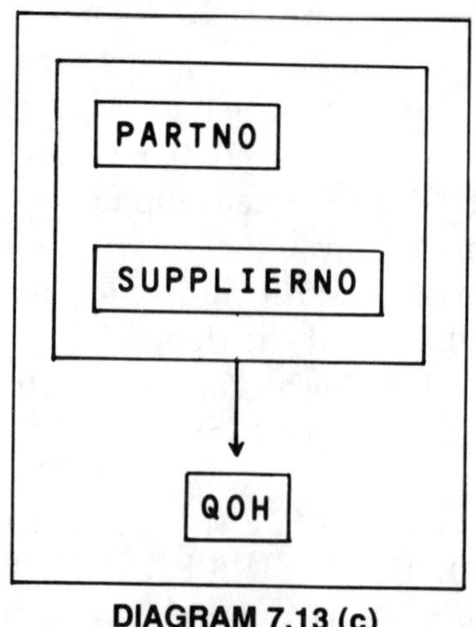

DIAGRAM 7.13 (c)

Each of the separate diagrams (7.13: a, b and c) would correspond to separate Paradox files. The key of the first is PARTNO, the key of the second is SUPPLIERNO, and the key of the third is the combination of PARTNO and SUPPLIERNO. The data given in Diagram 7.12 now look like the following:

PARTNO	DESCRIPTION	ITEM WEIGHT
P1	COMPUTER	55
P2	PRINTER	35
.	.	.
.	.	.
.	.	.

DIAGRAM 7.14 (a)

SUPPLIERNO	SUPPLIERNAME	ADDRESS
S1	OFFICE MACH.	NEW YORK
S2	BUSINESS SUP.	CHICAGO
.	.	.
.	.	.
.	.	.

DIAGRAM 7.14 (b)

PARTNO	SUPPLIERNO	QOH
P1	S1	5
P1	S2	3
P2	S1	2
P2	S2	4
.	.	.
.	.	.
.	.	.

DIAGRAM 7.14 (c)

When we create the Paradox files to match our dependency diagrams, we do not use a key in the sense of the dependency diagrams. We always use indexes to facilitate the accesses needed. The term *key*, as used in the discussions of dependency diagrams, is employed to help us identify the type of data that we are working with. In this example, we were able to identify three distinct types of data (part, supplier, and quantity). This helped us to construct the final choice of files. Only after the files have been chosen do we consider the indexes.

7.2.2.2 Over-decomposition

Whenever we construct files, there is a danger of over-decomposition. To over-decompose is to break up a file into too many pieces. For example, consider an employee file that contains SSN, NAME, and ADDRESS. Even if the only dependencies in the file are of NAME and ADDRESS on SSN, we might still decompose the file into two files, each having SSN as the key. Then the first file would have the fields SSN and NAME, and the second file would have the fields SSN and ADDRESS. What, if anything, have we gained and what have we lost?

This type of decomposition *never* gains us anything and is always expensive in terms of time. Over-decomposition has no advantages and, if we wish to determine both the name and the address from the social security number, then it is quite time-consuming. The general rule to avoid over-decomposition is: if two files have exactly the same key, and if the combination of the two files introduces no bad dependencies, then the two files *must* be combined.

7.2.3 Data Clustering: A Speed Technique

In previous sections in this chapter, we have seen how to construct a collection of data and determine the indexes that will give us the greatest degree of flexibility. Using files constructed in this manner, we will be able to access all the data, we will easily be able to add (or delete) both fields and records (files), and we will easily be able to add (or delete) indexes as needed. This type of file system also helps us see the real nature of the data that we are working with, since it is as simple as we can make it. At this point, our collection of files has little or no redundancy. The lack of redundancy will simplify file maintenance, but it will probably make certain types of processing slow.

To understand this problem, let us look at a collection of files constructed in the manner described earlier in this chapter.

A personnel department keeps records on all their employees, present and past. The type of information maintained by this department includes each of the following data items:

EMPLOYEE FILE

1. Name
2. Address
3. Social security number

DEPARTMENT

1. Department name
2. Department number

WORK HISTORY FILE

1. Social security number
2. Department number
3. Date started work in department
4. Date terminated work in department

These three files really have no unnecessary redundancy, since both the social security number and the department number are necessary for identification purposes in the WORK HISTORY file (in fact, the combination of these two fields constitutes the key for this file). These three files satisfy all the rules previously given in this chapter for the construction of a good file system, but there may still be some speed problems.

If we wish to print a report that shows, for a single department, a list of all the employees that have ever worked in that department in order by starting date, we will probably perform the following steps:

1. Obtain the number of the department.
2. Find all the records in the WORK HISTORY file for this department (access the records in date order or sort to put in the proper date order).
3. For each record selected from the WORK HISTORY file, print the employee name and the starting data.

In order to perform step 3, we will need the name of the employee for each record selected. The records that we are looking at are in the WORK HISTORY file, but the employee names are in the EMPLOYEE file. Thus, for each record selected from the WORK HISTORY file, we will have to make a separate access to the EMPLOYEE file. If we are working with large files, it might take 1 second to find each required name. If the number of employees that have worked in a specific department is 1000, then the amount of time required to print this simple report is at least 1000 seconds, or almost 17 minutes.

Note that just about all the time required for the report came from accessing the EMPLOYEE file to obtain the names of the employees. If, whenever we enter a new record into the WORK HISTORY file, we take the name of the employee from the EMPLOYEE file and copy it into the WORK HISTORY file record, we will save about 17 minutes each time the above-mentioned report is produced.

What have we really done in the above example? We have a process that can be performed with our current collection of files (and indexes), but it is too slow. We decide to speed up this process by carefully duplicating selected information. By doing so, we break some of the rules presented earlier in this chapter, since we have a field in the new EMPLOYEE WORK file that is dependent only on part of the key: the key consists of the combination of SOCIAL SECURITY NUMBER and DEPARTMENT NUMBER, but the EMPLOYEE NAME is dependent only on part of the key, the SOCIAL SECURITY NUMBER.

The *careful* duplication of fields in order to speed up selected processes is called *data clustering*. Since data clustering forces us to break some of the rules that we have set for ourselves, we must now examine the consequences of doing so. The duplication of the employee name in the WORK HISTORY file will:

1. Take extra space.
2. Make name changes more difficult.

In general, because data clustering forces us to change our collection of files and to put them into a form in which file maintenance is more difficult, we must carefully decide if we wish to use data clustering.

I recommend the following approach to file design:

1. First design the files so that they are in the best form.
2. Determine from the prospective users (the clients) which operations will be performed frequently.
3. Use data clustering and the other speed techniques introduced in this book to speed up those processes that you know will be so time-consuming that the users cannot live with them.
4. As the users gain familiarity with the system that you have constructed for them and as the size of each of the files grows, more speed problems may appear. Make the appropriate modifications to speed up the system.

CHAPTER

8

A LARGE SYSTEM IN PAL

8.1 INTRODUCTION TO THE SYSTEM

The following example is a working system. The user documentation, each of the Paradox database files, and each of the PAL programs is listed. The programs have been listed in alphabetical order for convenience in locating them. A chart showing the procedure dependencies has also been included.

In the programs you will note that some of the code has been duplicated, rather than having been placed in a separate file and executed as needed. This is because of the restriction on the number of files available on floppy disks.

The following application system has been tested on an IBM PC-XT using Paradox Version 1.00.

8.2 AN OUTLINE SHOWING THE LOGICAL STRUCTURE OF THE PAYABLES SYSTEM

```
PAYABLES                     Main driver and menu

    INVENTER                 Enter an invoice record

    INVCHANG                 Change an invoice record

    COMENTER                 Enter a company record

    COMCHANG                 Change a company record

    COMLIST                  Produce  a list of all  compa-

                             nies on file

    INVREPOR                 Produce  a report showing  all

                             invoices to be paid

        INVRHEAD             Heading for report

    INVPAY                   Mark invoices for future  pay-

                             ment
```

INVPREPO	Produce pre-payment report
INVPRHEA	Heading for pre-payment report
CHECKPRI	Print checks and update payment file
INVFIND	Locate invoices and display on screen
INVFHEAD	Heading for screen display of invoices
PAYFIND	Locate payments and display on screen
INVDELET	Delete record from the system
INVCHECK	Change the last check number used
INDEXES	Reindex the database files

8.3 THE DATABASE FILES USED IN THE SYSTEM

Checks table

STRUCT	Field Name	Field Type
1	CHLNAME	A20
2	CHFNAME	A15
3	CHCOMPANY	A25
4	CHPOBOX	A10
5	CHSTREET	A20
6	CHCITY	A15
7	CHSTATE	A2
8	CHZIP	A9
9	CHCHECKNO	A6
10	CHDATE	D
11	CHAMOUNT	$
12	CHDESC	A30

Checks Table (continued)

STRUCT	Field Name	Field Type
13	CHINVNO	A25
14	CHDEPT	A2
15	CHSERVTYP	A3

Company table

STRUCT	Field Name	Field Type
1	COMNO	A4*
2	COMLNAME	A20
3	COMFNAME	A15
4	COMCOMPANY	A25
5	COMPOBOX	A10
6	COMSTREET	A20
7	COMCITY	A15
8	COMSTATE	A2
9	COMZIP	A9

Invoice table

STRUCT	Field Name	Field Type
1	INVIDNO	A5*
2	INVLNAME	A20
3	INVFNAME	A15
4	INVCOMPANY	A25
5	INVPOBOX	A10
6	INVSTREET	A20
7	INVCITY	A15
8	INVSTATE	A2
9	INVZIP	A9
10	INVPAYTYPE	A1
11	INVCHECKNO	A6
12	INVDATEDUE	D
13	INVAMTDUE	$
14	INVDISCAMT	$
15	INVDISCDAT	D

Invoice Table (continued)

STRUCT	Field Name	Field Type
16	INVPAIDDAT	D
17	INVPAIDAMT	$
18	INVREASON	A25
19	INVINVNO	A25
20	INVSERVTYP	A3
21	INVDEPT	A2
22	INVPAYAMT	$
23	INVPAYDATE	D
24	INVPDINFUL	A1
25	INVDESC	A30

Invmisc table

STRUCT	Field Name	Field Type
1	INVMIDNO	N
2	INVMB1CHNO	N
3	INVMB2CHNO	N
4	INVMCOMNO	N

Invpayme table

STRUCT	Field Name	Field Type
1	INVPIDNO	A5
2	INVPCHECKNO	A6
3	INVPPAYDATE	D
4	INVPAMT	$

8.4 DOCUMENTATION FOR THE PAYABLES SYSTEM

Introduction

The purpose of this software system is to allow a greater degree of control over accounts payable. The complete system, hardware and software, consists of the following:

1. The computer is the IBM PC–XT.
2. The printer is the EPSON MX–100 III (it really is an OKIDATA Microline 84 with the PLUG'N PLAY ROMS).
3. The payables software is delivered on two disks. One disk contains the programs (written in PAL) and the other disk contains the data files.
4. The Paradox system is delivered separately, on several other disks. It is recommended that you use a hard disk machine for this application.

One type of paper is necessary: 14″ x 11″.

The appropriate disk type for backup of programs and data is: 5 1/4″, dual sided, double density.

The disks may be purchased in boxes of ten. The recommended disk type is: DYSAN, 104/2D.

Even the best quality new disks may not work. If a new disk does not work, it usually can be returned to the seller for a refund.

It is strongly recommended that backup copies of database files be made on a regular basis. These backups are required, since there are several situations that might destroy the data on the disk. Some, but not all, of the situations that might destroy the data on the disk are a power failure or a reboot while writing on the disk.

It is also recommended that a backup of the database files be made each time immediately before the actual payment routine is run. This insures that the payment process can be rerun in case of system failure, such as power failure or paper jamming in the printer.

Follow the appropriate procedures for backup of database files. If you are to use a floppy disk for purposes of backup, remember to format new disks before their first use. Be careful not to format the hard disk, since this will cause the loss of all programs and data on the disk.

The Payables System

The system is run as follows:

1. Turn on your machine.
2. When prompted by the operating system (when C> appears on the screen), key in PARADOX PAYABLES.

A menu will then appear on the screen. The purpose of the menu is to display the major functional areas on the screen and allow you to select the desired function. If a request for data is displayed on the screen with a white (or green) background, then your response will be limited to this area. If your entry does not entirely fill the area, you will need to enter a carriage return at the end of the data to indicate that you have completed the entry. If your entry completely fills the area, a tone will sound and the computer will acknowledge the completion of the entry. In all other cases, when you are prompted for input, i.e., when there is no white (or green) background, you must enter the required information and then press the RETURN button (the carriage return). You may then be presented with another menu in order to further refine the choice of action, or the selected action may start immediately, depending on the function selected.

The main menu allows the choice of the following major functional areas:

A. EXIT FROM SYSTEM
B. INVOICE, ENTER
C. INVOICE, CHANGE
D. COMPANY, ENTER
E. COMPANY, CHANGE
F. COMPANIES, LIST
G. INVOICES TO BE PAID REPORT
H. REVIEW AND MARK INVOICES FOR LATER PAYMENT
I. PRINT PRE-PAYMENT REPORT
J. PROCESS PAYMENTS AND PRINT CHECKS
K. FIND AND DISPLAY INVOICES
L. FIND AND DISPLAY PAYMENTS
M. DELETE RECORDS
N. CHANGE LAST CHECK NUMBER
O. REINDEX FILES

EXIT FROM SYSTEM

Terminate operation of the PAYABLES SYSTEM.

INVOICE, ENTER

Enter a new invoice. A unique identification code will be automatically assigned to each invoice at the time that it is entered. This unique code may be obtained at any time through the use of the FIND module, item K. You will be asked if the company name is already on file. If so, after you enter the company number, the company name and address will be automatically transferred from the company file to the invoice for you. If not, you will be asked for the company information.

INVOICE, CHANGE

Used to change information on an invoice already in the system. You will need to know the unique system ID for the invoice before it can be changed.

COMPANY, ENTER

Enter a record for a company. This record will contain name and address information for use when entering invoices. A unique company code is automatically assigned by the system.

COMPANY, CHANGE

Change information about a company. You will need to know the unique code for the company before the company record can be changed. The code for the company may be obtained from the lists of companies provided by function F, listing the company names.

COMPANIES, LIST

List the company records in order by company name or by company number.

INVOICES TO BE PAID REPORT

You will be prompted for the beginning date of the period. All the invoices not already paid in full, i.e., those not actually paid in full and not marked as paid in full if a discount is applicable, will be reported, if either the due date or the discount date is not greater than 7 days from the beginning date. Use this report to determine which invoices to pay, the amount to be paid, and the payment date. This report presents the invoices in order by due date, and provides both the total amount due each day and a grand total due for the indicated period.

REVIEW AND MARK INVOICES FOR LATER PAYMENT

Select either a single invoice to be marked for payment or review all the ones listed on the INVOICES TO BE PAID REPORT. Enter payment amounts to be made and payment dates. Actual payments may be partial or full, but the total payment amount (the sum of any previous amounts and the current amount) cannot be greater than the invoice amount. If you apply a discount, be sure to mark the invoice as paid in full, if appropriate.

PRINT PRE-PAYMENT REPORT

Use this report to verify the amount to be paid on all invoices selected for payment on a particular date. If an error is found, use the REVIEW AND MARK INVOICES FOR LATER PAYMENT module to select the individual invoices and to change the payment date or amount. If any changes are made, you may run this report again to verify that the changes were performed correctly. This report presents the invoices in order by service type within department and provides a total of payments to be made for each service type in each department, for each department, and for all invoices to be paid on the given date.

PROCESS PAYMENTS AND PRINT CHECKS

For each invoice to be paid on the selected date, update the INVOICE record to reflect the actual payment made and record the payment in the PAYMENT file. In addition, print one check for each invoice to be paid. The information for the printing of the checks is actually stored in a separate file, independent of both the INVOICE and the PAYMENT file. This technique will allow you to reprint the checks, if necessary. You will want to reprint the checks, for example, if the check stock jams in the printer.

FIND AND DISPLAY INVOICES

Find invoices by unique ID, company invoice number, last name of individual, company name, or date. Display part of the invoice on the screen. This module may be used to determine the unique ID for the invoice or to determine its status (how much paid so far).

FIND AND DISPLAY PAYMENTS

The invoice is identified by its unique ID number. Information from the invoice and the associated payments are displayed on the screen.

DELETE RECORDS

Mark records for deletion. Physically remove and reformat the files upon actual exit from this module. Delete invoice, payment, or company records. If you delete an invoice, all associated payments will also be deleted. You may delete invoices by unique ID (whether paid or not) or you may delete all old paid invoices. Individual payments are deleted by unique ID. If an individual payment is deleted, the amount of the payment is subtracted from the appropriate invoice so that the amount paid so far matches the records in the payment file. Companies are deleted by unique ID.

CHANGE LAST CHECK NUMBER

Change the last check number used on either or both banks. This is particularly useful when the system is first initialized, so that the check numbering may be continued from the previous manual system.

REINDEX FILES

Used to reindex the secondary indexes if you suspect that the index information for the system is incorrect.

Recommended Order of Operation

1. Establish the beginning numbers to be used on the checks for each of the two bank accounts.
2. Enter information for companies or individuals to whom you regularly make payments.
3. Print a listing of the information entered in step 2. Make changes in this information as appropriate.
4. Enter invoices as necessary. You may use the INVOICE, CHANGE module, if desired, to view the invoices to determine that the information is recorded correctly.
5. Print the INVOICES TO BE PAID REPORT to determine which invoices are to be paid during the next 7 days.
6. Enter information concerning the amounts of the invoices and dates that they are to be paid. You may select a single invoice for payment or you may view all the invoices for payment. When viewing all the invoices for payment, the system will present only those that are not yet paid in full (or marked as paid in full) and whose payment dates (or discount dates) are less than or equal to the end of the payment period. You may elect to make no payment, make a partial payment, or to pay in full. The system will not let you pay more than the original amount due.
7. Print the prepayment report to review the payments to be made on the date(s) that you have selected. If you catch any errors in the payment dates or amounts, use the REVIEW AND MARK INVOICES FOR LATER PAYMENT module to correct them. Then print the prepayment report again to verify that the changes were performed correctly.
8. Make a backup copy of the INVOICE and PAYMENT files before processing payments and printing checks.
9. Process payments and print the checks. The module to process payments and print the checks will allow you either to process the payments and then print the checks, or to print the checks only. This means that you may reprint the checks if, for example, the check stock jams in the printer. When you process the payments, you destroy any previous check information. This is a protection feature

to insure that checks do not accidentally get printed twice. Unfortunately, if you process payments and then do not print the checks, then the first check information is destroyed the next time that you process payments. Therefore, if you process payments and then accidentally process payments again, you will not be able to print the checks associated with the first processing. It is therefore imperative that you print the checks immediately after each processing of payments. If, for some reason, you actually do process payments without printing the checks and the check information is destroyed, you will need to copy the files from your backup disk(s). Each time that you mark invoices for payment, you can select only one payment date. Thus, each time that you process your invoices for payment, all the checks for the payment of the selected invoices will be printed on one day and all of them will have the same date on them.

Starting Up the System

Because of the complexity of a software system such as this one, it is desirable to try the system first with a limited amount of data. This gives you the opportunity to be able to verify manually that the system does or does not work correctly. Then, when you are convinced that the system works correctly with a limited amount of data, gradually increase the amount of data in the system and verify again that the system works correctly. Finally, increase the amount of the data in the system to full capacity. This technique will help you to determine personally that the system works in the manner that you desire. Many organizations take three full accounting cycles (usually 3 months) to test out a new system and have the errors removed.

Warranty

Because of the nature of software construction, it must be assumed that any newly delivered software system will contain some errors, even though every effort has been made by the programmer to insure that the software is as error free as possible. In the event of errors or problems, feel free to contact me at any time. My current work telephone number is 555-1212. In case of errors, I will make every reasonable effort to correct the problem as quickly as possible.

8.5 THE PROGRAMS

; CHECKPRI.SC

```
; PROCESS ACTUAL PAYMENTS AND PRINT THE CHECKS
; MEMPROCFLG = INDICATES WHETHER PAYMENTS WERE PROCESSED THIS
;              TIME OR NOT
VIEW "INVOICE"
VIEW "INVMISC"
VIEW "CHECKS"
EDIT "INVPAYME"
CLEAR
@ 1,0 TEXT
  THIS PROGRAM WILL PROCESS PAYMENTS AND/OR PRINT PAYMENT CHECKS.

  EACH TIME YOU RUN THIS PROGRAM TO PROCESS PAYMENTS, THE TEMPORARY
  INFORMATION FROM WHICH CHECKS ARE PRINTED IS DESTROYED.  THIS
  MEANS THAT YOU NEED TO PRINT THE CHECKS FOR THE PREVIOUSLY
  PROCESSED PAYMENTS BEFORE YOU PROCESS MORE PAYMENTS.

  IF YOU PROCESS PAYMENTS AND HAVE DIFFICULTY PRINTING THE CHECKS,
  YOU MAY RUN THIS PROGRAM AGAIN, WITHOUT PROCESSING MORE PAYMENTS,
  IN ORDER TO PRINT THE CHECKS AGAIN.  IF YOU RE-PRINT THE CHECKS,
  MAKE SURE THAT YOU DESTROY ALL OLD COPIES OF THE CHECKS.

  THIS PROGRAM MAY BE USED TO PROCESS PAYMENTS AND/OR PRINT CHECKS.

ENDTEXT
```

```
MESSAGE "CONTINUE WITH THIS PROGRAM (Y/N)"
ACCEPT "A1" PICTURE "&" TO ANSWER
IF ANSWER <> "Y" THEN
  RETURN
ENDIF
MEMCOUNT = 0
MEMPROCFLG = FALSE
IF NRECORDS("INVPAYME") = 0
  THEN FIRSTPAY = TRUE
  ELSE FIRSTPAY = FALSE
ENDIF
CLEAR
@ 1,1 ?? "DO YOU WISH TO PROCESS INVOICES FOR PAYMENT (Y/N):"
ACCEPT "A1" PICTURE "&" TO ANSWER
IF ANSWER <> "Y" THEN
  MEMPROCFLG = FALSE
ELSE
  CLEAR
  @ 0,0
  ? "THE PAYMENT DATE IS THE DATE THAT YOU HAVE SPECIFIED TO"
  ? "ACTUALLY PROCESS THE PAYMENT AND PRINT THE CHECK."
  ? "ENTER THE PAYMENT DATE IN THE FORM MM/DD/YY:"
  @ 8,0 ACCEPT "D" TO MEMDATE
  CLEAR
  MEMMB1CHNO = [INVMISC -> INVMB1CHNO]
  MEMMB2CHNO = [INVMISC -> INVMB2CHNO]
  ? "NOW DESTROYING PREVIOUS TEMPORARY CHECK INFORMATION"
```

```
? "IN PREPARATION FOR PROCESSING THE CURRENT PAYMENTS."
CANCELEDIT
EMPTY("CHECKS")
EDITKEY
FIRSTCHECK = TRUE
; CREATE RECORD FROM WHICH CHECK WILL BE PRINTED
CLEAR
? "TODAY'S DATE WILL APPEAR ON THE CHECK AS THE ACTUAL PAYMENT "
?? "DATE."
MESSAGE "PRESS ANY KEY TO CONTINUE"
BEEP
X = GETCHAR()
IF NRECORDS("INVOICE") = 0 THEN
  CLEAR
  @ 1,0 ?? "INVOICE FILE IS EMPTY"
  MESSAGE "PRESS ANY KEY TO CONTINUE"
  BEEP
  SLEEP 2000
  CLEARALL
  RETURN
ENDIF
MOVETO [INVOICE ->]
SCAN
  IF [INVDEPT] <> "01" AND [INVDEPT] <> "02" AND [INVDEPT] <> "03"
    THEN
        ? "ERROR IN DEPARTMENT NUMBER FOR INVOICE=", [INVIDNO]
        ? "CAN NOT PAY THIS INVOICE"
        BEEP
```

```
     SLEEP 2000
     LOOP
ENDIF
IF [INVPAYDATE] <> MEMDATE THEN
  LOOP
ENDIF
MOVETO [CHECKS ->]
END
IF FIRSTCHECK
  THEN
    FIRSTCHECK = FALSE
  ELSE
    DOWN
ENDIF
[CHLNAME] = [INVOICE -> INVLNAME]
[CHFNAME] = [INVOICE -> INVFNAME]
[CHCOMPANY] = [INVOICE -> INVCOMPANY]
[CHPOBOX] = [INVOICE -> INVPOBOX]
[CHSTREET] = [INVOICE -> INVSTREET]
[CHCITY] = [INVOICE -> INVCITY]
[CHSTATE] = [INVOICE -> INVSTATE]
[CHZIP] = [INVOICE -> INVZIP]
[CHDATE] = TODAY()
[CHAMOUNT] = [INVOICE -> INVPAYAMT]
[CHDESC] = [INVOICE -> INVDESC]
[CHINVNO] = [INVOICE -> INVINVNO]
[CHDEPT] = [INVOICE -> INVDEPT]
```

```
    [CHSERVTYP] = [INVOICE -> INVSERVTYP]
    IF [INVOICE -> INVDEPT] = "01" THEN
      MEMMB1CHNO = MEMMB1CHNO+1
      MEMCHNO = STRVAL(MEMMB1CHNO)
      [CHCHECKNO] = MEMCHNO
    ELSE
      MEMMB2CHNO = MEMMB2CHNO+1
      MEMCHNO = STRVAL(MEMMB2CHNO)
      [CHCHECKNO] = MEMCHNO
    ENDIF
    MOVETO [INVOICE ->]
    [INVCHECKNO] = MEMCHNO
    MEMCOUNT = MEMCOUNT+1
ENDSCAN
MEMTDATE = TODAY()
MOVETO [INVOICE ->]
; STORE PAYMENT RECORD AND UPDATE INVOICE USING TODAY'S DATE
; AS ACTUAL PAYMENT DATE
SCAN
  IF [INVPAYDATE] <> MEMDATE THEN
    LOOP
  ENDIF
  MOVETO [INVPAYME ->]
  END
  IF FIRSTPAY
    THEN
      FIRSTPAY = FALSE
    ELSE
```

```
        DOWN
      ENDIF
      [INVPIDNO] = [INVOICE -> INVIDNO]
      [INVPPAYDATE] = MEMTDATE
      [INVPAMT] = [INVOICE -> INVPAYAMT]
      [INVPCHECKN] = [INVOICE -> INVCHECKNO]
      MOVETO [INVOICE ->]
      [INVPAIDDAT] = TODAY()
      [INVPAIDAMT]= [INVPAIDAMT]+[INVPAYAMT]
      [INVPAYAMT] = 0
      [INVPAYDATE] = BLANKDATE()
    ENDSCAN
    MEMPROCFLG = TRUE
  ENDIF
  IF (NOT MEMPROCFLG) AND ANSWER = "Y" THEN
    CLEAR
    @ 1,0
    ? "EITHER NO PAYMENTS TO BE MADE ON THE SPECIFIED DATE,"
    ? "OR ALL OF THE PAYMENTS FOR THIS DATE HAVE ALREADY BEEN PROCESSED."
    MESSAGE "PRESS ANY KEY TO CONTINUE"
    X = GETCHAR()
  ENDIF
  ; UPDATE MISC FILE WITH NEW CHECK NUMBERS
  IF MEMPROCFLG THEN
    MOVETO [INVMISC ->]
    [INVMB1CHNO] = MEMMB1CHNO
    [INVMB2CHNO] = MEMMB2CHNO
```

```
ENDIF
; PRINT CHECKS
CLEAR
IF MEMCOUNT <> 0 THEN
  MEMDATE = TODAY()
ELSE
  CLEAR
  @ 1,0
  ? "SINCE NO PAYMENTS WERE PROCESSED DURING THIS EXECUTION OF THE"
  ? "PROGRAM, YOU NEED TO ENTER THE DATE THAT THE PAYMENTS WERE"
  ? "ACTUALLY PROCESSED."
  ?
  ? "ENTER THE DATE OF PROCESSING"
  ?
  ACCEPT "D" TO MEMDATE
ENDIF
; PROCESS FOR DEPARTMENT 1
MOVETO [CHECKS ->]
MEMDEPTCNT= 0
SCAN
  IF [CHDEPT] = "01" THEN
     MEMDEPTCNT = MEMDEPTCNT + 1
   ENDIF
ENDSCAN
IF MEMDEPTCNT = 0 THEN
  CLEAR
  ? "NO CHECKS DRAWN ON FIRST BANK"
  MESSAGE "PRESS ANY KEY TO CONTINUE"
```

```
    X = GETCHAR()
  ELSE
    CLEAR
    @ 1,0
    ? "IN PREPARATION FOR PRINTING OF CHECKS"
    ? "    1. TURN THE PRINTER OFF"
    ? "    2. SET ROTARY DIAL TO 1"
    ? "    3. INSERT THE CHECK STOCK FOR FIRST BANK"
    ? "       SO THAT THE TOP OF THE PRINT GUIDE IS ALIGNED"
    ? "       WITH THE HORIZONTAL PERFORATION AND SO THAT"
    ? "       THE PRINT GUIDE IS BISECTED BY THE "
    ? "       VERTICAL PERFORATION"
    ? "    4. TURN THE PRINTER ON."
    ?
    MESSAGE "PRESS ANY KEY TO CONTINUE"
    X = GETCHAR()
    CLEAR
    PRINTOK = FALSE
    WHILE NOT PRINTOK
      PRINTER ON
      ? SPACES(20), "XXXXXX",
        SPACES(29-COL()), "XXXXXXXX",
        SPACES(57-COL()), "XXXXXX",
        SPACES(65-COL()), "XXXXXXXX"
      ?
      ? SPACES(57), "AMT: XXXXXXX.XX"
      ? SPACES(57), "INV#: XXXXXXXXXXXXXXXXXXXXXXXXX"
```

```
  ? SPACES(57), "DESC: XXXXXXXXXXXXXXXXXXXXXXXXXXXXXX"
  ? "XXXXXXXXXXXXXXXXXXXXXXXXXXXXXX"
  ? "XXXXXXXXXXXXXXXXXXXXXXXXXXXXXX"
  ? "XXXXXXXXXXXXXXXXXXXXXXXXXXXXXX"
  ? "XXXXXXXXXXXXXXXXXXXXXXXXXXXXXX"
  ? SPACES(44), "XXXXXXX.XX"
  PRINT "\f"
  CLEAR
  PRINTER OFF
  @ 1,0 ?? "PRINTING ALIGNMENT OK (Y/N):"
  ACCEPT "A1" PICTURE "&" TO ANSWER
  IF ANSWER = "Y" THEN
    PRINTOK = TRUE
  ENDIF
ENDWHILE
PRINTER ON
SCAN
  IF [CHDEPT] <> "01"
    THEN
       LOOP
  ELSE IF [CHDATE] <> MEMDATE
    THEN
       MESSAGE "DATE OF CHECK = ", [CHDATE],
               " DOES NOT MATCH GIVEN DATE."
       BEEP
       SLEEP 2000
       LOOP
  ENDIF
```

```
ENDIF
; PRINT CHECK HERE
MEMPAMT = FALSE
? SPACES(20), [CHCHECKNO],
  SPACES(29-COL()), [CHDATE],
  SPACES(57-COL()), [CHCHECKNO],
  SPACES(65-COL()), [CHDATE]
?
? SPACES(56), "AMT:",
  SPACES(61-COL()), [CHAMOUNT]
? SPACES(56), "INV#:"+[CHINVNO]
? SPACES(56), "DESC:"+[CHDESC]
MYROW = 4
IF NOT ISBLANK([CHLNAME]) THEN
  MYROW = MYROW + 1
  ? [CHLNAME]+", "+[CHFNAME]
ENDIF
IF NOT ISBLANK([CHCOMPANY]) THEN
  MYROW = MYROW + 1
  ? [CHCOMPANY]    ENDIF
IF NOT ISBLANK([CHPOBOX]) THEN
  MYROW = MYROW + 1
  ? "PO BOX "+[CHPOBOX]
ENDIF
IF NOT ISBLANK([CHSTREET]) THEN
  MYROW = MYROW + 1
  ? [CHSTREET]
```

```
    ENDIF
    IF MYROW=8 THEN
      MEMPAMT = TRUE
      ?? SPACES(45-COL()), FORMAT("W10.2, E*", [CHAMOUNT])
    ENDIF
    MYROW = MYROW+1
    MEMADDRESS = [CHCITY]+", "+[CHSTATE]+", "+[CHZIP]
    ? FORMAT("W44", MEMADDRESS)
    IF NOT MEMPAMT THEN
      WHILE ROW() < 8
        ?
      ENDWHILE
      ?? SPACES(45-COL()), FORMAT("W10.2, E*", [CHAMOUNT])
    ENDIF
    PRINT "\f"
  ENDSCAN
ENDIF
; PROCESS FOR DEPARTMENTS 2 AND 3
PRINTER OFF
MEMDEPTCNT= 0
SCAN
  IF [CHDEPT] = "01" OR [CHDEPT] = "02" THEN
     MEMDEPTCNT = MEMDEPTCNT + 1
  ENDIF
ENDSCAN
IF MEMDEPTCNT = 0 THEN
  CLEAR
  ? "NO CHECKS DRAWN ON SECOND BANK"
```

```
  MESSAGE "PRESS ANY KEY TO CONTINUE"
  X = GETCHAR()
ELSE
  CLEAR
  @ 1,0
  ? "IN PREPARATION FOR PRINTING OF CHECKS"
  ? "    1. TURN THE PRINTER OFF"
  ? "    2. SET ROTARY DIAL TO 1"
  ? "    3. INSERT THE CHECK STOCK FOR SECOND BANK"
  ? "       SO THAT THE TOP OF THE PRINT GUIDE IS ALIGNED"
  ? "       WITH THE HORIZONTAL PERFORATION AND SO THAT"
  ? "       THE PRINT GUIDE IS BISECTED BY THE "
  ? "       VERTICAL PERFORATION"
  ? "    4. TURN THE PRINTER ON."
  ?
  MESSAGE "PRESS ANY KEY TO CONTINUE"
  X = GETCHAR()
  CLEAR
  PRINTOK = FALSE
  WHILE NOT PRINTOK
    PRINTER ON
    ? SPACES(20), "XXXXXX",
      SPACES(29-COL()), "XXXXXXXX",
      SPACES(57-COL()), "XXXXXX",
      SPACES(65-COL()), "XXXXXXXX"
    ?
    ? SPACES(57), "AMT: XXXXXXX.XX"
```

```
    ? SPACES(57), "INV#: XXXXXXXXXXXXXXXXXXXXXXXXX"
    ? SPACES(57), "DESC: XXXXXXXXXXXXXXXXXXXXXXXXXXXXXX"
    ? "XXXXXXXXXXXXXXXXXXXXXXXXXXXXXX"
    ? "XXXXXXXXXXXXXXXXXXXXXXXXXXXXXX"
    ? "XXXXXXXXXXXXXXXXXXXXXXXXXXXXXX"
    ? "XXXXXXXXXXXXXXXXXXXXXXXXXXXXXX"
    ? SPACES(44), "XXXXXXX.XX"
    PRINT "\f"
    CLEAR
    PRINTER OFF
    @ 1,0 ?? "PRINTING ALIGNMENT OK (Y/N):"
    ACCEPT "A1" PICTURE "&" TO ANSWER
    IF ANSWER = "Y" THEN
      PRINTOK = TRUE
    ENDIF
ENDWHILE
PRINTER ON
SCAN
  IF [CHDEPT] <> "01"
    THEN
       LOOP
  ELSE IF [CHDATE] <> MEMDATE
    THEN
       MESSAGE "DATE OF CHECK = ", [CHDATE],
               " DOES NOT MATCH GIVEN DATE."
       BEEP
       SLEEP 2000
       LOOP
```

```
ENDIF
ENDIF
; PRINT CHECK HERE
MEMPAMT = FALSE
? SPACES(20), [CHCHECKNO],
  SPACES(29-COL()), [CHDATE],
  SPACES(57-COL()), [CHCHECKNO],
  SPACES(65-COL()), [CHDATE]
?
? SPACES(56), "AMT:",
  SPACES(61-COL()), [CHAMOUNT]
? SPACES(56), "INV#:"+[CHINVNO]
? SPACES(56), "DESC:"+[CHDESC]
MYROW = 4
IF NOT ISBLANK([CHLNAME]) THEN
  MYROW = MYROW + 1
  ? [CHLNAME]+", "+[CHFNAME]
ENDIF
IF NOT ISBLANK([CHCOMPANY]) THEN
  MYROW = MYROW + 1
  ? [CHCOMPANY]    ENDIF
IF NOT ISBLANK([CHPOBOX]) THEN
  MYROW = MYROW + 1
  ? "PO BOX "+[CHPOBOX]
ENDIF
IF NOT ISBLANK([CHSTREET]) THEN
  MYROW = MYROW + 1
```

```
      ? [CHSTREET]
    ENDIF
    IF MYROW=8 THEN
      MEMPAMT = TRUE
      ?? SPACES(45-COL()), FORMAT("W10.2, E*", [CHAMOUNT])
    ENDIF
    MYROW = MYROW+1
    MEMADDRESS = [CHCITY]+", "+[CHSTATE]+", "+[CHZIP]
    ? FORMAT("W44", MEMADDRESS)
    IF NOT MEMPAMT THEN
      WHILE ROW() < 8
        ?
      ENDWHILE
      ?? SPACES(45-COL()), FORMAT("W10.2, E*", [CHAMOUNT])
    ENDIF
    PRINT "\f"
  ENDSCAN
ENDIF
PRINT "\f"
PRINTER OFF
CLEAR
@ 1,0
? "IF THE CHECKS HAVE BEEN PROPERLY PRINTED"
? "   1. TURN THE PRINTER OFF"
? "   2. REMOVE THE CHECK STOCK"
? "   3. INSERT THE DESIRED PAPER"
? "   4. TURN THE ROTARY KNOB TO 7"
? "   5. TURN THE PRINTER ON, IF DESIRED."
```

```
MESSAGE "PRESS ANY KEY TO CONTINUE"
X = GETCHAR()
DO_IT!
CLEARALL
RETURN
```

; **COMCHANG.SC**

```
EDIT "COMPANY"
WHILE TRUE
  CLEAR
  @ 2,0 ?? "ENTER THE NUMBER OF THE COMPANY TO BE CHANGED - ",
           "0 TO QUIT:"
  ACCEPT "N" TO MEMCOMNO
  IF MEMCOMNO = 0 THEN
     QUITLOOP
  ENDIF
  MOVETO [COMPANY -> COMNO]
  LOCATE STRVAL(MEMCOMNO)
  IF NOT RETVAL THEN
    MESSAGE "NO COMPANY ON FILE FOR THE GIVEN NUMBER"
    BEEP
    SLEEP 2000
    LOOP
  ENDIF
  PICKFORM "1"
  WAIT RECORD
```

```
      MESSAGE "PRESS F2 WHEN EDITING HAS BEEN COMPLETED"
   UNTIL "F2"
   KEYPRESS "F7"
ENDWHILE
DO_IT!
CLEARALL
RETURN
```

; **COMENTER.SC**

```
CLEAR
IF NRECORDS("INVMISC") = 0 THEN
    MESSAGE "DATABASE ERROR - UNABLE TO GENERATE UNIQUE ID FOR COMPANIES."
    BEEP
    SLEEP 2000
    RETURN
ENDIF
VIEW "INVMISC"
MOVETO RECORD 1
MEMCOMNO = [INVMCOMNO]
IF NRECORDS("COMPANY") = 0
    THEN
        FIRST = TRUE
    ELSE
        FIRST = FALSE
ENDIF
EDIT "COMPANY"
WHILE TRUE
```

```
CLEAR
MESSAGE "DO YOU WISH TO ENTER ANOTHER COMPANY (Y/N):"
@ 22,79 ACCEPT "A1" PICTURE "&" TO ANSWER
IF ANSWER <> "Y" THEN
  MOVETO [INVMISC ->]
  IF [INVMCOMNO] <> MEMCOMNO THEN
    [INVMCOMNO] = MEMCOMNO
  ENDIF
  QUITLOOP
ENDIF
MEMCOMNO = MEMCOMNO+1
IF FIRST
   THEN
      FIRST = FALSE
      END
   ELSE
      END
      DOWN
ENDIF
[COMNO] = STRVAL(MEMCOMNO)
PICKFORM "1"
WAIT RECORD
    MESSAGE "Press F2 when entry has been completed."
UNTIL "F2"
KEYPRESS "F7"
IF ISBLANK([COMCOMPANY]) THEN
  DEL
```

```
    MESSAGE "THIS RECORD WILL NOT BE ENTERED"
    BEEP
    SLEEP 2000
  ENDIF
ENDWHILE
DO_IT!
CLEARALL
RETURN
```

; **COMLIST.SC**

```
WHILE TRUE
  CLEAR
  @ 5, 5 ?? "COMPANY LIST SELECTION MODES"
  @ 6, 5 ?? "----------------------------"
  @ 7,10 ?? "A. EXIT"
  @ 8,10 ?? "B. BY COMPANY NAME"
  @ 9,10 ?? "C. BY COMPANY NUMBER"
  MESSAGE "ENTER A SELECTION CODE"
  @ 12,0 ACCEPT "A1" TO CODE1
  SWITCH
    CASE CODE1 = "A":
      QUITLOOP
    CASE CODE1 = "B":
      CLEAR
      @ 5,0 ?? "INSERT WIDE PAPER IN THE PRINTER, THEN"
      @ 6,0 ?? "TYPE ANY KEY TO CONTINUE."
```

```
      X = GETCHAR()
      CLEAR
      REPORT "COMPANY" "1"
       ;  Note:  You can either sort the data in the table COMPANY
       ;         before you use the REPORT statement, or you
       ;         can use the sort function that is internal to
       ;         the report system to produce this report.  If you
       ;         use the sort in the report writer, the bode of the
       ;         report will be double spaced.
    CASE CODE1 = "C":
      CLEAR
      @ 5,0 ?? "INSERT WIDE PAPER IN THE PRINTER, THEN"
      @ 6,0 ?? "TYPE ANY KEY TO CONTINUE."
      X = GETCHAR()
      CLEAR
      REPORT "COMPANY" "2"
       ;  Note:  It is not necessary to sort the data in the table COMPANY
       ;         for this report, since COMNO (company number) is the
       ;         field used for the primary index.
    OTHERWISE:
      MESSAGE "ILLEGAL SELECTION CODE"
      BEEP
      SLEEP 2000
  ENDSWITCH
ENDWHILE
CLEARALL
RETURN
```

```
; FILEEMPT.SC
EMPTY("COMPANY")
EMPTY("INVOICE")
EMPTY("INVPAYME")
EMPTY("INVMISC")
EDIT "INVMISC"
   END
   [INVMIDNO] =   1
   [INVMB1CHNO] = 0
   [INVMB2CHNO] = 0
   [INVMCOMNO]  = 0
DO_IT!
EMPTY("CHECKS")
CLEARALL
RETURN

; INDEXES.SC FOR THE PAYABLES SYSTEM
; COMNO IS THE PRIMARY INDEX FOR THE COMPANY FILE
; INVIDNO IS THE PRIMARY INDEX FOR THE INVOICE FILE
INDEX "INVPAYME" ON "INVPIDNO"
INDEX "INVOICE"  ON "INVLNAME"
INDEX "INVOICE"  ON "INVCOMPANY"
INDEX "INVOICE"  ON "INVDATEDUE"
RETURN

; INVCHANG.SC
EDIT "INVOICE"
WHILE TRUE
  CLEAR
```

```
@ 2,0 ?? "ENTER THE NUMBER OF THE INVOICE TO BE CHANGED - ",
          "0 TO QUIT:"
ACCEPT "N" TO MEMIDNO
IF MEMIDNO = 0 THEN
   QUITLOOP
ENDIF
MOVETO [INVOICE -> INVIDNO]
LOCATE STRVAL(MEMIDNO)
IF NOT RETVAL THEN
  MESSAGE "NO INVOICE ON FILE FOR THE GIVEN NUMBER"
  BEEP
  SLEEP 2000
  LOOP
ENDIF
OKTYPE = FALSE
WHILE NOT OKTYPE
   PICKFORM "1"
   WAIT RECORD
     MESSAGE "PRESS F2 WHEN EDITING HAS BEEN COMPLETED"
   UNTIL "F2"
   KEYPRESS "F7"
   IF [INVPAYTYPE] <> "A" AND [INVPAYTYPE] <> "a" AND
      [INVPAYTYPE] <> "M" AND [INVPAYTYPE] <> "m"
     THEN
        MESSAGE "Type of payment must be A(uto) or M(anual)"
        BEEP
        SLEEP 2000
     ELSE
```

```
            OKTYPE = TRUE
         ENDIF
      ENDWHILE
ENDWHILE
DO_IT!
CLEARALL
RETURN
```

; **INVCHECK.SC**

```
; CHANGE THE NUMBER OF THE LAST CHECK USED
CLEAR
IF NRECORDS("INVMISC")= 0 THEN
  ? "ERROR IN DATA BASE CONTAINING LAST CHECK NUMBER"
  ? "UNABLE TO CHANGE IT"
  BEEP
  SLEEP 2000
  RETURN
ENDIF
@ 5,1 ?? "DO YOU WISH TO CHANGE THE NUMBER OF THE LAST CHECK USED (Y/N):"
ACCEPT  "A1" PICTURE "&" TO ANSWER
IF ANSWER <> "Y" THEN
  RETURN
ENDIF
EDIT "INVMISC"
MOVETO RECORD 1
OKNUMBER = FALSE
WHILE NOT OKNUMBER
```

```
  CLEAR
  @ 5,5 ?? "CHECK NUMBER FOR ACCOUNT #1:", [INVMB1CHNO]
  @ 6,5 ?? "NEW CHECK NUMBER           :" ACCEPT "N" TO MEMB1CHNO
  @ 8,5 ?? "CHECK NUMBER FOR ACCOUNT #2:", [INVMB2CHNO]
  @ 9,5 ?? "NEW CHECK NUMBER           :" ACCEPT "N" TO MEMB2CHNO
  MESSAGE "IS THE CHECK NUMBER OK NOW (Y/N):"
  @ 12,0  ACCEPT "A1" PICTURE "&" TO ANSWER
  IF ANSWER = "Y" THEN
    OKNUMBER = TRUE
  ENDIF
ENDWHILE
[INVMB1CHNO] = MEMB1CHNO
[INVMB2CHNO] = MEMB2CHNO
DO_IT!
CLEARALL
RETURN
```

; **INVDELETE.SC**

```
VIEW "INVOICE"
VIEW "COMPANY"
EDIT "INVPAYME"
WHILE TRUE
  CLEAR
  @ 5, 5 ?? "RECORD DELETION MODES"
  @ 6, 5 ?? "---------------------"
  @  7,10 ?? "A. RETURN TO MAIN MENU"
  @  8,10 ?? "B. INVOICE (AND ALL ASSOCIATED PAYMENTS)"
```

```
@  9,10 ?? "C. PAYMENT (FOR A SPECIFIC INVOICE)"
@ 10,10 ?? "D. COMPANY"
MESSAGE "SELECT A CODE"
@ 12,0 CODE1 = CHR(GETCHAR())
?? CODE1
SWITCH
  CASE CODE1 = "A":
    CLEAR
    QUITLOOP
  CASE CODE1 = "B":
    ; DELETE INVOICES AND ASSOCIATED RECORDS
    WHILE TRUE
      CLEAR
      @ 5, 5 ?? "INVOICE DELETION TYPES"
      @ 6, 5 ?? "----------------------"
      @ 7,10 ?? "A. EXIT"
      @ 8,10 ?? "B. BY UNIQUE ID"
      @ 9,10 ?? "C. ALL OLD PAID INVOICES"
      MESSAGE "ENTER A CODE"
      @ 12,0 CODE2 = CHR(GETCHAR())
      ?? CODE2
      IF CODE2 <> "A" AND CODE2 <> "B" AND CODE2 <> "C" THEN
        MESSAGE "ILLEGAL SELECTION CODE"
        BEEP
        SLEEP 2000
        LOOP
      ENDIF
```

```
IF CODE2 = "A" THEN
  QUITLOOP
ENDIF
IF CODE2 = "B" THEN
  CLEAR
  @ 5, 1 ?? "ENTER INVOICE ID:"
  ACCEPT "N" TO MEMIDNO
  MEMIDNO = STRVAL(MEMIDNO)
  MOVETO [INVOICE -> INVIDNO]
  LOCATE MEMIDNO
  IF NOT RETVAL THEN
    MESSAGE "NO INVOICE ON FILE FOR GIVEN ID NUMBER"
    BEEP
    SLEEP 2000
    LOOP
  ENDIF
  CLEAR
  @ 1,0
  ? "ID NO              =", [INVIDNO]
  ? "NAME               =", [INVLNAME]+", "+[INVFNAME]
  ? "COMPANY            =", [INVCOMPANY]
  ? "DUE DATE           =", [INVDATEDUE]
  ? "ORIGINAL AMOUNT DUE=", [INVAMTDUE]
  ? "AMOUNT PAID SO FAR =", [INVPAIDAMT]
  ? "PAYMENT TYPE       =", [INVPAYTYPE]
  MESSAGE "DELETE THIS INVOICE (Y/N):"
  ?
```

```
  ACCEPT "A1" PICTURE "&" TO ANSWER
  IF ANSWER = "Y" THEN
    DEL
    MESSAGE "THIS RECORD WILL BE DELETED"
    SLEEP 2000
    MOVETO [INVPAYME -> INVPIDNO]
    LOCATE MEMIDNO
    IF NOT RETVAL THEN
      CLEARALL
      LOOP
    ENDIF
    WHILE  RETVAL
      DEL
      LOCATE NEXT MEMIDNO
    ENDWHILE
  ELSE
    MESSAGE  "THIS RECORD WILL NOT BE DELETED"
    SLEEP 2000
  ENDIF
ENDIF
IF CODE2 = "C" THEN
  CLEAR
  @ 5,1 ?? "ENTER DATE IN THE FORM MM/DD/YY:"
  ACCEPT "D" TO MEMDATE
  SCAN FOR [INVDATEDUE] <= MEMDATE
    IF [INVPDINFUL] = "Y" OR [INVPAIDAMT] >= [INVAMTDUE] THEN
      MEMIDNO = [INVIDNO]
      DEL
```

```
          MOVETO [INVPAYME -> INVPIDNO]
          LOCATE MEMIDNO
          IF NOT RETVAL THEN
            KEYPRESS "F8"
            MOVETO [INVOICE ->]
            LOOP
          ENDIF
          WHILE RETVAL
            DEL
            LOCATE NEXT MEMIDNO
          ENDWHILE
        ENDIF
        MOVETO [INVOICE ->]
      ENDSCAN
    ENDIF
  ENDWHILE
CASE CODE1 = "C":
  ; DELETE PAYMENTS
  CLEAR
  @ 5, 1 ?? "ENTER THE UNIQUE ID OF THE INVOICE:"
  ACCEPT "N" TO MEMIDNO
  MEMIDNO = STRVAL(MEMIDNO)
  MOVETO [INVOICE -> INVIDNO]
  LOCATE MEMIDNO
  IF NOT RETVAL THEN
    MESSAGE "NO INVOICE ON FILE FOR GIVEN ID NUMBER"
    BEEP
    SLEEP 2000
```

```
  LOOP
ENDIF
CLEAR
@ 1,0
? "ID NO                 =", [INVIDNO]
? "NAME                  =", [INVLNAME]+", "+[INVFNAME]
? "COMPANY               =", [INVCOMPANY]
? "DUE DATE              =", [INVDATEDUE]
? "ORIGINAL AMOUNT DUE=", [INVAMTDUE]
? "AMOUNT PAID SO FAR =", [INVPAIDAMT]
? "PAYMENT TYPE          =", [INVPAYTYPE]
MESSAGE "DO YOU WISH TO DELETE PAYMENTS FOR THIS INVOICE (Y/N)"
?
ACCEPT "A1" PICTURE "&" TO ANSWER
IF ANSWER <> "Y" THEN
  LOOP
ENDIF
CLEAR
? "IF THERE IS MORE THAN ONE PAYMENT, EACH WILL BE DISPLAYED"
? " ON THE SCREEN, ONE AT A TIME"
BEEP
SLEEP 2000
MOVETO [INVPAYME -> INVPIDNO]
LOCATE MEMIDNO
IF NOT RETVAL THEN
  MESSAGE  "NO PAYMENTS ON FILE FOR THIS ID"
  BEEP
  SLEEP 2000
```

```
  LOOP
ENDIF
WHILE RETVAL
  CLEAR
  MEMDATE = [INVPPAYDATE]
  @ 1,0
  ? "DATE           =", MEMDATE
  ? "CHECK   NUMBER=", [INVPCHECKN]
  ? "PAYMENT AMOUNT=", [INVPAMT]
  MESSAGE "DELETE THIS PAYMENT (Y/N)"
  ?
  ACCEPT "A1" PICTURE "&" TO ANSWER
  IF ANSWER = "Y" THEN
    IF ISBLANK([INVPAMT])
      THEN MEMAMT = 0
      ELSE MEMAMT = [INVPAMT]
    ENDIF
    DEL
    DIDDELETE = TRUE
    MOVETO [INVOICE ->]
    [INVPAIDAMT] = [INVPAIDAMT]-MEMAMT
    MESSAGE "THIS PAYMENT WILL BE DELETED"
    BEEP
    SLEEP 2000
  ELSE
    DIDDELETE = FALSE
    MESSAGE  "THIS PAYMENT WILL NOT BE DELETED"
    BEEP
```

```
        SLEEP 2000
      ENDIF
      MOVETO [INVPAYME -> INVPIDNO]
      IF NOT DIDDELETE THEN
         DOWN
      ENDIF
      LOCATE NEXT MEMIDNO
    ENDWHILE
CASE CODE1 = "D":
    ; DELETE COMPANIES
CLEAR
@ 5, 1 ?? "ENTER THE ID OF THE COMPANY TO BE DELETED:"
ACCEPT "N" TO MEMCOMNO
MEMCOMNO = STRVAL(MEMCOMNO)
MOVETO [COMPANY -> COMNO]
LOCATE MEMCOMNO
IF NOT RETVAL THEN
    MESSAGE "NO COMPANY ON FILE FOR GIVEN NUMBER"
    BEEP
    SLEEP 2000
    LOOP
ENDIF
CLEAR
@ 1,0
? "COMPANY NO=", [COMNO]
? "NAME      =", [COMLNAME]+", "+[COMFNAME]
? "COMPANY   =", [COMCOMPANY]
```

```
  ? "PO BOX     =", [COMPOBOX]
  ? "STREET     =", [COMSTREET]
  ? "CITY       =", [COMCITY]
  ? "STATE      =", [COMSTATE]
  ? "ZIP        =", [COMZIP]
  MESSAGE "DELETE THIS RECORD (Y/N)"
  ?
  ACCEPT "A1" PICTURE "&" TO ANSWER
  IF ANSWER = "Y" THEN
    DEL
    MESSAGE "THIS RECORD WILL BE DELETED"
    BEEP
    SLEEP 2000
  ELSE
    MESSAGE "THIS RECORD WILL NOT BE DELETED"
    BEEP
    SLEEP 2000
  ENDIF
OTHERWISE:
      MESSAGE "ILLEGAL CODE - PLEASE REENTER"
      BEEP
      SLEEP 2000
  ENDSWITCH
ENDWHILE
DO_IT!
CLEARALL
RETURN
```

```
; INVENTER.SC
CLEAR
IF NRECORDS("INVMISC") = 0 THEN
   MESSAGE "DATABASE ERROR - UNABLE TO GENERATE UNIQUE ID FOR INVOICES."
   BEEP
   SLEEP 2000
   RETURN
ENDIF
VIEW "INVMISC" ; IMAGE 1
MOVETO RECORD 1
MEMIDNO = [INVMIDNO]
MEMFIDNO = [INVMIDNO]
VIEW "COMPANY" ; IMAGE 2
IF NRECORDS ("INVOICE") = 0
  THEN
    FIRST = TRUE
  ELSE
    FIRST = FALSE
ENDIF
EDIT "INVOICE" ; IMAGE 3
WHILE TRUE
  CLEAR
  MOVETO [INVOICE-> ]
  MESSAGE "DO YOU WISH TO ENTER ANOTHER INVOICE (Y/N):"
  @ 22,79 ACCEPT "A1" PICTURE "&" TO ANSWER
  IF ANSWER <> "Y" THEN
    IF MEMFIDNO <> MEMIDNO
      THEN
```

```
      MOVETO [INVMISC ->]
      MOVETO RECORD 1
      [INVMIDNO] = MEMIDNO
  ENDIF
  QUITLOOP
ENDIF
OKNAME = FALSE
WHILE NOT OKNAME
  CLEAR
  MESSAGE "IS THE COMPANY NAME ON FILE (Y/N):"
  @ 22,79 ACCEPT "A1" PICTURE "&" TO ANSWER
  IF ANSWER = "Y" THEN
    CLEAR
    MESSAGE "ENTER THE COMPANY NUMBER"
    @ 5,1  ACCEPT "A4"  TO MEMCOMNO
    MOVETO [COMPANY -> COMNO]
    LOCATE MEMCOMNO
    IF NOT RETVAL OR ISBLANK(MEMCOMNO) THEN
      MESSAGE  "NO RECORD ON FILE FOR THIS COMPANY NUMBER"
      BEEP
      SLEEP 2000
    ELSE
      CLEAR
      @  0, 0 ?? "COMPANY NUMBER:", [COMNO]
      @  2, 0 ?? "NAME"
      @  3, 5 ?? "LAST :"
      @  3,15 ?? [COMLNAME]
      @  4, 5 ?? "FIRST:"
```

```
      @  4,15 ?? [COMFNAME]
      @  6, 0 ?? "COMPANY:"
      @  6,10 ?? [COMCOMPANY]
      @  8, 0 ?? "ADDRESS"
      @  9, 5 ?? "PO BOX:"
      @  9,15 ?? [COMPOBOX]
      @ 10, 5 ?? "STREET:"
      @ 10,15 ?? [COMSTREET]
      @ 11, 5 ?? "CITY  :"
      @ 11,15 ?? [COMCITY]
      @ 12, 5 ?? "STATE :"
      @ 12,15 ?? [COMSTATE]
      @ 13, 5 ?? "ZIP   :"
      @ 13,15 ?? [COMZIP]
      MESSAGE "IS THIS CORRECT (Y/N):"
      @ 15,0 ACCEPT "A1" PICTURE "&" TO ANSWER
      IF ANSWER = "Y" THEN
        OKNAME = TRUE
        HAVENAME = TRUE
      ENDIF
    ENDIF
  ELSE
    HAVENAME = FALSE
    OKNAME = TRUE
  ENDIF
ENDWHILE
MOVETO [INVOICE ->]
IF FIRST
```

```
  THEN
    FIRST = FALSE
    END
  ELSE
    END
    DOWN
ENDIF
[INVIDNO] = STRVAL(MEMIDNO)
IF HAVENAME THEN
  [INVLNAME]   = [COMPANY -> COMLNAME]
  [INVFNAME]   = [COMPANY -> COMFNAME]
  [INVCOMPANY] = [COMPANY -> COMCOMPANY]
  [INVPOBOX]   = [COMPANY -> COMPOBOX]
  [INVSTREET]  = [COMPANY -> COMSTREET]
  [INVCITY]    = [COMPANY -> COMCITY]
  [INVSTATE]   = [COMPANY -> COMSTATE]
  [INVZIP]     = [COMPANY -> COMZIP]
ENDIF
OKTYPE   = FALSE
OKRECORD = TRUE
WHILE NOT OKTYPE
   PICKFORM "1"
   WAIT RECORD
     MESSAGE "Press F2 when entry of the invoice has been completed"
   UNTIL "F2"
   KEYPRESS "F7"
   IF ISBLANK([INVCOMPANY]) THEN
         DEL
```

```
        OKRECORD = FALSE
        MESSAGE "THIS RECORD WILL NOT BE ENTERED"
        BEEP
        SLEEP 2000
        QUITLOOP
    ENDIF
    IF [INVPAYTYPE] <> "A" AND [INVPAYTYPE] <> "a" AND
       [INVPAYTYPE] <> "M" AND [INVPAYTYPE] <> "m"
      THEN
        MESSAGE "Type of payment must be A(uto) or M(anual)"
        BEEP
        SLEEP 2000
      ELSE
        OKTYPE = TRUE
    ENDIF
  ENDWHILE
  IF OKRECORD THEN
    MEMIDNO = MEMIDNO+1
  ENDIF
ENDWHILE
; RESUME HERE AFTER THE QUITLOOP
DO_IT!
CLEARALL
RETURN
```

; INVFHEAD.SC

```
CLEAR
@  1, 0 ?? "ID NUMBER                    CONTACT PERSON
```

```
@  1,52 ?? "AMOUNT DUE   DATE DUE"
@  2, 0 ?? "INVOICE NUMBER            COMPANY NAME
@  2,52 ?? "AMOUNT PAID  DATE PAID  PIF"
@  3, 0 ?? "DESCRIPTION"
@  4, 0 ?? "---------------------------------------------------
@  4,52 ?? "---------------------------"
RETURN
```

; **INVFIND.SC**

```
MAXLINES = 18
EDIT "INVOICE"
WHILE TRUE
  CLEAR
  @  5, 5 ?? "INVOICE DISPLAY MODES"
  @  6, 5 ?? "---------------------"
  @  7,10 ?? "A. EXIT"
  @  8,10 ?? "B. BY UNIQUE ID"
  @  9,10 ?? "C. BY INVOICE NUMBER"
  @ 10,10 ?? "D. BY LAST NAME OF INDIVIDUAL"
  @ 11,10 ?? "E. BY COMPANY NAME"
  @ 12,10 ?? "F. BY DUE DATE"
  MESSAGE "ENTER A CODE:"
  @ 14,0 CODE = CHR(GETCHAR())
  @ 14,0 ?? CODE
  SWITCH
    CASE CODE = "A":
      QUITLOOP
    CASE CODE = "B":
```

```
; BY UNIQUE ID
CLEAR
@ 5, 1 ?? "ENTER THE UNIQUE ID:" ACCEPT "A5" TO MEMIDNO
MOVETO RECORD 1
MOVETO [INVIDNO]
LOCATE MEMIDNO
IF NOT RETVAL
  THEN
     MESSAGE "NO INVOICE ON FILE FOR GIVEN ID"
     BEEP
     SLEEP 2000
  ELSE
     PLAY "INVFHEAD"
     ;  *** DISPLAY DETAIL LINE HERE ***
     @ 6, 0 ?? [INVIDNO]
     @ 6,26 ?? FORMAT("W25", [INVLNAME]+", "+[INVFNAME])
     @ 6,52 ?? [INVAMTDUE]
     @ 6,65 ?? [INVDATEDUE]
     @ 7, 0 ?? [INVINVNO]
     @ 7,26 ?? [INVCOMPANY]
     @ 7,52 ?? [INVPAIDAMT]
     @ 7,65 ?? [INVPAIDDAT]
     @ 7,76 ?? [INVPDINFUL]
     @ 8, 0 ?? [INVDESC]
     ?
     MESSAGE "PRESS ANY KEY TO CONTINUE"
     X = GETCHAR()
ENDIF
```

```
CASE CODE = "C":
  ; BY INVOICE NUMBER
  MOVETO RECORD 1
  MOVETO [INVINVNO]
  CLEAR
  @ 5, 1 ?? "ENTER INVOICE NUMBER:" ACCEPT "A25" TO MEMINVNO
  LOCATE MEMINVNO
  IF NOT RETVAL
     THEN
       MESSAGE "NO INVOICE ON FILE FOR GIVEN INVOICE NO"
       BEEP
       SLEEP 2000
     ELSE
       PLAY "INVFHEAD"
       MYROW = 4
       WHILE RETVAL
         MYROW = MYROW+1
         IF MYROW > MAXLINES THEN
           MESSAGE "TYPE ANY KEY TO CONTINUE"
           X = GETCHAR()
           CLEAR
           PLAY "INVFHEAD"
           MYROW = 5
         ENDIF
         ;  *** DISPLAY DETAIL LINE HERE ***
         @ MYROW, 0 ?? [INVIDNO]
         @ MYROW,26 ?? FORMAT("W25", [INVLNAME]+", "+[INVFNAME])
         @ MYROW,52 ?? [INVAMTDUE]
```

```
          @ MYROW,65 ?? [INVDATEDUE]
          MYROW  = MYROW + 1
          @ MYROW, 0 ?? [INVINVNO]
          @ MYROW,26 ?? [INVCOMPANY]
          @ MYROW,52 ?? [INVPAIDAMT]
          @ MYROW,65 ?? [INVPAIDDAT]
          @ MYROW,76 ?? [INVPDINFUL]
          MYROW = MYROW+1
          @ MYROW, 0 ?? [INVDESC]
          MYROW = MYROW+1
          DOWN
          MOVETO [INVINVNO]
          LOCATE NEXT MEMINVNO
        ENDWHILE
        MESSAGE "PRESS ANY KEY TO CONTINUE"
        X = GETCHAR()
  ENDIF
CASE CODE = "D":
  ; BY NAME OF INDIVIDUAL
  MOVETO RECORD 1
  MOVETO [INVLNAME]
  CLEAR
  @ 5, 1 ?? "ENTER LAST NAME:" ACCEPT "A20" TO MEMLNAME
  LOCATE MEMLNAME
  IF NOT RETVAL THEN
    MESSAGE "NO INVOICE ON FILE FOR GIVEN LAST NAME"
    BEEP
    SLEEP 2000
```

```
ELSE
  PLAY "INVFHEAD"
  MYROW = 4
  WHILE RETVAL
    MYROW = MYROW+1
    IF MYROW > MAXLINES THEN
      MESSAGE "PRESS ANY KEY TO CONTINUE"
      X = GETCHAR()
      CLEAR
      PLAY "INVFHEAD"
      MYROW = 5
    ENDIF
    ; *** DISPLAY DETAIL LINE HERE ***
    @ MYROW, 0 ?? [INVIDNO]
    @ MYROW,26 ?? FORMAT("W25", [INVLNAME]+", "+[INVFNAME])
    @ MYROW,52 ?? [INVAMTDUE]
    @ MYROW,65 ?? [INVDATEDUE]
    MYROW  = MYROW + 1
    @ MYROW, 0 ?? [INVINVNO]
    @ MYROW,26 ?? [INVCOMPANY]
    @ MYROW,52 ?? [INVPAIDAMT]
    @ MYROW,65 ?? [INVPAIDDAT]
    @ MYROW,76 ?? [INVPDINFUL]
    MYROW = MYROW+1
    @ MYROW, 0 ?? [INVDESC]
    MYROW = MYROW+1
    DOWN
    MOVETO [INVLNAME]
```

```
      LOCATE NEXT MEMLNAME
    ENDWHILE
    MESSAGE "PRESS ANY KEY TO CONTINUE"
    X = GETCHAR()
  ENDIF
CASE CODE = "E":
  ; BY COMPANY NAME
  MOVETO RECORD 1
  MOVETO [INVCOMPANY]
  CLEAR
  @ 5, 1 ?? "ENTER COMPANY NAME:" ACCEPT "A25" TO MEMCOMPANY
  LOCATE MEMCOMPANY
  IF NOT RETVAL THEN
    MESSAGE "NO INVOICE ON FILE FOR GIVEN COMPANY NAME"
    BEEP
    SLEEP 2000
  ELSE
    PLAY "INVFHEAD"
    MYROW = 4
    WHILE RETVAL
      MYROW = MYROW+1
      IF MYROW > MAXLINES THEN
        MESSAGE "PRESS ANY KEY TO CONTINUE"
        X = GETCHAR()
        CLEAR
        PLAY "INVFHEAD"
        MYROW = 5
```

```
      ENDIF
      ; *** DISPLAY DETAIL LINE HERE ***
      @ MYROW, 0 ?? [INVIDNO]
      @ MYROW,26 ?? FORMAT("W25", [INVLNAME]+", "+[INVFNAME])
      @ MYROW,52 ?? [INVAMTDUE]
      @ MYROW,65 ?? [INVDATEDUE]
      MYROW  = MYROW + 1
      @ MYROW, 0 ?? [INVINVNO]
      @ MYROW,26 ?? [INVCOMPANY]
      @ MYROW,52 ?? [INVPAIDAMT]
      @ MYROW,65 ?? [INVPAIDDAT]
      @ MYROW,76 ?? [INVPDINFUL]
      MYROW = MYROW+1
      @ MYROW, 0 ?? [INVDESC]
      MYROW = MYROW+1
      DOWN
      MOVETO [INVCOMPANY]
      LOCATE NEXT MEMCOMPANY
    ENDWHILE
    MESSAGE "PRESS ANY KEY TO CONTINUE"
    X = GETCHAR()
  ENDIF
CASE CODE = "F":
  ; BY DUE DATE
  CLEAR
  MOVETO RECORD 1
  MOVETO [INVDATEDUE]
```

```
@ 5, 1 ?? "ENTER THE DUE DATE:" ACCEPT "D" TO MEMDATE
LOCATE MEMDATE
IF NOT RETVAL THEN
  MESSAGE "NO INVOICE ON FILE FOR GIVEN DATE"
  BEEP
  SLEEP 2000
ELSE
  PLAY "INVFHEAD"
  MYROW = 4
  WHILE RETVAL
    MYROW = MYROW+1
    IF MYROW > MAXLINES THEN
      MESSAGE "PRESS ANY KEY TO CONTINUE"
      X = GETCHAR()
      CLEAR
      PLAY "INVFHEAD"
      MYROW = 5
    ENDIF
    ; *** DISPLAY DETAIL LINE HERE ***
    @ MYROW, 0 ?? [INVIDNO]
    @ MYROW,26 ?? FORMAT("W25", [INVLNAME]+", "+[INVFNAME])
    @ MYROW,52 ?? [INVAMTDUE]
    @ MYROW,65 ?? [INVDATEDUE]
    MYROW  = MYROW + 1
    @ MYROW, 0 ?? [INVINVNO]
    @ MYROW,26 ?? [INVCOMPANY]
    @ MYROW,52 ?? [INVPAIDAMT]
```

```
        @ MYROW,65 ?? [INVPAIDDAT]
        @ MYROW,76 ?? [INVPDINFUL]
        MYROW = MYROW+1
        @ MYROW, 0 ?? [INVDESC]
        MYROW = MYROW+1
        DOWN
        MOVETO [INVDATEDUE]
        LOCATE NEXT MEMDATE
      ENDWHILE
      MESSAGE "PRESS ANY KEY TO CONTINUE"
      X = GETCHAR()
    ENDIF
  OTHERWISE:
    MESSAGE "ILLEGAL CODE - PLEASE REENTER"
    BEEP
    SLEEP 2000
 ENDSWITCH
ENDWHILE
CANCELEDIT
CLEARALL
RETURN
```

; **INVPAY.SC**

```
EDIT "INVOICE"
WHILE TRUE
  CLEAR
  @ 5, 5 ?? "PAYMENT SELECTION MODES"
```

```
@ 6, 5 ?? "----------------------"
@ 7,10 ?? "A. EXIT"
@ 8,10 ?? "B. REVIEW A SPECIFIC INVOICE  FOR PAYMENT"
@ 9,10 ?? "C. REVIEW ALL        INVOICES FOR PAYMENT"
MESSAGE "ENTER A SELECTION CODE:"
@ 11,1 CODE1 = CHR(GETCHAR())
?? CODE1
SWITCH
  CASE CODE1 = "A":
    QUITLOOP
  CASE CODE1 = "B":
    WHILE TRUE
      CLEAR
      @ 5, 1 ?? "ENTER ID NUMBER OF INVOICE TO BE REVIEWED - 0 TO QUIT:"
      ACCEPT "N" TO MEMIDNO
      IF MEMIDNO = 0 THEN
         QUITLOOP
      ENDIF
      MOVETO [INVIDNO]
      LOCATE STRVAL(MEMIDNO)
      IF NOT RETVAL THEN
        MESSAGE "NO INVOICE ON FILE FOR GIVEN ID"
        BEEP
        SLEEP 2000
        LOOP
      ENDIF
      IF [INVPAYTYPE] <> "A" THEN
```

```
  MESSAGE "THIS INVOICE HAS NOT BEEN DESIGNATED FOR SYSTEM PAYMENT"
  BEEP
  SLEEP 2000
  LOOP
ENDIF
OKPDINFUL = FALSE
OKAMT     = FALSE
WHILE  (NOT OKAMT) OR (NOT OKPDINFUL)
  PICKFORM "2"
  WAIT RECORD
     MESSAGE "PRESS F2 WHEN YOU ARE THROUGH WITH YOUR CHANGES"
  UNTIL "F2"
  KEYPRESS "F7"
  IF ISBLANK([INVPAIDAMT]) THEN
    [INVPAIDAMT] = 0
  ENDIF
  IF ISBLANK([INVPAYAMT]) THEN
    [INVPAYAMT] = 0
  ENDIF
  IF [INVPAIDAMT]+[INVPAYAMT] > [INVAMTDUE] THEN
    OKAMT = FALSE
    MESSAGE "AMOUNT TO BE PAID IS TOO LARGE"
    BEEP
    SLEEP 2000
  ELSE
    OKAMT = TRUE
  ENDIF
```

```
      IF [INVPDINFUL] = "Y" OR [INVPDINFUL] = "y"  OR
         [INVPDINFUL] = "N" OR [INVPDINFUL] = "n"  OR
         ISBLANK([INVPDINFUL])
      THEN
         OKPDINFUL = TRUE
      ELSE
        OKPDINFUL = FALSE
        MESSAGE "YOU MUST DESIGNATE 'PAID IN FULL' AS Y, N OR SPACE."
        BEEP
        SLEEP 2000
      ENDIF
    ENDWHILE
    KEYPRESS "F7"
  ENDWHILE
CASE CODE1 = "C":
  CLEAR
  MESSAGE "ENDING DATE WILL BE 7 DAYS AFTER BEGINNING DATE"
  @ 5,0 ?? "ENTER THE BEGINNING DATE:" ACCEPT "D" TO MEMBDATE
  MEMEDATE = MEMBDATE+7
  SCAN FOR ([INVDATEDUE] <= MEMEDATE OR [INVDISCDAT] <= MEMEDATE) AND
            [INVPAIDAMT] < [INVAMTDUE] AND [INVPAYTYPE] = "A" AND
            [INVPDINFUL] <> "Y" AND [INVPDINFUL] <> "y"
    OKPDINFUL = FALSE
    OKAMT     = FALSE
    WHILE  (NOT OKAMT) OR (NOT OKPDINFUL)
      PICKFORM "2"
      WAIT RECORD
```

```
  MESSAGE "PRESS F2 WHEN YOU ARE THROUGH WITH YOUR CHANGES"
UNTIL "F2"
KEYPRESS "F7"
IF ISBLANK([INVPAIDAMT]) THEN
   [INVPAIDAMT] = 0
ENDIF
IF ISBLANK([INVPAYAMT]) THEN
   [INVPAYAMT] = 0
ENDIF
IF [INVPAIDAMT]+[INVPAYAMT] > [INVAMTDUE] THEN
  OKAMT = FALSE
  MESSAGE "AMOUNT TO BE PAID IS TOO LARGE"
  BEEP
  SLEEP 2000
ELSE
  OKAMT = TRUE
ENDIF
IF [INVPDINFUL] = "Y" OR [INVPDINFUL] = "y" OR
   [INVPDINFUL] = "N" OR [INVPDINFUL] = "n" OR
   ISBLANK([INVPDINFUL]) THEN
  OKPDINFUL = TRUE
ELSE
  OKPDINFUL = FALSE
  MESSAGE "YOU MUST DESIGNATE 'PAID IN FULL'",
          " AS Y, N OR SPACE."
  BEEP
  SLEEP 2000
```

```
          ENDIF
        ENDWHILE
        KEYPRESS "F7"
      ENDSCAN
    OTHERWISE:
      MESSAGE "ILLEGAL SELECTION CODE"
      BEEP
      SLEEP 2000
  ENDSWITCH
ENDWHILE
DO_IT!
CLEARALL
RETURN
```

; **INVPREPO.SC**

```
CLEAR
@ 5,1 ?? "DO YOU WISH TO PRINT THE INVOICE PRE-PAYMENT REPORT (Y/N):"
ACCEPT "A1" PICTURE "&" TO ANSWER
IF ANSWER <> "Y" THEN
  RETURN
ENDIF
MESSAGE "INSERT WIDE PAPER IN THE PRINTER - TYPE ANY KEY TO CONTINUE"
X = GETCHAR()
CLEAR
@ 5,1 ?? "ENTER THE PAYMENT DATE IN THE FORM MM/DD/YY:"
ACCEPT "D" TO MEMDATE ; MEMDATE IS THE DATE THAT THE CHECKS ARE TO BE PRINTED
SORT "INVOICE" ON "INVDEPT", "INVSERVTYP" TO "SINVOICE"
EDIT "SINVOICE"
```

```
MAXLINES = 50
MYPAGENO = 1
MEMSERVTOT = 0
MEMDEPTTOT = 0
MEMGTOT = 0
PRINTER ON
PRINT CHR(15)
PLAY "INVPRHEA"
MYROW = 6
MOVETO RECORD 1
MEMDEPT = [INVDEPT]
MEMSERVTYP = [INVSERVTYP]
SCAN
  IF [INVPAYDATE]  <> MEMDATE THEN
    MEMDEPT = [INVDEPT]
    MEMSERVTYP = [INVSERVTYP]
    LOOP
  ENDIF
  ?
  MYROW = MYROW + 1
  IF MYROW > MAXLINES THEN
    PRINT "\f"
    MYPAGENO = MYPAGENO+1
    PLAY "INVPRHEA"
    MYROW = 7
  ENDIF
  IF MEMDEPT <> [INVDEPT] THEN
    MYROW = MYROW + 1
```

```
    ? SPACES(129), MEMSERVTYP,
      SPACES(55-COL()),"SERVICE TYPE TOTAL:",
      SPACES(76-COL()), FORMAT("W9.2",MEMSERVTOT)
    MYROW = MYROW + 1
    ? SPACES(129), MEMDEPT,
      SPACES(55-COL()), "DEPARTMENT   TOTAL:",
      SPACES(76-COL()), FORMAT("W9.2",MEMDEPTTOT)
    MEMSERVTOT = 0
    MEMDEPTTOT = 0
    ?
    MYROW = MYROW + 1
  ELSE
  IF MEMSERVTYP <> [INVSERVTYP] THEN
    MYROW = MYROW + 1
    ? SPACES(129), MEMSERVTYP,
      SPACES(55-COL()), "SERVICE TYPE TOTAL:",
      SPACES(76-COL()), FORMAT("W9.2",MEMSERVTOT)
    MEMSERVTOT = 0
    ?
    MYROW = MYROW + 1
  ENDIF
  ENDIF
  ;   *** PRINT DETAIL LINE
  MEMLNAME = [INVLNAME]
  MEMFNAME = [INVFNAME]
  MEMNAME = MEMLNAME+", "+MEMFNAME
  MEMADDRESS = SPACES(1)
```

```
  IF NOT ISBLANK([INVPOBOX]) THEN
    MEMADDRESS = "PO BOX:"+[INVPOBOX]
  ENDIF
  IF NOT ISBLANK([INVSTREET]) AND LEN(MEMADDRESS) >= 1 THEN
        MEMADDRESS = MEMADDRESS+", "+[INVSTREET]
  ENDIF
  IF NOT ISBLANK([INVSTREET]) AND LEN(MEMADDRESS) = 0 THEN
        MEMADDRESS = [INVSTREET]
  ENDIF
  MEMADDRESS = MEMADDRESS+", "+[INVCITY]+", "+[INVSTATE]+", "+[INVZIP]
  MYROW = MYROW + 1
  ? [INVIDNO],
     SPACES(7-COL()), FORMAT("W30", MEMNAME),
     SPACES(39-COL()), [INVCOMPANY],
     SPACES(65-COL()), FORMAT("W49", MEMADDRESS),
     SPACES(35-COL()), [INVDATEDUE],
     SPACES(45-COL()), FORMAT("W9.2",[INVAMTDUE]),
     SPACES(55-COL()), FORMAT("W9.2",[INVPAIDAMT]),
     SPACES(65-COL()), FORMAT("W9.2", [INVAMTDUE]-[INVPAIDAMT]),
     SPACES(76-COL()), FORMAT("W9.2", [INVPAYAMT])
  MEMSERVTOT = MEMSERVTOT+[INVPAYAMT]
  MEMDEPTTOT = MEMDEPTTOT+[INVPAYAMT]
  MEMGTOT = MEMGTOT+[INVPAYAMT]
  MEMDEPT = [INVDEPT]
  MEMSERVTYP = [INVSERVTYP]
ENDSCAN
?
```

```
? SPACES(129), MEMSERVTYP,
  SPACES(55-COL()), "SERVICE TYPE TOTAL:",
  SPACES(76-COL()), FORMAT("W9.2",MEMSERVTOT)
? SPACES(129), MEMDEPT,
  SPACES(55-COL()), "DEPARTMENT   TOTAL:",
  SPACES(76-COL()), FORMAT("W9.2",MEMDEPTTOT)
?
? SPACES(135-COL()),"GRAND        TOTAL:",
  SPACES(76-COL()), FORMAT("W9.2",MEMGTOT)
PRINT CHR(18)
PRINT "\f"
PRINTER OFF
CANCELEDIT
CLEARALL
RETURN
```

; **INVPRHEA.SC**

```
? SPACES(99), "INVOICE PRE-PAYMENT REPORT",
  SPACES(70-COL()), "PAGE NO:", FORMAT("W3", MYPAGENO)
? SPACES(99), "PAYMENT DATE:",
  SPACES(34-COL()), MEMDATE
?
? "ID NO",
   SPACES(7-COL()), "NAME",
   SPACES(39-COL()), "COMPANY",
   SPACES(65-COL()), "ADDRESS",
   SPACES(115-COL()), "DATE DUE",
   SPACES(45-COL()), "ORIG AMT",
```

```
   SPACES(55-COL()), "PD SO FAR",
   SPACES(65-COL()), "TO BE PAID",
   SPACES(76-COL()), "PAYMENT"
? "-----",
   SPACES(7-COL()),  "------------------------------",
   SPACES(39-COL()), "-------------------------",
   SPACES(65-COL()), "-------------------------------------------------",
   SPACES(35-COL()), "--------",
   SPACES(45-COL()), "---------",
   SPACES(55-COL()), "---------",
   SPACES(65-COL()), "----------",
   SPACES(76-COL()), "----------"
RETURN
```

; **INVREPOR.SC**

```
CLEAR
MESSAGE "DO YOU WISH TO PRINT THE UNPAID INVOICE REPORT (Y/N):"
@ 22,79 ACCEPT "A1" PICTURE "&" TO ANSWER @ 22,79
IF ANSWER <> "Y" THEN
  RETURN
ENDIF
CLEAR
MESSAGE "INSERT WIDE PAPER IN THE PRINTER-PRESS ANY KEY TO CONTINUE"
X = GETCHAR()
CLEAR
@ 5,0 ?? "ENTER THE BEGINNING DATE FOR THE PAYMENT PERIOD IN THE FORM"
  ?? " MM/DD/YY:" ACCEPT "D" TO MEMBDATE
MEMDATE = MEMBDATE+7
```

```
SORT "INVOICE" ON "INVDATEDUE" TO "TEMP"
EDIT "TEMP"
SCAN
   FOR ([INVDATEDUE] > MEMDATE AND [INVDISCDAT] > MEMDATE) OR
       [INVPAIDAMT] >= [INVAMTDUE] OR [INVPAYTYPE] <> "A" OR
       [INVPDINFUL] = "Y" OR [INVPDINFUL] = "y"
   KEYPRESS "DEL"
ENDSCAN
MAXLINES = 50
MYPAGENO = 1
MEMDAYTOT = 0
MEMGTOT = 0
PRINTER ON
PRINT CHR(15)
PLAY "INVRHEAD"
MYROW = 5
MEMDAY = [INVDATEDUE]
PRINTER ON
SCAN
   IF MYROW > MAXLINES THEN
       ? "\f"
       MYPAGENO = MYPAGENO + 1
       PLAY "INVRHEAD"
       ?
       MYROW = 6
   ENDIF
   IF ISBLANK([INVPAIDAMT]) THEN
      [INVPAIDAMT] = 0
```

```
ENDIF
IF [INVDATEDUE] <> MEMDAY AND MEMDAYTOT <> 0 THEN
   MYROW = MYROW + 1
   ? SPACES(199), "TOTAL FOR DAY    ", FORMAT("W9.2", MEMDAYTOT)
   MEMDAYTOT = 0
   ?
   MYROW = MYROW + 1
ENDIF
MEMLNAME = [INVLNAME]
MEMFNAME = [INVFNAME]
MEMNAME = MEMLNAME+", "+MEMFNAME
MEMADDRESS = SPACES(1)
IF NOT ISBLANK([INVPOBOX]) THEN
    MEMADDRESS = "PO BOX "+[INVPOBOX]
ENDIF
IF NOT ISBLANK([INVSTREET]) AND NOT ISBLANK(MEMADDRESS) THEN
   MEMADDRESS = MEMADDRESS+", "+[INVSTREET]
ENDIF
IF NOT ISBLANK([INVSTREET]) AND ISBLANK(MEMADDRESS) THEN
   MEMADDRESS = [INVSTREET]
ENDIF
MEMADDRESS = MEMADDRESS+", "+[INVCITY]+", "+[INVSTATE]+", "+[INVZIP]
? [INVIDNO],                                ; IN COLUMN 1
   SPACES(7-COL()-1), [INVINVNO],              ; IN COLUMN 7
   SPACES(33-COL()-1),FORMAT("W31", MEMNAME), ; IN COLUMN 33
   SPACES(64-COL()-1), [INVCOMPANY],           ; IN COLUMN 64
   SPACES(MOD(80-COL(),80)),    ; GO TO THE NEXT LINE ON THE SCREEN
   SPACES(10-COL()-1), ; ADVANCE TO SCREEN COLUMN 10, PAGE COLUMN 90
```

```
        FORMAT("W49", MEMADDRESS),
        SPACES(60-COL()-1), [INVDATEDUE] ,          ; IN COL 140
        SPACES(70-COL()-1), FORMAT("W9.2",[INVAMTDUE]),  ; IN COL 150
        SPACES(80-COL()-1), FORMAT("W9.2",[INVDISCAMT]), ; IN COL 160
        SPACES(10-COL()-1), [INVDISCDAT],                ; IN COL 170
        SPACES(20-COL()-1), FORMAT("W9.2",[INVPAIDAMT]), ; IN COL 180
        SPACES(30-COL()-1), FORMAT("W25",[INVREASON]),   ; IN COL 190
        SPACES(57-COL()-1), FORMAT("W9.2", [INVAMTDUE]-[INVPAIDAMT]); COL 217
    MEMDAYTOT = MEMDAYTOT + [INVAMTDUE] - [INVPAIDAMT]
    MEMGTOT   = MEMGTOT   + [INVAMTDUE] - [INVPAIDAMT]
    IF [INVDISCAMT] > 0 AND [INVDISCDAT] < MEMDATE THEN
      ?? SPACES(67-COL()-1), "*"                         ; IN COL 227
    ENDIF
    MYROW = MYROW + 1
    ? [INVDESC]
    MEMDAY = [INVDATEDUE]
ENDSCAN
?
? SPACES(199), "TOTAL FOR DAY     ", FORMAT("W9.2", MEMDAYTOT)
?
? SPACES(199), "GRAND TOTAL       ", FORMAT("W9.2", MEMGTOT)
PRINT CHR(18)
PRINT "\f"
PRINTER OFF
DO_IT!
CLEARALL
RETURN
```

; INVRHEAD.SC

```
      ; ROW 1
? SPACES(99),"INVOICES TO BE PAID REPORT",SPACES(25),"PAGE NO:",
  FORMAT("W3",MYPAGENO)
      ; ROW 2
? SPACES(109), TODAY()
      ; ROW 3
?
      ; ROW 4
? "ID NO INVOICE NO                NAME                         "
?? "COMPANY                  ADDRESS                            "
?? "              DATE DUE  ORIG AMT  DISC AMT  DISC DATE PD SO FAR "
?? "REASON FOR NON-PAYMENT    TO BE PAID DISC"
      ; ROW 5
? "DESCRIPTION"
      ; ROW 6
? "----- ------------------------- ------------------------------ "
?? "------------------------- ------------------------------------"
?? "------------- --------- --------- --------- --------- --------- "
?? "------------------------- ---------- ----"
RETURN
```

; PAYABLES.SC

```
; MAIN DRIVER FOR THE PAYABLES SYSTEM
ECHO OFF
WHILE TRUE
  PRINTER OFF
  CLEAR
```

```
CLEARALL
@    0, 5 ?? "PAYABLES SYSTEM"
@    1, 5 ?? "---------------"
@    2,10 ?? "A. EXIT FROM SYSTEM"
@    3,10 ?? "B. INVOICE, ENTER"
@    4,10 ?? "C. INVOICE, CHANGE"
@    5,10 ?? "D. COMPANY, ENTER"
@    6,10 ?? "E. COMPANY, CHANGE"
@    7,10 ?? "F. COMPANIES, LIST"
@    8,10 ?? "G. INVOICES TO BE PAID REPORT"
@    9,10 ?? "H. REVIEW AND MARK INVOICES FOR LATER PAYMENT"
@   10,10 ?? "I. PRINT PRE-PAYMENT REPORT"
@   11,10 ?? "J. PROCESS PAYMENTS AND PRINT CHECKS"
@   12,10 ?? "K. FIND AND DISPLAY INVOICES"
@   13,10 ?? "L. FIND AND DISPLAY PAYMENTS"
@   14,10 ?? "M. DELETE RECORDS"
@   15,10 ?? "N. CHANGE LAST CHECK NUMBER"
@   16,10 ?? "O. REINDEX FILES"
@   18, 0
MESSAGE "ENTER A SELECTION CODE"
CODE = CHR(GETCHAR())
?? CODE
SWITCH
  CASE CODE = "A":
    CLEAR
    MESSAGE "NORMAL TERMINATION OF PAYABLES SYSTEM"
    SLEEP 1000
```

```
  EXIT
CASE CODE = "B":
  PLAY "INVENTER"
CASE CODE = "C":
  PLAY "INVCHANG"
CASE CODE = "D":
  PLAY "COMENTER"
CASE CODE = "E":
  PLAY "COMCHANG"
CASE CODE = "F":
  PLAY "COMLIST"
CASE CODE = "G":
  PLAY "INVREPOR"
CASE CODE = "H":
  PLAY "INVPAY"
CASE CODE = "I":
  PLAY "INVPREPO"
CASE CODE = "J":
  PLAY "CHECKPRI"
CASE CODE = "K":
  PLAY "INVFIND"
CASE CODE = "L":
  PLAY "PAYFIND"
CASE CODE = "M":
  PLAY "INVDELET"
CASE CODE = "N":
  PLAY "INVCHECK"
CASE CODE = "O":
```

```
        PLAY "INDEXES"
      OTHERWISE:
        MESSAGE "ILLEGAL SELECTION CODE"
        BEEP
        SLEEP 2000
    ENDSWITCH
    RELEASE VARS ALL
ENDWHILE
RETURN
```

; **PAYFIND.SC**

```
MAXLINES = 18
VIEW "INVOICE"
EDIT "INVPAYME"
WHILE TRUE
  CLEAR
  @ 5,1 ?? "ENTER THE SYSTEM ASSIGNED ID FOR THE INVOICE - BLANK TO QUIT:"
  ACCEPT "A5" TO MEMIDNO
  IF ISBLANK(MEMIDNO) THEN
     QUITLOOP
  ENDIF
  MOVETO [INVOICE -> INVIDNO]
  LOCATE MEMIDNO
  IF NOT RETVAL THEN
    MESSAGE "NO INVOICE ON FILE FOR GIVEN ID NUMBER"
    BEEP
    SLEEP 2000
    LOOP
```

```
ENDIF
CLEAR
PLAY "INVFHEAD"
; *** DISPLAY INVOICE HERE ***
@ 6, 0 ?? [INVIDNO]
@ 6,26 ?? FORMAT("W25", [INVLNAME]+", "+[INVFNAME] )
@ 6,52 ?? [INVAMTDUE]
@ 6,65 ?? [INVDATEDUE]
@ 7, 0 ?? [INVINVNO]
@ 7,26 ?? [INVCOMPANY]
@ 7,52 ?? [INVPAIDAMT]
@ 7,65 ?? [INVPAIDDAT]
@ 7,76 ?? [INVPDINFUL]
@ 8, 0 ?? [INVDESC]
@ 10, 1 ?? "DATE"
@ 10,10 ?? "AMOUNT"
@ 11, 1 ?? "--------"
@ 11,10 ?? "---------"
MYROW = 11
MOVETO RECORD 1
MOVETO [INVPAYME -> INVPIDNO]
LOCATE MEMIDNO
IF NOT RETVAL THEN
  @ 12, 1 ?? "NO PAYMENTS ON FILE"
  MESSAGE "PRESS ANY KEY TO CONTINUE"
  BEEP
  SLEEP 2000
```

```
  ENDIF
  WHILE RETVAL
    MYROW = MYROW+1
    IF MYROW > MAXLINES THEN
      MESSAGE "PRESS ANY KEY TO CONTINUE"
      BEEP
      SLEEP 2000
      MEMLINE = 12
      @ MEMLINE,0 CLEAR EOS
      MYROW = 12
    ENDIF
    @ MYROW, 1 ?? [INVPPAYDATE]
    @ MYROW,10 ?? FORMAT("W9.2", [INVPAMT])
    DOWN
    MOVETO [INVPAYME -> INVPIDNO]
    LOCATE NEXT MEMIDNO
  ENDWHILE
  MESSAGE "PRESS ANY KEY TO CONTINUE"
  BEEP
  X = GETCHAR()
ENDWHILE
CANCELEDIT
CLEARALL
RETURN
```

APPENDIX

A

MENU COMMANDS

Paradox has two types of commands that allow the user to perform functions that appear in a Paradox menu: a sequence of recorded keystrokes and PAL statements. A PAL statement that allows the selection of a function from a Paradox menu can be thought of as an abbreviated menu command, since it usually has fewer elements in it than does the corresponding sequence of keystrokes.

For any desired operation, you can record the sequence of keystrokes in the following manner: enter ALT–F3 to initiate the INSTANT SCRIPT RECORD, enter the desired sequence of keystrokes interactively, select the Scripts function from the Paradox main menu, and then stop the INSTANT SCRIPT RECORD. The sequence of keystrokes (together with a few extra keystrokes at the end of the file) will be recorded in a file named INSTANT.SC. Note that a new INSTANT.SC file is created each time that you use the ALT–F3 keystroke. You can modify the contents of the INSTANT.SC file and/or copy it into a program of your own, using the Read function in the editor. Once you see how keystrokes can be incorporated into your program, you might wish to enter them directly into your programs just as you would enter a PAL statement in your program.

Let's examine a common operation both as a sequence of keystrokes and as a PAL statement to see the differences between the two approaches. If we wish to display a table on the screen (access the records in a table), the interactive steps are:

1. Go to the main menu.
2. Select item VIEW.
3. Enter the name of the table to be displayed on the screen.

You can enter these operations directly in your PAL program by including the following

```
MENU {VIEW} {MYTABLE}
```

where MYTABLE is the name of the table to be displayed on the screen.

NOTE: When you run a PAL program, the table is copied to your workspace, but usually does not appear on the screen. This allows you to access the records in the table as needed, leaving the display of the table up to the discretion of the programmer. The keyword MENU tells Paradox that you wish to enter a sequence of menu selections, rather than enter a PAL statement. The individual menu selections and data items that would be entered by the user are passed to Paradox enclosed in { }. Note that both VIEW, the menu function to be selected, and MYTABLE, the name of the database table, are included in { }. Each separate entry must be enclosed in its own set of { }. The same sequence of operations performed through the use of a PAL statement looks like the following

```
VIEW "MYTABLE"
```

Note here that neither the keyword MENU nor the { } are used in the PAL statement. The PAL keyword VIEW designates that a PAL statement, not a sequence of Paradox keystrokes, is to be used. The syntax of this PAL statement requires a character string constant or variable to follow the keyword VIEW. This allows you to enter either a constant (in quotation marks as shown above) or a variable that contains a character string. The ability to use a variable dramatically increases the usefulness of the PAL statement over the sequence of keystrokes, as shown by the following code

```
@ 1,0 ?? "Enter the name of the table:"
ACCEPT "A8" TO FILENAME
VIEW FILENAME
```

This code obtains the desired table and places a copy of it in the workspace. To make it visible to the user for the purposes of editing, after it has been placed in the workspace, use the following code

```
@ 1,0 ?? "Enter the name of the table:"
ACCEPT "A8" TO FILENAME
VIEW FILENAME
  EDITKEY
```

Alternatively, you could use the following code to accomplish the same task

```
@ 1,0 ?? "Enter the name of the table:"
ACCEPT "A8" TO FILENAME
EDIT FILENAME
```

The following table lists the abbreviated menu commands.

Table A.1

PAL COMMAND	PURPOSE
ADD	Copy records from one table to another
CANCELEDIT	Exit Edit mode and discard changes
COPY	Make a copy of a database table and its associated auxiliary files
CREATE	Create a new database table
DELETE	Delete a database table and its auxiliary tables
EDIT	Place an image of a table on the screen and enter Edit mode
EMPTY	Remove all the records from a table
EXIT	Exit Paradox and return to DOS
PICKFORM	Select a form to be used when an image is viewed
PLAY	Execute a program
PROTECT	Encrypt a table and assign a password to it
RENAME	Change the name of a database table and all its auxiliary files
REPORT	Print a report
SORT	Sort the records in a database table
SUBTRACT	Delete records from a database table that already exist in another database table
UNPASSWORD	Take back a password
VIEW	Place a table in the workspace

APPENDIX
B SPECIAL KEYS USED IN PAL PROGRAMS

On your keyboard you will find a number of keys that have special names. Examples are: HOME, PGUP, PGDN, and END. Each of these keys has a special meaning when used in a PAL program. In addition to these keys, additional keys and keystrokes have been designated as special keys for use in Paradox. When you use the name of the key in a PAL program, it is interpreted as if the keystroke had been entered at the keyboard. These keystrokes and their PAL names are given in alphabetical order by their PAL Names in Table B.1.

Table B.1

PAL NAME	KEYSTROKE	PAL NAME	KEYSTROKE
Backspace	BACKSPACE	Esc	ESC
Check	F6	Example	F5
CheckPlus	ALT-F6	FieldView	ALT-F5
ClearAll	ALT-F8	FieldView	CTRL-F
ClearImage	F8	FormKey	F7
CtrlBackspace	CTRL-BACKSPACE	Help	F1
CtrlBreak	CTRL-BREAK	Home	HOME
CtrlEnd	CTRL-END	Ins	INS
CtrlHome	CTRL-HOME	InstantPlay	ALT-F4
CtrlLeft	CTRL- ←	InstantRecord	ALT-F3
CtrlRight	CTRL- →	InstantReport	ALT-F7
CtrlPgDn	CTRL-PGDN	Left	← (left arrow)
CtrlPgUp	CTRL-PGUP	Menu	F10
Del	DEL	PalMenu	ALT-F10
DeleteLine	CTRL-Y	PgDn	PGDN
Ditto	CTRL-D	PgUp	PGUP
Do_it!	F2	Right	→ (right arrow)
Down	↓ (down arrow)	ReverseTab	SHIFT-TAB
DownImage	F4	Rotate	CTRL-R
EditKey	F9	Tab	TAB
Editor	CTRL-E	Up	↑ (up arrow)
End	END	UpImage	F3
Enter	RETURN	VertRuler	CTRL-V

These keystrokes and their PAL names are given in alphabetical order by their keystroke names in Table B.2.

Table B.2

PAL NAME	KEYSTROKE	PAL NAME	KEYSTROKE
Left	← (left arrow)	VertRuler	CTRL-V
Right	→ (right arrow)	DeleteLine	CTRL-Y
Up	↑ (up arrow)	Del	DEL
Down	↓ (down arrow)	End	END
InstantRecord	ALT-F3	Enter	ENTER
InstantPlay	ALT-F4	Esc	ESC
FieldView	ALT-F5	Help	F1
CheckPlus	ALT-F6	Do_it!	F2
InstantReport	ALT-F7	UpImage	F3
ClearAll	ALT-F8	DownImage	F4
PalMenu	ALT-F10	Example	F5
Backspace	BACKSPACE	Check	F6
CtrlLeft	CTRL- ←	FormKey	F7
CtrlRight	CTRL- →	ClearImage	F8
CtrlBackspace	CTRL-BACKSPACE	EditKey	F9
CtrlBreak	CTRL-BREAK	Menu	F10
Ditto	CTRL-D	Home	HOME
Editor	CTRL-E	Ins	INS
CtrlEnd	CTRL-END	PgDn	PGDN
FieldView	CTRL-F	PgUp	PGUP
CtrlHome	CTRL-HOME	Enter	RETURN
CtrlPgDn	CTRL-PGDN	ReverseTab	SHIFT-TAB
CtrlPgUp	CTRL-PGUP	Tab	TAB
Rotate	CTRL-R		

APPENDIX

C TECHNICAL SPECIFICATIONS

Maximum Number of Variables	Limited only by main memory
Maximum Number of Bytes in a Table	260,000,000
Maximum Number of Records in a Table	65,000
Maximum Number of Bytes in a Record	4,000
Maximum Number of Characters in a Field	255
Maximum Number of Fields in a Record	255
Maximum Number of Open Database Tables	No limit
Maximum Number of Open Files (All Types)	No limit
Maximum Number of Forms/Table	10
Maximum Number of Secondary Indexes/Table	255
Numeric Accuracy (Real Number)	$\pm 10^{-307}$ to $\pm 10^{308}$
Numeric Accuracy (in Digits):	15
Numeric Accuracy (Short Integers)	-32,767 to 32,767
Bounds for Dates	Jan 1, 100 through Dec 31, 9999
Maximum Length of a Character String	255
Number of Dimensions in an Array	1
Maximum Length of a Variable Name	132
Maximum Length of a Field Name	25
Maximum Length of a Table Name	8

APPENDIX

D

CONVERTING A dBASE III SYSTEM TO PARADOX

If you have a good editor (like WordStar in nondocument mode), many of the following changes are easily made.

1. Identify which asterisks(*) are used to start a comment, and replace each one with a semicolon (;).
2. Replace SAY with ??.
3. You may replace WAIT either with GETCHAR( ) or with SLEEP. The GETCHAR( ) can be used to freeze the screen and the SLEEP can be used to insert a pause.
4. Replace DO CASE with SWITCH and ENDCASE with END-SWITCH.
5. Replace SET TALK OFF with ECHO OFF.
6. Replace SET DEVICE TO SCREEN with PRINTER OFF, and SET DEVICE TO PRINT with PRINTER ON.
7. Replace .T. with TRUE, and .F. with FALSE.
8. Replace DO WHILE with WHILE, and ENDDO with ENDWHILE.
9. Replace CLEAR ALL with RELEASE VARS ALL and CLEARALL.
10. Replace CLEAR with CLEAR and CLEARALL.
11. You may wish to replace some of the ? statements with TEXT, ?, or ?? statements, depending on where the output is to go and the form of the output. The PICTURE clause in output is also replaced with a FORMAT function.
12. Replace APPEND BLANK with a DOWN (if in Table view) or a PGDN (if in Forms view).
13. Replace USE either with VIEW or EDIT.
14. The SEEK and the FIND are replaced by the LOCATE or LOCATE NEXT statements.
15. The TRIM is not needed, since PAL automatically removes both leading and trailing blanks.
16. Replace SELECT with MOVETO.
17. Replace EJECT with PRINT "\f".
18. The SKIP 1 might be replaced by a DOWN (if in Table view), a PGDN (if in Forms view), or a MOVETO RECORD RECORD( )+1.
19. Replace QUIT with EXIT.

20. Add the word THEN after the condition in each IF statement.
21. Replace DATE( ) with TODAY( ).
22. Replace each STORE statement with a statement of the type

```
X = Y
```

The above list is not exhaustive. It merely is a list that I compiled when I converted a dBASE III program to PAL. Note that many of the above steps apply equally well to dBASE II.

Since the structure of a dBASE III program is almost the same as the structure of a PAL program, you will probably find the conversion relatively straightforward. Nevertheless, there is one aspect of the conversion that you might wish to look at carefully. When a sequential scan of an entire database file is performed, starting with the first record in the file, you might wish to use a SCAN loop rather than a WHILE loop. An associated problem is the order in which the records are encountered. In dBASE II and III, the records are presented in order by primary index and you can change the primary index through the use of the SET INDEX statement. In Paradox, when you access the data using a secondary index, the data is not presented to you in order by secondary index values. Rather, it is still presented in order by primary index values, if there is a primary index for the file. If there is no primary index, the data is presented in stored record order. This can present some ordering problems for reports. In such a situation, I recommend that you sort the file and place the result of the sort into a temporary file to be used for the report. This is not a particularly good solution if the file is large, but it appears to be the only viable solution. The reason that I recommend a temporary file is that a table (file) with a primary index cannot be directly sorted. Remember that a Paradox file with a primary index cannot contain duplicate primary index values, so, in many cases, you cannot use the primary index to keep the records in the desired (sorted) order.

I am sure that there are a number of additional replacements that can be made when a dBASE program is converted to PAL. The list in this appendix depends on my own particular programming style in both dBASE and in PAL. If you have a significantly different style, your conversion list might contain a few more items.

APPENDIX

E

SUMMARY OF CHANGES FROM PARADOX VERSION 1.0 TO 1.1

1. **INSTALLATION:**
   Place the INSTALLATION DISK in drive A and enter the DOS command

   A:INSTALL C:

   When prompted, insert the requested disks in drive A. When you first install PARADOX you will be asked for your name and the name of your organization. This information is recorded on your distribution disk. Subsequent uses of PARADOX automatically display your name and the name of your organization (you need not enter this information again). This version is not copy protected. If you have already created a directory named /PARADOX, the installation procedure will use it. If there is no such directory on your hard disk, the installation procedure will create one for you.

2. **NEW IMPORT/EXPORT FEATURES:**
   The new files handled by PARADOX are SYMPHONY 1.1, Lotus 1-2-3 2.0, and dBASE III PLUS. The IMPORT function has been enhanced to allow Paradox to scan an ASCII file and create a new table based upon the structure of this file.

3. **CHANGES IN UNDO:**
   As you UNDO an editing or data entry operation, you can return, in increments, to a previous step.

4. **MENU USAGE:**
   You can scroll to the right or left when a large selection of menu items is displayed on the screen. Press UP ARROW or CTRL-RIGHT ARROW to scroll right and DOWN ARROW or CTRL-LEFT ARROW to scroll to the left. If you select a menu item by entry of the first letter of the name of the item, and if more than one item in the menu starts its name with that letter, then the names beginning with other letters are removed from the screen, allowing you to more easily select your item. To select the desired item, highlight it and press RETURN.

5. **REPORTS:**
   Records can be grouped by date. In particular, records can be grouped by day, week, month, or year.

6. **ABILITY TO ENTER DATA INTO TWO OR MORE TABLES:**
   Select MODIFY followed by MULTIENTRY to use a single table

(the source table) to enter records in one data entry form but add the records to two or more (target) tables. Select TOOLS, then MORE, and then MULTIADD to modify records in more than one table. Before you can use these two features, you must first create the source table used for the entry or modification of the data, the target tables that will receive the data, and the information (mapping) that instructs Paradox how to transfer the data. Use the MODIFY/MULTIENTRY/ENTRY option to enter the data and the MODIFY/MULTIENTRY/SETUP option to create the mapping. After the data has been entered, press Do_It! (F2) to copy the data to the target tables. The records are placed in their proper positions (merged) in the target tables but are not merged with records in the source table.

7. **TEMPORARY EXIT TO DOS AND SUBSEQUENT RETURN:** Select TOOLS, MORE, and TODOS to suspend Paradox and invoke DOS. Note that Paradox saves some information for its own use (when you reenter Paradox) including main memory mappings, so it is important that you do not perform any operations in DOS that might disturb the reentry to Paradox. In particular, do not run any memory-resident programs; do not use the DOS PRINT or MODE commands; and if you change the directory, change it back before returning to Paradox. When you have completed the desired DOS operations, enter the command

   ```
   EXIT
   ```

   to return to PARADOX. An alternative to TOOLS/MORE/TODOS is to enter the keystroke CTRL-0. This operation is complicated somewhat if you are not using a hard disk, since you must have COMMAND.COM on the floppy disk in drive A if you are using a dual-floppy system.

8. **A SCRIPT CAN NOW BE PRINTED FROM THE EDITOR —NO NEED TO EXIT FROM PARADOX TO PRINT THE SCRIPT:** Use SCRIPTS/EDITOR/WRITE or EDIT/PRINT.

9. **SUPPORT OF A PROCEDURE LIBRARY:** A procedure library allows you to speed up access to frequently used procedures and minimizes the number of disk accesses. The procedures in a library are stored in a form that is different from normal

script form. The following commands are used to create and maintain the procedure library:

CREATELIB: used to create the library file
WRITELIB: used to store additional scripts in the library file
READLIB: used to load a procedure from the library
INFOLIB: used to list the names of the procedures in a library

Because a procedure is not stored in a format that can be edited, Paradox also stores the name of the original script in the library. When you use the debugger for a procedure, Paradox automatically accesses the original script for editing purposes.

10. **NEW PAL COMMANDS (STATEMENTS):**

CREATELIB: create a new procedure library
DOS: temporarily suspend Paradox and invoke DOS. You must use the EXIT command to leave DOS and return to Paradox.
INFOLIB: list the name of the procedures in the library
READLIB: load a procedure from a library
RUN: invoke a DOS command. When the DOS command has been completed, Paradox automatically returns to execution of the current script
SETDIR: change the current directory
WRITELIB: add a procedure to a library

11. **NEW PAL FUNCTIONS:**

BOT: test for the beginning of the file
EOT: test for the end of the file
DRIVESPACE: check for available space on the disk
MENUCHOICE: return a character string containing the current menu selection

WINDOW: return a character string containing the current window message.

12. MODIFIED STATEMENTS:

WAIT: ability to display a message that stays at the top of the screen until the current operation has been completed.

INDEX

K

L

M

N

O

P

W

Y

To order,
contact your local bookstore or computer store, or send the order form to

Scott, Foresman and Company
Professional Publishing Group
1900 East Lake Avenue
Glenview, IL 60025

In Canada, contact
Macmillan of Canada
164 Commander Blvd.
Agincourt, Ontario
M1S 3C7

Please check method of payment:

☐ Check/Money Order ☐ MasterCard ☐ VISA

Amount Enclosed $__________

Credit Card No. __________

Exp. Date __________

Signature __________

Name (please print) __________

Address __________

City __________ State _____ Zip _____

Add applicable sales tax, plus 6% of Total for shipping.

Full payment must accompany your order.

A18569